LEGAL REALISM
to
LAW IN ACTION

LEGAL REALISM
to
LAW IN ACTION

INNOVATIVE LAW COURSES AT UW-MADISON

Edited by William Clune

Foreword by Lawrence M. Friedman

qp

QUID PRO BOOKS
New Orleans, Louisiana

Published in 2021 by Quid Pro Books.

ISBN 978-1-61027-437-1 (pbk.)
ISBN 978-1-61027-438-8 (hbk.)
ISBN 978-1-61027-439-5 (ePUB)

QUID PRO BOOKS
5860 Citrus Blvd., Suite D
New Orleans, Louisiana 70123
www.quidprobooks.com

Publisher's Cataloging-in-Publication

Clune, William.

Legal realism to law in action : innovative law courses at UW-Madison / ed. by William Clune.

p. cm. — (Contemporary Society)

Includes bibliographical references.

1. Law—Study and teaching—Wisconsin—History. 2. University of Wisconsin System—History. 3. Legal education—Wisconsin—History. I. Title.

KF273 .H512 2021 2021317258

CONTENTS

Foreword:
The Wisconsin Idea in Perspective

Lawrence M. Friedman

For many years, I taught a survey course on American legal history at my school. When we came to discuss the second half of the twentieth century (ancient history as far as the students were concerned), I would tell the class, jokingly, that I was now old enough to be a primary source. It was a joke, but it had a certain amount of truth. I *lived* through periods before the students were born, and that means I have a sense of what the period actually felt like. Of course, periods surely felt different to different people; nonetheless, I can claim to be a primary source—a data point. A source for what the McCarthy period felt like; what the Cold War period felt like, what the civil rights era felt like; obviously, how you experienced these periods depended on who you were, where you lived, what your social status was, your race, your gender—all of those things. Nobody is ever truly "typical." Still, living through a period does give a person a privileged voice, a sense of the times, that the after-borns really do not have.

All this is by way of an introduction to an introduction. This book is a collection of essays and interviews about a particular period in the history of the University of Wisconsin Law School. A kind of golden age, an age of innovation in legal education; about what might be called the legal branch of the Wisconsin Idea; and the courses in the law school that reflected those innovations. In particular, it is about four "influential introductory courses," which were developed during that period; the essay by Bill Clune deals with these courses in detail, and describes the general "themes" that they exemplified; the other materials expand on the themes, and the personalities behind these particular courses. Wisconsin is still an important law school, and it can still be described as "innovative." But much of its strength, much of its ethos, can be traced to that golden age of the 1950s and the 1960s; the era of Willard Hurst and Frank Remington, very notably, and the other members of a strong faculty, who served during that period.

Willard Hurst was an important mentor for me personally. I first met him in the late 1950s, and I joined the faculty of the law school at the beginning of the 1960s. I cannot claim, of course, that I was present at the creation, as it were. When I arrived, the golden age was in full flow; Wisconsin was an exciting and heady place; a richly original and feisty law school. Alas, only a few of us are still around to testify about that period.

Stewart Macaulay, who became an important figure in legal scholarship, joined the Wisconsin faculty in 1957; Bill Whitford arrived in 1965. They too, along with me, can claim the status of primary source. They were witnesses to the atmosphere of the law school in those days: witnesses to what was different (and exhilarating) about Wisconsin.

At that time, it seems to me, Willard Hurst exercised tremendous influence—particularly, I think, on the younger faculty. Willard was a legal historian, of course; and the most obvious impact of his work was in that field. I will return to this theme. What I want to stress here is that his influence went far beyond legal history. New faculty members would be invited to lunch with Willard; and he would discuss with them their future plans: what kind of research they had in mind. After they spoke, he would gently but firmly urge them to do something bolder, more innovative, more long-term, more untraditional. We used to refer to these suggestions as Willard's "five-year plans." In his critique of Hurst's work, Dirk Hartog shocked me by using the word "arrogant" to describe Willard Hurst. In my view—and I knew him very well—this misrepresents his character. Yes, he was self-assured; yes, he was serious, and determined; yes, he had definite ideas about what counted as important legal research. But the word "arrogant" implies an attitude toward others which was completely alien to Willard Hurst. A more selfless scholar never existed. A more helpful mentor. His single-spaced comments on the work of his colleagues, pounded out on his battered old typewriter, were famous. He was unfailingly kind and cooperative. He was never too busy to help out, to encourage his fellow law-teachers.

I think this cooperative spirit pervaded the law school; and, I should add, the spirit of cooperation went beyond the law school. Elsewhere in legal academia, law schools—at least this is my impression—were basically walled off from the universities they were supposed to be part of. Law professors tended to be contemptuous of outsiders, to look down on scholars who did not know how to think like a lawyer. My own school since the late 1960s, Stanford, was no exception. For example, until recently, the law school at Stanford was on the semester system; the rest of the university was on the quarter system. This discouraged, to say the least, interaction with students and faculty outside the law school. The very calendar stood in the way.

The golden age in Wisconsin, in short, was a cooperative effort, in the law school, and among scholars in other departments who studied the legal system. And, although I am convinced that Wisconsin was in many ways unique, bits and pieces of its ethos could be found in other schools as well. Empirical research on law was not a Madison monopoly. The legal realist movement, in the 1920s and 1930s, professed a belief in law in action, in studying the real world; realists expressed skepticism about the impact and meaning of legal rules and doctrines outside the courtroom.

Some of the realists actually went out and counted this or that. I was a student at the University of Chicago Law School; Chicago can claim to its credit the great study of the American jury, carried out by Harry Kalven and Hans Zeisel. But I can assure you (again as an eyewitness) that such things were a sideshow at Chicago; legal education at the school was, on the whole, thoroughly conventional—in some cases almost ludicrously so (courses in criminal law and property law especially). I suspect this was true almost everywhere. Empirical research was marginalized, if there was any such research in the first place. In Wisconsin, what became the law and society movement was not a sideshow at all: it was the dominant ethos of the school.

Much of the material in this book is about criminal justice; Frank Remington and Herman Goldstein, and the teams they assembled, did pathbreaking and influential work. Willard Hurst's own work, to be sure, has almost nothing to say about criminal justice. Dirk Hartog's critique of Hurst hits hard on the theme that the work was cramped, ingrown, narrow in its range. Hurst's writings dealt mainly with the market, with law and the economy. True enough; but his influence was felt in many other fields. He helped create the atmosphere in which Remington and Goldstein flourished; he encouraged their approach, and—this should not be overlooked—helped them to get funding, as Herman Goldstein points out in his interview. This was at a time when funds for empirical research in law were very hard to come by. Summer funds, which Willard Hurst had scraped up, gave me my first introduction to his brand of historical research.

Wisconsin, during the days of Hurst and company, definitely marched to its own drummer. It was not in the mainstream of legal education, and in some ways it was proud of this fact. Its uniqueness was a tremendous source of strength. So many law schools slavishly followed the lead of schools like Harvard and Yale. They hired graduates of these schools for their faculty; they used casebooks written by their professors; they followed the methods and the teaching techniques these schools were noted for. Wisconsin was an exception. Not entirely, of course—that would have been almost impossible. But it cared much less about what the mainstream was doing than perhaps most or even all the other schools. It was this independence that made it an incredibly exciting place.

The Wisconsin Idea: Criminal Justice

To be honest, uniqueness was also a weakness. Wisconsin, as an outlier, never had the influence on the legal academy that it should have had. Most notably on law school teaching. Take criminal justice—here the Frank Remington school arguably made a real difference, in research, and in the formation of policy. It should have made a bigger difference in *teaching* as well. But did it? Probably not. When I read the interview with Cecelia Klingele and Keith Findley, in this book, I couldn't help thinking, what a wonderful course they teach. What a wonderful experience for the students. Do they realize how different this course is, how rich in experiential learning? I am sure the instructors do. But their course, as they admit, is hardly typical of law school teaching on criminal law and criminal procedure. Law teachers, they admit, still tend to be "very doctrinal," still tend to be "very, very far removed from reality."

Alas, that seems to be all too true. Much of my own work has been about the history of criminal justice, and I was called upon for a few years to teach the course called "Criminal Law." I had never taken courses in the subject, and I had little or no experience with modern criminal justice. Nobody in my law school (Chicago) rode around on police cars, or looked at anything at all at the level of trial courts, let alone at such issues as plea bargaining. Hence, I felt somewhat unqualified to teach the course, but I did it anyway. When I tried to get ready to teach the course, I explored the big, popular casebooks, the ones everybody else was using. I was frankly appalled. That these casebooks were "far removed from reality" was completely obvious. On the whole, they ignored mass incarceration, the drug wars, prisons, police brutality, domestic violence, plea bargaining and so many aspects of criminal justice. When I feebly pointed this out, colleagues told me, oh, those things are covered in the course on criminal procedure. But criminal procedure courses were equally unreal; they were about big Supreme Court cases; they were heavily doctrinal, and they never seemed to ask, what impact did these big cases have? Did the *Miranda* case, and the Miranda warning, make any difference to police behavior? How important were Supreme Court decisions in the stationhouse, or at the level of trial courts?

Meanwhile, the criminal law course was a farrago of pop political philosophy, case-parsing, and such non-issues as the distinction between justification and excuse; there was material on the difference between first degree and second-degree murder; but nothing on homicide rates, on who murdered whom and why, and other related issues. And, by the way, almost nothing on race and class. It might be that professors supplemented the casebooks with other materials; I certainly hope so. But, at the time I taught the course, the casebooks were, to my way of thinking, barren deserts. They were collections of appellate cases exclusively, except for endless dithering about the text of the Model Penal Code. Criminology and its findings were invisible. The great work of the Remington school, the great work of Frank Zimring at Berkeley, the corpus of empirical research on crime and punishment; anything about the politics, history, and sociology of criminal justice: these were basically ignored. Perhaps this situation is changing. Change is badly needed. Courses like Klingele and Findley's could serve as valuable models.

The Wisconsin Idea: Contracts

The course on contracts is one of the four innovative courses the book discusses. In contract law and contract teaching, the dominant figure is Stewart Macaulay (full disclosure: he is both a friend and a collaborator), along with his associates, notably Bill Whitford. The interview with Macaulay and Whitford is extremely illuminating. This is another area where the Wisconsin Law School has gone its own way. Gone the *right* way, in my opinion. To me, there is no question but that the Macaulay approach to contract law—or, more accurately, to contract *behavior*—is as superior to classical law teaching as astrophysics is to the study of horoscopes. While the criminal justice people were riding around in police cars, and observing the real world, other law professors, as I said, were debating some phrase in the Model Penal Code, or dissecting some obscure point in an appellate case. In the world of contract, Stewart Macaulay was doing something just as enlightening, and just as revolutionary: he went out and actually talked to businesspeople in Wisconsin; he asked them questions about their use and non-use of contract doctrine.

Here too the Wisconsin idea has great strength, but also a weakness. The strength is that it confronts the real world—of lawyers, businesspeople, and consumers—and not the imaginary world of hairy hands, Carbolic smoke balls, and people halfway up a pole who are told not to go on climbing. Remember, the contracts course is considered fundamental. Legal education as we know it is the child of Christopher Columbus Langdell and his Harvard revolution of 1870. Langdell's field was contract law; he invented the modern casebook, and the first of his casebooks was his *Cases on Contracts*. Macaulay was thus a real rebel; he was attacking the citadel, which was old, tightly guarded, and defended by moats and dragons. The Macaulay approach was not without influence. I think the whole idea of "relational contracts" owes a good deal to his work. But his influence, in my opinion, should have been greater. Why is it that only a few law schools have adopted the Wisconsin casebook on contracts? In an ideal world, it, or something like it, almost everybody would be using it.

Mainstream law schools are incredibly difficult to move in any direction; they are extremely self-satisfied; and they are rigidly hierarchical. One or two schools have exercised inordinate influence over the other law schools. Their professors learned law the traditional way; as students, the future professors were labeled the cream of the crop, the brightest of the bright. Now they are professors themselves: why on earth should they change the way things are done? Why should they challenge the system which put them where they are?

On the other hand, legal scholarship—*real* scholarship—does not only come out of law schools. Perhaps I should say, scholarship about law, rather than legal scholarship. Many, perhaps even most, of the members of the Law and Society Association are not law professors at all. They are sociologists, anthropologists, psychologists, political scientists, and even a few maverick economists. In the law and society world, Wisconsin has a high reputation. It has been that way since the beginning of the movement. Sociologists from Wisconsin were among the founders of the Law and Society Association: Harry Ball and Jack Ladinsky, for example. And, from the early days, the Wisconsin Law School made a significant contribution. No single article in the field has been more discussed, cited, praised, and replicated, than Stewart Macaulay's seminal study of Wisconsin businesspeople—how they used, and didn't use, formal contract doctrine. A whole world of research flows out of that single source, written by a young member of the faculty of the Wisconsin Law School.

In the law school world, the pinnacle of prestige tends to go to constitutional pundits. They appear on television, and they publish essays on such topics as originalism, on what the Fourteenth Amendment "really" means (in their opinion); they follow breathlessly every emanation from the United States Supreme Court. Their work is earnest, self-centered, and highly normative. Some of it (the originalists, for example) write essays that remind me of essays produced by the flat earth society. They write with assurance, but without evidence. In the law and society world, values and techniques are entirely different. There is a commitment to actual research, research in the world, empirical research; a commitment to asking questions about the sources of law, the meaning of law, the impact of law; work based not on ideology (hopefully) but on honest observation and measurement. In that world, Wisconsin Law School in the Hurst days was at the very cutting edge, and is still among the leaders.

The Wisconsin Idea: Legal History

Wisconsin has, as I said, made an important contribution to two areas of legal scholarship: legal history, and law and society. As to legal history, the field has been on the whole a story of growth and success—particularly in the law schools. During the early years—in the 1950s, say—there was very little teaching and very little research on the subject in the legal academy. At the school I attended, the University of Chicago, American legal history was almost totally neglected. Of course, constitutional law had to pay some attention to the founding fathers and the constitutional convention and the like. And various courses mentioned this or that nugget of history; but there was nothing systematic. My property law course was in a way an exception. The professor seemed enamored of a few crushingly dull aspects of old English land law. He said absolutely nothing about the American experience. Nothing, for example, about public land law, or about the way American legislatures and courts transformed and adapted inherited land law. Today there are dozens and dozens of courses on American legal history in the law schools. The literature is rich.

I brought out a general history of American law in 1973; last year (2019) the fourth edition was published. Working on these successive editions has given me something of a bird's eye view of the way the field has developed. The Hurst school has certainly made a mark. It influenced a generation of legal historians. Legal history was once basically a dreary and unprofitable history of doctrines, focused on reported cases in high courts, and pretty much divorced from social and economic history. Hurst's huge book on the lumber industry in Wisconsin was a revolutionary move: essentially a study of one industry in a Middle-Western state, on the way law impacted the industry, and the way the industry impacted the law. No such thing could have come out of, say, the Harvard Law School. And Willard sponsored, or encouraged, or directed, a series of monographs and articles on Wisconsin legal history. Full disclosure: I wrote one of the monographs, *Contract Law in America*. Some of the monographs and articles were better than others. But, taken together, they gave a rich picture of the role of law in one particular state, in the nineteenth century. (The "America" in the title of my book was really Wisconsin, and only Wisconsin). This exploration of the role of law in a single state was unique, as far as I know. Certainly there was nothing like it at the time.

Legal history has changed greatly since Hurst's day: that much is clear. But history in general has also changed. If, say, in 1950—the year Willard published his seminal work on the growth of American law—a young graduate student in history, searching for a topic, had proposed doing a dissertation on pre-Civil war cookbooks, or on the sex life of Brazilians in the colonial period, I think his mentor (quite properly) would have told him to look for some other topic. (And, at the time, both mentor and disciple would have likely been a "him" and not a "her.") History has fashions like many other fields. Yes, Willard left out all sorts of things in his own work. He encouraged others, though, to fill in some of the gaps.

Today, what Hurst wrote about has come to seem narrow. It was, for one thing, confined to the nineteenth century and a bit of the twentieth. He had almost nothing to say about the colonial period. Moreover—here I have to agree with Dirk Hartog—the "we" in his writing is jarring. All the talk about what "we" did, and what "we" Americans thought, and what "we" accomplished. This "we," Hartog tells us, has been "a subject of ridicule" among his graduate students. Ridicule, and perhaps anger, I imagine; because this "we" excluded most of the population. The "we" consisted of "white men . . . those he recognized as striving individuals and consumers of law." I can appreciate why, in this day and age, the "we" in Willard Hurst's writing might seem jarring. Perhaps it should have been jarring to people even back then. But I must say this: when I came to Wisconsin, and while I was there, and while I was very much under

Willard's spell, I simply do not remember any such feeling. I do not recall that the "we" offended me, or that I found it inappropriate. Yet the "we" was a term of exclusion, rather than inclusion. It excluded *me,* for one thing; and the millions of others who were children and grandchildren of immigrants from southern and eastern Europe. My grandmother, who lived with us after her husband died, was illiterate, and spoke broken English. Absolutely nobody in my family qualified as one of the "we." And of course, the "we" also left out African Americans, Latinos, Native Americans, or for that matter, women.

But you have to consider Hurst in context. History has its own history. American history, as I remember it from high school, was all about this "we." The teachers and the textbooks told us that "we" settled on Plymouth Rock, that "we" left England to find more freedom, and that "we" fought the British and gained independence; afterwards "we" drafted and adopted a Constitution. Yet probably not a single person in my class had any claim to be part of this group of "we" people; they came from immigrant stock. They did not qualify as "we" people—and neither did the teacher. Why, then, did this "we" not bother me at the time? Perhaps I should have been bothered. But I was not. Nor was I bothered to be part of Willard's team; nor did it bother me when, way back then, I first read *Law and the Conditions of Freedom,* the book that Hartog's students find so jarring. Actually, I loved the book.

Yet, admittedly, times have changed, and this "we" is now offensive—and obsolete. I understand the feeling of Hartog's students. But the change in attitude, the sensitivity to the "we," reflects a real change in the culture. When I was growing up, many of us accepted the "we," because we assumed that this was a country which, for better or worse, had majorities and minorities. The majority owned the country; the rest of us were here basically as guests. We had to speak English, of course, because that was the language of the majority. We had to behave like Americans. We had to accept American values. For immigrants, it was worth the effort. This was America, the land of opportunity, the golden land; it was better than any of the alternatives, whatever its flaws (and nobody bothered in high school textbooks, for example, to dwell on any of these flaws). Millions of us were children and grandchildren of fairly recent immigrants. Nobody made us feel particularly welcome, just as the Irish were not really welcome in the 1840s. The Statute of Liberty was supposed to honor the "huddled masses, yearning to be free." In fact, nobody was particularly anxious to have huddled masses. But the huddled masses did get into the country, by the millions, before strict and racist immigration laws put a stop to this. The old-line American (for the most part) tolerated certain aspects of the huddled masses. They could practice their religions, for example. My family consisted of Jews from the Russian empire. Life on the east side of New York, or the west side of Chicago, seemed a lot better than life in the land of poverty and pogroms. Italians, Poles, and Greeks undoubtedly felt the same way.

Or perhaps we simply swallowed the Kool-Aid of establishment history; history in which the country was always right, in which Washington and Jefferson and Lincoln were heroes, and the Constitution was a model admired by freedom-lovers all over the world. We absorbed a view of Southern history from *Gone with the Wind* (or, even worse, from *Birth of a Nation*). We learned about the West from cowboy movies, in which the "Indians" were villainous savages and the heroes were white men riding horses. We learned about women's roles from the way Hollywood and the popular press presented them. I remember how shocked I was, the first time I visited Mexico City, to see what our southern neighbors thought about the Mexican War. What, this was an unjust war? But that's when America acquired California and the Southwest, how could that be bad? Nobody in my high school class questioned the morality of this war, as far as I can remember. Certainly the teacher never did. No suggestion that this was perhaps a war of aggression, an imperialist war, against a weaker nation to the south. Did we learn anything in school about how the Hawaiian kingdom became an American territory? Was there anything about Puerto Rico and the Philippines? The occupation of Haiti? Did we ever hear a word of criticism of any aspect of American foreign policy? No: we were not only a blessed nation, we were a country that had never lost a war; and we were, moreover, a moral beacon to the world.

In any event, things are different now (I hope). My high school days are in the distant, hazy past. No doubt many Americans (most, perhaps?) still believe in the fairytale history of the United States; but historians do not. African Americans always knew the story was untrue. So did the Cherokees and the other Native peoples. So did the Chinese in California and the West; and the Hispanics in Texas and elsewhere. Today, all of these are speaking up more loudly; they have demanded rights, recognition, a place at the table. Legal history, and history in general, has become much more inclusive. Historians pay attention to women, to sexual minorities, and to history's victims in general. This is an age of what I call plural equality. Minorities are not simply "tolerated;" they are entitled to equality of respect, and it does not matter that they are outnumbered. Numbers are important, but they are certainly not everything. We expect the President (well, not Trump) to greet Muslim citizens on Ramadan, perhaps to hold a Passover seder in the White House. A prominent Mormon ran for President—that would have once been unthinkable. Indeed, a Catholic president was unthinkable, until Kennedy. Even a divorced president was unthinkable. This was and is a majority Protestant country. Yet, at one point, fairly recent, of the nine justices of the United States Supreme Court, there was not a single Protestant. All this amounts to a massive cultural change.

I have no doubt that Willard Hurst, if we could bring him back from the grave, would approve of much or even all of these developments, and wholeheartedly. Of course, later generations will surely point out *our* blind spots, our prejudices and misconceptions. Willard Hurst's work, despite the "we," was a giant step forward. His "we" may have been mostly about white males. But he was writing about ordinary people, doing ordinary things, and using ordinary law to make a living and craft a life for themselves. Old-style doctrinal history never tried to do that. Hurst's legal history was real history, history connected to context, to real life. Hurst's legal history may not have been, in itself, inclusive, but it helped to lay the foundations that made a new, more inclusive legal history possible. It freed legal history from the deadweight of arid tradition. It joined legal history to the mainstream of historical research—made it a kind of tributary stream. As the mainstream shifted, so did legal history. Now, many years later, it is fitting and proper to read Hurst as a classic: not as the last word, or the latest word, but as himself part of a historical moment; we can look at his work as if frozen in amber. The dead cannot come back to revise their work. They have no way to bring it up to date. In that regard, Dirk Hartog is right to read Hurst as a product of Hurst's own period; any classic historian has to be read and understood that way. Hartog's essay is brilliant and thought-provoking. But, it too is a product of its time—our own time—and I found its tone (to be perfectly honest) somewhat jarring; as jarring, perhaps, as the "we" that makes his students so uncomfortable.

Willard's *The Growth of American Law,* his first major book, came out in 1950. That was seventy years ago. Since then, a great deal has happened to the field. A great deal, of course, has happened in America. And what happens in American life determines what historians are interested in; it shapes their point of view, whether they know it or not. The current crop of legal historians—a pretty impressive bunch, I must say—are no longer Willard Hurst's children or grandchildren. Not merely because they have broadened the field, not merely because of their deep involvement with people and subjects he left out or minimized: issues of race and gender, issues of sexual behavior, immigration and immigrants, Native peoples, and all of the rest. More fundamentally, because they are *historians,* not men and women with law degrees who were somehow attracted to legal history. They have PhDs; they were trained as historians; compared to the older generation, they have a different reference group, look to different models, have different mentors, and different criteria. The older generation of non-PhDs is dying out. They did a good job, they laid a foundation; now it's time to turn the job over to the newcomers. The new historians tend to have law degrees as well. They are comfortable in two worlds, like people who carry two passports. They understand the trends and ideas of academic history. At the same time, they have the technical skill to handle legal materials; and they understand the law school world. On the whole, this is a wholesome development. On the whole. Not entirely, of course, but for the most part yes.

The Wisconsin Idea: Law and Society

Willard Hurst's work was essentially about the nineteenth century, with special emphasis on Wisconsin. But at the law school, as I mentioned, he had a broad influence, and not just on legal history. He exercised what today might be called soft power. He influenced, in the first place, simply by being incredibly helpful and collegial. But also through the power of his ideas, attitudes, and methods. The law and society movement owes a great deal to him. Frank Remington and his team, encouraged and nurtured at Wisconsin, had an impact on criminology and the empirical study of criminal justice, as this book demonstrates in detail. The legal process course was historical; but it was socio-legal history, and the socio part was absolutely crucial.

The law and society movement, as I said, was much indebted to Wisconsin. In the law school, Stewart Macaulay was a young star. I mentioned the sociology department, where Jack Ladinsky, Harry Ball, and others were active. Indeed, sociologists were behind the founding of the Law and Society Association; sociologists began the practice of annual meetings. It was a small band of scholars, at first; but since the 1950s and the 1960s, LSA has grown greatly. In terms of numbers, the movement is more of a success story than the legal history movement. Thousands of participants attend the annual meetings of LSA; hundreds attend the annual meetings of the American Society for Legal History. Yet in the law schools, in many ways, the opposite situation holds true. Legal history has found a home in dozens of law schools. At least four faculty members at my own school, Stanford, are primarily identified as legal historians. Legal history is well represented at all of the elite law schools. But law and society, or the sociology of law, makes a much weaker showing in the legal academy. At least that is my impression. To be sure, empirical research, quantitative and qualitative studies, and the findings of social scientists have percolated into the teaching of many law professors, and are well represented in the major law reviews. Like the character in Moliere, who hadn't realized he had been speaking prose all his life, there are droves of law professors who do law and society work, or make use of it, without pinning the label on themselves.

Moreover, as is well known, law and economics made a big splash in the law school world. The early devotees were, if anything, hostile to the other social sciences, and thus hostile to the law and society movement. Their work was largely theoretical. Still, it was a rejection of orthodox legal scholarship. The current generation of economists is more behavioral and empirical. Many schools have courses in law and economics, or economic analysis of law. And yet, in these same law schools, despite all the new hires with PhDs, there are few courses frankly labeled "law and society" or "sociology of law." Here too it would nice if the Wisconsin Idea had more traction.

To sum up: the four innovative courses, which this book celebrates, richly deserve the praise. They remind us of the soundness of the Wisconsin Idea. What the school did, what it accomplished, and what it stood for during its golden age remains impressive, after all these years. The materials in this book illustrate an important chapter in the history of legal education. And in the history of legal research and legal thought. I hope that it will give, to this remarkable period of a remarkable school, something of the credit it deserves.

Stanford, California
August, 2021

Preface

William Clune

This book is a collection of papers and interviews written for an event honoring Professor Herman Goldstein who has since passed away.[1] It is about four innovative courses, including Goldstein's, developed by faculty of the Wisconsin Law School from 1950-1970.[2] These courses reflected the goals of legal realism, an emphasis on law in action, and the growing importance of social science and empirical research (law and social science).

Legal realism was a movement among law professors in the 1920s and 1930s that criticized legal education for its exclusive focus on appellate judicial decisions and legal reasoning. One criticism was that the logical method of legal reasoning in decisions of that time obscured reactionary political agendas. Realists urged equally logical but more progressive and fact-oriented analysis (progressive in the sense of more tolerant of worker protection, etc.). Another was that the narrow perspective of appellate cases left out the greatest part of the legal system. Omitted aspects included how lawyers and clients actually made decisions at the ground level considering law on the books as one aspect of their decisions. How much law weighs in decisions where it is relevant differs greatly depending on other pressures and incentives operating in very different contexts. A lawyer who specializes in financial transactions said that it is more about

---

[1] See the paper by Michael Scott in this volume. Herman Goldstein recently passed at age 88. In Malcolm Feeley's words, "We have lost a treasure."

In a career that spanned more than five decades, Goldstein would go on to change the way police look at crime. His contributions to modern policing — outlined in the books *Policing a Free Society* (1977) and *Problem-Oriented Policing* (1990), as well as many articles — won worldwide acclaim. Most recently, he received the 2018 Stockholm Prize in Criminology, an international award that has been called the Nobel Prize of criminology. "We want to move more and more to … where we don't do unnecessary damage in the course of trying to do good," Goldstein said in 2017. "And we reach out to people and to the community in ways that ultimately have an effect that is both effective and fair." https://news.wisc.edu/policing-pioneer-law-school-professor-herman-goldstein-dies-at-88/

[2] (1) Legal History by Willard Hurst
(2) Criminal Justice Administration by Frank Remington, Herman Goldstein and colleagues
(3) The Wisconsin Contracts course by Stewart Macaulay, Bill Whitford and colleagues
(4) Legal Process by Willard Hurst, Lloyd Garrison, Carl Auerbach and colleagues.

All four courses continued at Wisconsin or nationally from that early time to the present.

"lore" than the law, referring to the customs and norms of various kinds of deal making (which are learned by lawyers on the job).

It was as if the traditional method of legal instruction took place in the penthouse of a tall building, with a limited view of the ground below, and consisted of logical discussions between law professors, rather an expanded view based on empirical knowledge. It is true that legal reasoning is the "language" for lawyers and judges involved in appellate arguments. Moot court arguments in law schools are realistic for that kind of practice. Trial courts are close to the ground and are strongly influenced by the facts before them and local context. But court decisions as a whole offer a narrow perspective, for example, on how most contracts are made and enforced, how the criminal justice system operates and affects the public, and how the policies affecting our lives are made and change over time.

Why decisions are made is an empirical question, a question about facts, which cannot be understood through the logical method of legal reasoning. Research is one way to acquire empirical knowledge (legal practice being another), and the realists did some empirical research funded by grants. Early research on bankruptcy found that bankruptcy trial courts did not seize the assets of farmers who required credit, instead extending credit to harvest time, but did promptly seize the assets to pay debts accrued through stock speculation or gambling. Early studies of the criminal justice system found that the overwhelming majority of cases were resolved through expedited plea bargaining before trial, contrary to the initial assumptions of the researchers that the main problem with the criminal justice system was delay from inefficient administration of criminal trials.

The early tradition of empirical research on the legal system has been greatly expanded in modern times both in law schools and social science departments. In this way early legal realism evolved into the modern tradition of research on law in action, sociology of law, law and social sciences. Malcolm Feeley, one of the authors in this book and a former member of the UW Political Science department, is a good example of the transition with his book *The Process is the Punishment* (Russell Sage Foundation, 1992), which found that the greatest punishment for those accused of lesser crimes was not fines and imprisonment, but rather pretrial costs, like lost wages, commissions to bail bondsmen, and attorneys' fees. He found that the most important goal of those accused, and for criminal justice, was to minimize the time and money spent dealing with criminal justice administration before trial.

The shift toward law and social science was momentous. The realist view of how lawyers and clients actually make decisions (taking the law into account) is a view both from inside and outside the legal system. Introduction of something "beyond the text" can be experienced by students and professors as "not law" or "sociology not law." (See the interviews for discussion of this point.) And yet realism/law and social science has profoundly influenced legal instruction, and "text only" now seems like a barren alternative. Many traditional law professors will venture outside the text for an explanation of the historical background and policy arguments surrounding a particular rule without worrying about inside and outside the text.[3]

The four courses described in this book were developed during a time of extraordinary policy innovation following the New Deal and the end of World War II. The New Deal was in its own way a culmination of legal realism, with its many administrative agencies staffed by experts with detailed knowledge of the regulated industries, and its sweeping progressive emphasis. Administrative agencies are closer to the ground than appellate judicial decisions. Several New Dealers taught on the UW faculty during this period, including Nathan Feinsinger (associate general counsel to the National War Labor Board and general counsel to the Wisconsin Labor Relations Board), Jake Beuscher (Office of Price Administration, later teaching land use and environment), Carl Auerbach (Office of Price Stabilization), Samuel Mermin (Bituminous Coal Act), and Willard Hurst who worked with the Department of the Navy and the Justice Department during WWII on the law of treason, and in typical Hurst fashion published the results in three *Harvard Law Review* articles and a book.

Hurst considered his Legal Process materials and book (first named *Law in Society*) both as his first work in economic legal history *and* as one of the pioneers in legal process/administrative law. He developed the course with Dean Lloyd Garrison and coauthored a later edition with Carl Auerbach and Samuel Mermin. Garrison had hired Hurst and encouraged him to work on something different. This was innovation as a conscious policy, which was true of the other courses as well. The Legal Process book traced legal decision-making across areas of law over time around a common problem, the allocation of the burden of industrial accidents. The book told the story from nineteenth-century England until the birth of workers' compensation (in Wisconsin) through materials for study that included cases, legislation, and administrative regulations and practice. The problem of industrial accidents was addressed first by courts, then legislatures, then by administrative agencies, and finally by the manifold interactions across agencies, courts, legislature, and the executive. Early

3 Professor Hartog adds: Inside/outside is a heuristic and an extraordinarily helpful one, even as the realists always knew that nothing stayed on one or the other side of the line. Contract law is incomprehensible without a moral and political economy of values and assumptions. See the addendum to Hartog's paper and the summary below. A constitutive theory of law seeks to avoid the view that law is either autonomous from or completely determined by society in favor of an interactive relationship between law and society in which each has influence on but is not reducible to the other. Michael Osborne, "Explorations in Law and Society: Toward a Constitutive Theory of Law" (1995), 4 *Dal J Leg Stud* 293.

judicial cases such as the fellow servant rule recognized the problem but were administratively cumbersome and riddled with impractical exceptions. Thus, the enormous number of accidents created by the industrial revolution were eventually addressed with a more flexible and speedy administrative process.

Hurst was in many ways the godfather of the innovative period, for example, obtaining foundation grants for other faculty members. But each of the other teachers had their own lineage and established their own traditions of law school teaching. Herman Goldstein started work with Frank Remington on the American Bar Foundation survey of criminal justice in 1956. That study had a large influence on the Criminal Justice Administration course at Wisconsin and Goldstein's later work on problem-oriented policing. Stewart Macaulay was teaching contracts and working on the supplement that became the Contracts Law in Action course when Bill Whitford was hired in 1965 and joined him in that effort.

The rest of this book consists of four papers and five interviews conducted by me. I wondered if the interviews were too rambling and chatty. But they add an element of freshness and dialogue. More important, they overflow with essential and illuminating details about points made in a more general way in the papers and about how the courses are taught. A compelling example is the long interview with Professors Macaulay and Whitford about their course Contracts Law in Action. General points I make in my paper about that course are vividly illustrated, and many aspects of contract law which I did not understand are clarified. For me the interview was a mini-course in this innovative approach to contracts law. Regarding the current version of the Remington/Goldstein approach being taught currently at Wisconsin Law School, Professor Lawrence Friedman says in his Foreword to this book:

> When I read the interview with Cecelia Klingele and Keith Findley, in this book, I couldn't help thinking, what a wonderful course they teach. What a wonderful experience for the students. Do they realize how different this course is, how rich in experiential learning? I am sure the instructors do. But their course, as they admit, is hardly typical of law school teaching on criminal law and criminal procedure. Law teachers, they admit, still tend to be "very doctrinal," still tend to be "very, very far removed from reality."

Summaries of the papers and interviews are given below.

Paper by Emeritus Professor Clune. My paper is an overview of the four courses and the influence of legal realism/law in action. It is organized around eight crosscutting themes characteristic of legal realism, with examples, such as the importance of practical remedies over theoretical rights, how private actors take account of law in their decisions, the growth of legal policies over time, the gap between legal outcomes and social needs (progressivism), and the importance of empirical and interdisciplinary research.

Paper by Professor Malcolm Feeley. Malcolm Feeley's paper is about the significance and impact of Frank Remington and Herman Goldstein's research on criminal justice administration flowing from the large American Bar Foundation project on the administration of national justice in the 1950s (funded by the Ford Foundation). The focus of the project was revolutionary for its time: a study of the discretion exercised by public officials at every stage of the criminal justice system: police, prosecutors, bail bondsmen, probation officers, lawyers, and judges. The goals of the project, to produce a new type of scholar of criminal law and to improve the administration of justice, were richly achieved.

Paper by Professor Dirk Hartog. This paper has three fragments or parts: first, an overview of what is it like to do legal history today, second, Willard Hurst's distinctive and innovative view of legal history, with its omissions and flaws, and, third, notwithstanding these flaws, the reasons why Hurst's work is admired and relevant to this day. Hartog taught legal history at Wisconsin while Hurst was an emeritus professor, considers Hurst a mentor, and has regularly assigned readings from Hurst in his own courses. In an addendum to his paper, Hartog urges thinking of legal history as an "accompaniment" rather than as a part of academic law, a perspective that he sees as compatible with Hurst. Hurst's work did not express an inside or outside view of law. Rather, he saw law as ever an expression of culture, law as constitutive of society, and society constitutive of law (in this way prefiguring critical legal studies). His great study of the lumber industry was meant to describe a particular set of legal and social practices but also to represent a fragment of the larger culture. Even apparently oppositional and resistant legal episodes contain both hegemonic and oppositional cultures, for example, the modern tradition of constitutional rights as counter-majoritarian (as does the simple exercise of legal representation in criminal prosecutions).

Paper by Professor Michael Scott. A fitting tribute to Herman Goldstein, this paper traces the influence of Goldstein on Professor Michael Scott himself, legal education, the police, and society. Scott began his contact with Goldstein while writing an undergraduate thesis at University of Wisconsin-Madison and subsequently taught Goldstein's courses at UW Law School including Problem-Oriented Policing. He is presently the Director of the Center for Problem-Oriented Policing at Arizona State

University, a research center that produces and disseminates information about how police can effectively and fairly address specific public-safety problems. The center has published guidebooks on seventy-five different problems each with its own analysis of references, situational criminology, and suggested problem-solving. Regarding impact on the police, the goal of problem-oriented policing (POP) is to make policing more effective and fair without over-reliance on law enforcement and the exercise of coercive authority. In terms of legal education, the courses taught at UW Law School by Goldstein and Scott recognized that police treated formal law (on the books) as a tool used to achieve particular goals of policing. Students need to know the nature of police business, the various goals and objectives of police, and the multitude of incentives and disincentives that push and pull police officers toward some actions and away from others. In terms of impact on society, especially in these days of Black Lives Matter, Goldstein well understood that fair treatment of all people was fundamental to policing and that citizens' quality of life depended on it. He noted the numerous ways in which police commonly mistreated members of minority communities. Problem-oriented policing itself is a valuable approach to police reform, for example, as it encourages police to seek and out and listen to the concerns of minority communities and to think of responses beyond criminal law enforcement, such as informal conflict resolution, conveying information to discourage problem behavior, issuing warnings, reinforcing informal social control, altering the physical environment, bringing in needed social services and other community resources, and protecting high-risk victims. In this, it draws heavily from the criminological field of situational crime prevention.

Interview with Professor Dirk Hartog. The interview with Dirk Hartog, which supplements his paper, discusses how the field of legal history has changed since Hurst. A large secondary literature has appeared within and outside law schools, and many more legal historians have been appointed. The field has also moved in new directions such as gender and sexuality, race and the significance of the Civil War, borderland citizenship, and viewing legal history through the lens of imperialism, colonialism, and Atlantic World studies. Over the last thirty years, Hurst's interest in the history of capitalism and economic growth diminished, but in the last ten years it has become central again through the lens of slavery studies, particularly the debate over whether slavery and slave law were capitalist or anti-capitalist. Interestingly, some of Professor Hartog's Indian students see his work as relevant to post-colonial history in India. In retrospect, Hurst's work has strengths and weaknesses. In framing the history of capitalism, he largely ignored oppressed and unrepresented groups, but he did recognize the ruthless greed of the communal "we" that plundered the northern forest. His brilliance came in framing lawmaking as an exercise of improvised social construction cutting across doctrinal areas guided by an underlying consensus of economic liberty and constraints. At the deepest level, Hurst posed a social consensus around middle-class goals and constitutionalism encompassing the entire regulatory legal process which while full of contradiction and drift did have a common vector around these goals. Both sides of the consensus, middle-class goals and regulation, still exist to this day, for example, freed slaves and later generations of African Americans strove and succeeded in becoming middle class in a legal environment which alternatively blocked and enabled them.

Interview with the late Professor Herman Goldstein. Herman Goldstein's interview is the first of three in the criminal justice areas. The interview discusses the impact of the American Bar Foundation study of the criminal justice system on the innovative criminal law courses developed at Wisconsin. Four radical changes from the previous model of teaching criminal procedure (which mainly covered Supreme Court cases) were: (1) the idea of an interconnected system, from first contact with the police all the way through to parole and corrections, (2) the pervasive role of low visibility discretion at every stage, (3) the differential impact of police interventions on different groups of people (e.g., homosexuals, poor, and minorities), and (4) the importance of distinct behavioral problems as to what occurs in the criminal justice system (e.g., street prostitution and public intoxication).

Interview with Professors Macaulay and Whitford. This rich and extensive interview with Stewart Macaulay and Bill Whitford is about their Contracts Law in Action materials and course book. A law in action approach to contracts can be understood as an empirically oriented alternative to conventional casebooks that feature contract-formation (offer, acceptance, etc.) and doctrinal analysis. The Macaulay/Whitford book begins with remedies which severely constrain the empirical odds of successful litigation. Lawsuits based on lost profit ("you promised to give me money") or expectation damages almost never succeed because of a variety of defenses, such as the obligation to mitigate damages, reasonably foreseeable damages, and others. The rule that successful parties do not recover the costs of litigation means that many recoveries are not financially worthwhile. Restitution as a remedy is based on a distinct conception of damages (restoration of losses). Other law in action themes are relational contracts (e.g., long-term supply contracts), inconsistency of doctrines (doctrine and counter-doctrine), the contextual background of cases, and the dominance of more powerful parties. Relational contracts between parties whose transactions are embedded in ongoing relationships, such as employment, marriage, and commercial supply agreements, are based on trust rather than legalities, and disputes are usually resolved through negotiation rather than litigation. At the other extreme is unequal bargaining power. The dominance of one party to contracts over the other party, characteristic of consumer transactions and employment, means that consent of the less powerful party is a formality, and the more powerful party has virtually all practical rights and remedies (including binding arbitration). The Wisconsin Progressive tradition can be seen in attention to cases and legislation that attempted to redress imbalances of power (e.g., restrictions on do-not-compete clauses and automotive lemon laws) which are sometimes successful but often unsuccessful because of the legislative and judicial influence of powerful elites in legislatures and courts.

Interview with Professors Klingele and Findley. The interview with Professors Cecelia Klingele and Keith Findley, the second on criminal justice, is about the course they teach, Introduction to Criminal Procedure, which is the modern version of the course on Criminal Justice Administration developed by Remington and Goldstein. Whereas traditional courses in criminal procedure are organized doctrinally (Fourth Amendment, Fifth Amendment, and Sixth Amendment), this course is organized sequentially and introduces Supreme Court cases as they relate to each phase. The course covers the important Supreme Court cases as they relate to the chronological stages, but fewer cases are included than in traditional courses because these cases are considered as remote from the real practice of criminal law and are rarely encountered in discussions with practitioners. The course emphasizes the central role of discretionary decision-making. Discretionary decision-making feels uncertain for students, as discretion is a difficult concept involving reasoned judgment between competing legal principles, as opposed to arbitrary, unmoored or biased judgments. In the final examination for the course, students must engage with the legal sources that guide discretion, such as the supplemental statute pack, ethical principles, and ABA standards. Students have direct experience of how discretion operates through non-classroom activities such as police ride-alongs and simulated plea bargaining. Practice plea bargaining is assisted by the observations and commentary of prosecutors, judges, and defense lawyers. In addition, four evening discussion panels are mandatory—on policing (with police chiefs), prosecutors, defense attorneys, and judges. Panelists discuss their roles and the exercise of discretion. Students ask questions.

Interview with Emeritus Professor Walter Dickey. Walter Dickey's interview is the third on criminal justice. Dickey took Remington's Criminal Justice Administration course as a student and taught the updated version when he joined the faculty in 1976 and began collaborating with Frank Remington and Herman Goldstein. Dickey observes that both Remington and Goldstein were interested in teaching the course as a study of how to make the criminal justice system more fair and effective in reducing threats to public safety with the least possible harmful side effects. The starting place was the behaviors that came to the attention of law enforcement. The course was organized to encourage analysis of a set of common questions: what is the behavior that attracts law enforcement, how does law enforcement learn of the behavior, what is the response, how fair and effective is the response, and how authority could be conferred in a more effective manner.

Madison, Wisconsin
August, 2021

LEGAL REALISM
to
LAW IN ACTION

INNOVATIVE LAW COURSES AT UW-MADISON

Legal Realist Innovation in the Wisconsin Law School Curriculum 1950–1970: Four Influential Introductory Courses

William Clune

Abstract

This paper is about four courses developed by faculty of the Wisconsin Law School from about 1950–1970 that reflected the law in action instructional goals of American legal realism: Legal History by Willard Hurst; Criminal Justice Administration by Frank Remington, Herman Goldstein and colleagues; The Wisconsin Contracts course by Stewart Macaulay, Bill Whitford and colleagues; and Legal Process by Willard Hurst, Lloyd Garrison, Carl Auerbach and colleagues. Eight themes in the courses are discussed:

1. Major flaws in the legal reasoning of appellate decisions (e.g., as internally incoherent, un-predictive of later results, politically biased under the guise of formal reasoning)

2. The importance of practical remedies over theoretical rights

3. The importance of legal agencies and law practice beyond appellate and other court decisions (e.g., legislation and administrative law)

4. The importance and impact of discretionary decisions of lower-level public officials (for lawyers and citizens)

5. How private actors react to law and influence outcomes (and the role of lawyers in advising them)

6. Growth of legal policies over time in relationship to the wider society and economy (legal history)

7. The gap between social needs and justice in the outcomes of law, as compared to workable legal reforms (political progressivism)

8. The importance of empirical research on law, interdisciplinary research, and social scientists on law school faculties or in collaboration with law faculty members.

Legal Realist Innovation in the Wisconsin Law School Curriculum 1950–1970: Four Influential Introductory Courses

This paper is about four courses developed by faculty of the Wisconsin Law School from about 1950–1970 that reflected the law in action instructional goals of American legal realism:

- Legal History by Willard Hurst
- Criminal Justice Administration by Frank Remington, Herman Goldstein, and colleagues
- The Wisconsin Contracts course by Stewart Macaulay, Bill Whitford, and colleagues
- Legal Process by Willard Hurst, Lloyd Garrison, Carl Auerbach, and colleagues.[1]

All four courses continued as offerings in the Wisconsin curriculum for many years, in two instances up to the present time (contracts and criminal justice), and have had widespread national influence.

It has been said that each new generation of children is an arrival by (adorable) little barbarians who must be civilized before it is too late. The same could be said of law professors. When I arrived as a new law professor in 1971, having come from the Russell Sage supported JD and PhD programs at Northwestern, I was more familiar with some of the teacher/scholars discussed here than others, and I definitely felt well placed in a supportive environment sympathetic to law and social science. But I had

[1] Course books used by the authors at various dates of publication are: Frank Remington, Donald Newman, Edward Kimball, Herman Goldstein & Walter Dickey, *Criminal Justice Administration* (1982) (1st edition was 1969, preceded by materials); Herman Goldstein, *Problem-Oriented Policing* (1990); James Willard Hurst, *The Growth of American Law* (1950), *Law and the Conditions of Freedom in the 19th Century United States* (1956); Carl Auerbach, Lloyd Garrison, Willard Hurst & Samuel Mermin, *The Legal Process, An Introduction to Decision-Making by Judicial, Legislative, Executive, and Administrative Agencies* (1961). The edition of the Remington course currently being taught at Wisconsin is Cecelia Klingele & Keith Findley, *Criminal Justice Administration*; Stewart Macaulay, William Whitford, Kathryn Hendley & Jonathan Lipson, *Contracts: Law in Action* (4th ed., Carolina Academic Press, 2016). Macaulay, John Kidwell, and Whitford were coeditors of three editions. Marc Galanter was a coeditor of the first edition, before his retirement. Jean Braucher, of Arizona Law School, was added as a coeditor of the third edition. Both Kidwell and Braucher have since passed away. Kathryn Hendley (Wisconsin) and Jonathan Lipson (Temple) have been added as editors for the fourth edition. Both have used the casebook for many years. The first edition of the casebook was published in 1995. The Wisconsin Supplement which preceded the casebook began in the late 1960s. See Macaulay & Whitford, "The Development of Contracts Law in Action," 47 *Temple L. Rev.* 793 (2015).

little sense of how the institution I was joining was built— not the achievements of Willard Hurst (never having had a course in legal history), nor of Frank Remington's path-breaking role in criminal justice, nor how a contracts course could be shaped by empirical legal studies. I knew vaguely of legal realism, having been assigned but barely understanding Karl Llewellyn's *Bramble Bush*[2] as a summer reading before law school (the importance of facts I still remember). To that extent, I was a highly educated barbarian. Doing the research for this article as an Emeritus Professor so long after arrival has been a pleasure, a revelation, and a source of appreciation. Not for nothing do educators speak of lifelong learning.

The wide-ranging scope of this paper has understably raised questions about its boundaries: e.g., why seemingly related things are not included. It is about the four courses as curriculum and instruction and not about the universe of related socio-legal research. The focus is the period 1950-1970 when the courses were created and not about faculty, research, and other developments post-1970.[3]

The paper is organized as follows: 1) a contrast between legal realist and traditional goals for legal instruction, 2) examples of the legal realist goals from the Wisconsin courses, 3) how Wisconsin became a realist-friendly environment, and 4) a conclusion about the extent of legal realist influence on the modern law school curriculum and the importance of legal history as a law school subject.

The contrast between legal realist and traditional goals for legal instruction

The traditional course and casebook that have been the mainstay of legal education from the time of Dean Christopher Columbus Langdell of the Harvard Law School around 1900 consist in pure form of appellate judicial cases that are analyzed doctrinally through the logic of legal reasoning aimed at understanding prevailing and alternative interpretations of legal rules. In the first half of the twentieth century, legal realists mounted a vigorous critique of the traditional casebook and doctrinal

[2] A recent edition is Karl N. Llewellyn, *The Bramble Bush: On Our Law and Its Study*, Foreword by Stewart Macaulay (Quid Pro Books, 2012).

[3] Exceptions beyond this scope but integral to this paper are: descriptions of more recent versions of the four courses and their instructors up to the present time; in the case of legal history, references to the kind of research that changed the focus of that course over time; references needed to clarify the relevance of legal realism to the four courses; and a few other closely related topics. For example, Professors David Trubek, Howard Erlanger, and Mitra Sharafi on the Institute for Legal Studies and Hurst Summer Institute, Malcolm Feeley on discretionary decision-making in the criminal justice system. See notes 14 and 43 below.

teaching.[4] Legal concepts and doctrines taught from appellate cases were seen as providing incomplete or misleading guidance about the situations actually encountered by lawyers, clients, and citizens. Doctrinal courses were seen as "law on the books," legal realism as "law in action." In an earlier blog, I said that law in action can be thought of as empirical study of the full range of legal and law-related decisions, appellate cases, trial cases, lawyers' strategies, clients' decisions, police conduct, corporate managers' decisions about litigation, lawyers' decisions about commercial transactions, and so forth.[5] Empirical analysis examines the decisions and their consequences and the full range of influences motivating and constraining them, such as more or less reliance on legal precedent and text, pragmatic assessment of facts, subjective values, cultural and organizational influences, economic incentives, and disparities in power and resources. Realism also had a normative element: the evaluation of decisions against policy goals, standards of justice, and social welfare—as when Roscoe Pound calledupon law to meet social needs in his coining of the term law in action[6] and when Llewellyn said that contract law should promote security of transactions.[7]

The practical irrelevance of traditional casebooks can be overstated. Jerome Frank quipped that teaching legal practice from appellate cases was like teaching dog training using stuffed dogs, but traditional casebooks would not have survived if they had no practical value. Doctrinal law courses are introductory surveys of areas of law that facilitate explanations of the policy objectives, purposes, and intent underlying the law and its sub-parts. The knowledge acquired can be thought of as a set of tools applicable in different situations. Many situations that arise in practice require an understanding of how different aspects of the same body of law interrelate in a coordinated fashion. One basic skill taught in law classes is the ability to distinguish the precise holding of a case as judicial precedent based on its facts from more expansive dicta on its significance for similar cases. A related skill is alternative interpretations of cases and statutes as

---

4 Llewellyn, "A Realistic Jurisprudence — The Next Step," *Columbia Law Review*, Vol. 30, No. 4 (Apr., 1930), pp. 431-465, stable URL: http://www.jstor.org/stable/1114548; Schlegel, J.H. (1995), *American Legal Realism and Empirical Social Science* (University of North Carolina Press, Chapel Hill & London); Kalman, Laura, *Legal Realism at Yale*_(University of North Carolina Press, 1986).

5 http://newlegalrealism.org/2013/06/12/law-in-action-and-law-on-the-books-a-primer/

6 R. Pound, "Law in Books and Law in Action," 44 *Am. L. Rev.* 12 (1910).

7 "I would not be understood thereby to deny that those three words are highly useful, or that they refer to very significant aspects of our life. But I am very eager to be understood as questioning how much is accomplished, for any given specific problem, by resting merely on the magic of those words." Llewellyn, op. cit. at 445.

applied to different fact patterns. In addition to these advantages, traditional courses have survived for pragmatic reasons, such as that they are suitable for large classes (e.g., economical compared to medical education), offer a structured narrative amenable for group discussion, and support a sense of shared professional identity among law professors and students.[8] As Professor Dirk Hartog said in his interview with me, appellate decisions can be an important part of legal history (e.g., *Brown v. Board of Education* and other civil rights cases).

The sharp contrast between traditional and realist instruction has been further blurred in contemporary times because many of the original realist goals have been absorbed and adopted. It is sometimes said that "we are all realists now." Realist skepticism about the formal autonomy of legal rules began quite early, for example, in the practice of counting votes on the Supreme Court rather than seeking overarching logical consistency.[9] Deconstruction of legal reasoning originally pioneered by legal realists as "cognitive relativism" was enormously extended by critical legal studies and has become one of the basic tools of legal analysis.[10] An emphasis on statutory and administrative law pervades the second and third-year curriculum. The first year of law school still mostly emphasizes judge-made common law with exceptions, such as the Uniform Commercial Code in contracts, statutory definitions of crimes in criminal law, and administrative rules governing police conduct in criminal procedure

---

[8] The Wisconsin approach to contracts taught over a 25-year period gives due consideration to the traditional approach by including leading cases, rules and policy considerations conventionally assigned for the rules, and economic efficiency as a policy consideration. Justifications for knowing traditional legal content (law on the books) include that it teaches the language and culture of the field and has some weight in resolving disputes and litigation. This and other information about the course is taken from Macaulay & Whitford, "The Development of Contracts Law in Action," 47 *Temple L. Rev.* 793 (2015), or from my interview with them.

[9] According to Kalman, op. cit., Thomas Reed Powell, who was teaching at Columbia and Harvard Law Schools in the 1920s, said that judicial decisions in cases like minimum wages were the result of economic biases and that there was no such thing as constitutional law, only split decisions of the Supreme Court.

[10] Morton J. Horwitz, The *Transformation of American Law, 1870-1960: The Crisis of Legal Orthodoxy.* A fundamental legal realist critique was that property is itself a creation of law, a bundle of different rights with no resemblance to the simple concept of natural law. Yale law professor Wesley Hohfeld was influential in developing the foundations of cognitive relativism with his 1913 article on jural opposites. https://en.wikipedia.org/wiki/Corelative. His analysis of the opposing elements of legal rights was an exercise of "cognitive relativism" used to deconstruct the idea of property as a monolithic right rooted in natural law (which was an important aspect of nineteenth-century conservative jurisprudence). E.g., the privilege to employ non-union labor did not imply a right to prevent unionization. Legal realist Yale contracts professor Arthur Corbin was supposedly greatly excited by the implication of Hohfeld's work for contracts law. http://www.kentlaw.edu/perritt/courses/property/Hohfeld.htm (link is to an article in the *Wis. L. Rev.*).

courses that take the Remington approach. Instructional innovations such as those pioneered at Wisconsin have become more common in other schools, for example, legal history and varieties of legal process. Most of the policies championed by the realists in their advocacy of progressive legislation have become regular parts of the curriculum (income tax, antitrust, labor law, administrative law, etc.). Law school today is not exactly like the "Euclidean Geometry" experienced by Willard Hurst in Harvard Law School.[11]

Despite these convergent trends, the presence of legal realism is stronger in some law courses than others and especially so in the four exemplary Wisconsin courses.

The instructional goals of legal realism and examples from the Wisconsin courses

The instructional goals of legal realism can be summarized as embodying eight themes:[12]

1. Major flaws in the legal reasoning of appellate decisions (e.g., as internally incoherent, un-predictive of later results, politically biased under the guise of formal reasoning)
2. The importance of practical remedies over theoretical rights
3. The importance of legal agencies and law practice beyond appellate and other court decisions (e.g., legislation and administrative law)
4. The importance and impact of discretionary decisions of lower-level public officials (for lawyers and citizens)
5. How private actors react to law and influence outcomes (and the role of lawyers in advising them)
6. Growth of legal policies over time, in relationship to the wider society & economy (legal history)

---

[11] Hurst graduated in 1935 at the top of his class, clerked for Justice Brandeis, and spent another year assisting Felix Frankfurter with a set of lectures. A courteous, contrarian, innovative, empirically oriented Midwesterner with regal law school credentials.

[12] A longer list from which this list was distilled was: (1) texts v. behavior (2) judicial decisions v. all interactions between government officials and citizens (3) rights v. remedies (4) rules v. application (5) logic v. empiricism (6) predictability of judicial decisions v. unpredictability based on facts, judicial preference, logic of countervailing precedents, etc. (7) single areas of law v. transactions involving multiple areas (8) law as controlling factor v. law with variable impact depending on context (9) policy intent v. implementation (10) regulation nominally applicable to all v. regulation mainly impacting specific groups (11) formal equality of law v. large differences in wealth, power, and access (12) isolated precedent v. continuous legal process (13) existing law v. law reform (14) current law v. historical change (15) library research v. field research and knowledge from practice (16) law professors only v. also professors from other disciplines (e.g., social sciences) (17) law degree only v. joint, specialized, and advanced degrees (18) classroom instruction v. clinical and simulation.

7. The gap between social needs and justice and real legal outcomes and workable legal reforms (political progressivism)
8. The importance of empirical research on law, interdisciplinary research, and social scientists on law school faculties or in collaboration with law faculty members.

Examples of legal-realist goals in the four Wisconsin courses

Here are examples of the eight themes from the four Wisconsin courses:

1. Major flaws in appellate court reasoning

Anti-formalism is one of the main purposes of the Wisconsin contracts course which, while it pays close attention to doctrine, also informs students that the most brilliant legal argument is only one factor in successful litigation.[13] The course includes examples of doctrine and counter-doctrine, such as that the words of the agreement must be honored vs. frustration of purpose. Many cases are "contextualized" by including background on the practical origins and ultimate outcomes of the litigation. In the area of legal history, teachers of legal history at Wisconsin following Hurst, such as Bob Gordon and Dirk Hartog, became national leaders in critical legal studies and critical race and gender research which strongly emphasized the covert policy bias of appellate and trial decisions and the real lived experience of excluded groups.

2. Remedies v. rights

Emphasis on remedies as a limitation of rights is a major aspect of the Wisconsin contracts course. The focus on remedies is a legacy of Lon Fuller's legal realist-oriented research and course book that was the one first taught by Macaulay at Wisconsin (because it had already been adopted when he arrived).

Factors that may limit remedies include:

- Influence of long-term relationships in deterring litigation, encouraging informal bargaining, and providing opportunities for favorable settlements
- Cost and uncertainty of litigation compared with damages expected from winning a case, making litigation a poor investment and hence unlikely

[13] See Macaulay & Whitford, op. cit. note 8 above.

- Considerations of economic efficiency and fairness that typically inform contract remedies and make results unpredictable before individual judges
- Qualitative doctrines common in contract law allowing for a wide range of possible outcomes before an individual judge (e.g., substantial impairment of contract, lack of good faith, basic or less basic conditions, requested damages more or less reasonable)
- Strength of losing parties' position and arguments often not acknowledged by majority opinions on appeal (hence importance of understanding context and history of cases)
- Standardized form contracts written by powerful parties that nullify or modify legal precedents when formally agreed to by less powerful parties

In criminal justice administration, avoidance of coercion, arrest, prosecution, and conviction is the "remedy" of greatest concern to most people.[14] The low-visibility discretion characteristic of all phases of criminal justice administration discussed below in #4 means that the letter of the law is an uncertain guide. Legal representation and financial resources are so important partly because of this pervasive empirical uncertainty. Professors Klingele and Findley say that they tell their students that even if they do not practice criminal law, they likely will receive worried calls from relatives and friends saying that someone has been justly or unjustly arrested (or harmed by police intervention). The statement "no one is above the law" is, as expected by legal realism, simultaneously an ideal of justice, a standard that can be evaded through improper influence, and when flouted, a frightening reminder of arbitrary power. For Klingele and Findley, a primary teaching objective for their students is how to make discretionary decisions guided by appropriate legal standards in every role (judge, prosecutor, defense lawyer, etc.).

3. Lawmaking beyond courts

The Hurst legal process course traces the development of workers' compensation from common law, where recovery was sometimes difficult under doctrines such as the fellow servant rule, through the enactment of workers' compensation legislation and administration. The book is credited by Peter Strauss in his law review article on "Langdell and the

---

14 See Malcolm Feeley, *The Process is the Punishment* (Russell Sage Foundation, 1992). The greatest punishment for those accused of lesser crimes is not fines and imprisonment but pretrial costs like lost wages, commissions to bail bondsmen, and attorneys' fees. Therefore, the most important goal of the accused is to minimize the time and money spent dealing with criminal justice administration before trial.

Public Law Curriculum"[15] with being among the few early examples, along with Hart and Sacks, of texts that included extensive non-judicial materials such as statutory law and administrative regulations. Strauss maintains that legislation, administrative rules, and administrative adjudications in their original form, not viewed through the lens of courts and appellate cases, are the bread and butter of legal practice for most lawyers. The Hurst tradition of legal process at Wisconsin was succeeded by another legal process book and course taught and coauthored by George Bunn.[16] Professor Mark Tushnet taught legal process while he was at Wisconsin and has coauthored a policy-oriented book in a course at Harvard Law School.[17]

4. Discretionary decisions of public officials

The importance and impact of discretionary decisions of lower-level public officials was virtually the main theme of the innovative Remington course in Criminal Justice Administration and remains so to this day in the course as presently taught by Professors Klingele and Findley. The Remington book and course, coauthored and taught by Professor Herman Goldstein, became the foundation of the closely related and immensely influential fields of problem-oriented and community policing, which deal with how police and other public officials can reduce the occurrence of crime through problem-solving rather than relying exclusively on law enforcement, and was, like the administration course itself, influential in both academic instruction and the real world of policy and practice.[18] A fundamental premise of the Criminal Justice Administration course is that the vast majority of encounters of the average person with the criminal justice system occur with police and prosecutors prior to trial, and the vast majority of formal charges that are brought end with a plea bargain. Only a tiny fraction go to trial. Topics include the decision to investigate, investigative methods, use of force by the police, plea bargaining, and the role of the lawyer in the decision to charge and plea negotiations. Like its predecessors, the current course explores "the many low visibility points at which discretion is exercised, a characteristic of the system at virtually

15 Peter L. Strauss, Review Essay: "Christopher Columbus Langdell and the Public Law Curriculum," *Journal of Legal Education*, vol. 66, no. 1 (2016), 157-185.

16 Hans A. Linde and George Bunn, *Legislative and Administrative Process* (Foundation Press, 1976).

17 Lisa Heinzerling & Mark Tushnet, *The Regulatory and Administrative State* (2006).

18 Herman Goldstein, *Problem-Oriented Policing* (McGraw-Hill, 1990); Herman Goldstein, *Policing a Free Society* (Ballinger Publishing, 1977).

every important decision-making point" and the critical role of lawyers in assuring the principled rather than untethered exercise of discretion.[19] Leading Supreme Court cases are included, but more attention is paid to other legal sources such as administrative rules governing police behavior. So great has been the impact of the Remington approach that it led to the enactment of administrative rules governing police discretion in law enforcement.

5. Private actors and the law

Private actors' reactions to law and lawyers' advising them is a major topic of the Wisconsin contracts course with its emphasis on relational contracting. Stewart Macaulay's pathbreaking research on this topic[20] led to its inclusion in the Wisconsin Supplement that eventually evolved into the contracts course book.[21] Relational contracts, which are formed and performed in a context in which the contract is only one aspect of the relationship between the parties, typically involve non-legal norms and sanctions that are respected by the parties, rarely lead to litigation, do not specify details which might undermine trust and interfere with subsequent flexible problem-solving, and present many implicit understandings not stated in writing (and problems for contract interpretation). Relational contracts appear everywhere in the business world, for example, long-term supply contracts dominated by either sellers or buyers. In his article on the new legal realism, Macaulay seems correct in saying that private actors' responses to law represent an additional "tier" of legal realism beyond the actions of public officials (part of Ehrlich's "living law").[22] That insight applies far beyond contracts, for example, in virtually every business transaction, which often implicate multiple areas of law (tax, antitrust, banking, sales, bankruptcy, etc.), but which are guided and governed as much by custom and context as by law. It also applies to the just mentioned universe of low-visibility discretionary decisions made by parties and lawyers as the paramount characteristic of the criminal justice system. Hence, contrary to the idea that this "living law tier of legal realism" does not involve lawyers, lawyers play an important role at least where citizens

---

19 Cecelia Klingele & Keith Findley, *Introduction to Criminal Procedure,* Preface (E-book at University of Wisconsin Law School).

20 Macaulay, S. (1963), "Non-Contractual Relations in Business: A Preliminary Study," *American Sociological Review,* vol. 28, no. 1.

21 Macaulay, S. & Whitford, W., "The Development of Contracts: Law in Action," 87 *Temple L. Rev.* 793 (2015).

22 Macaulay, S., The New Versus the Old Legal Realism: "Things Ain't What They Used to Be," *Wisconsin Law Review,* vol. 2005, no. 2, pp. 365-403 (2005).

can afford legal representation. On the other hand, vast areas of both contract and criminal law involve clients who are unrepresented and face powerful opposing parties, in the case of contracts of adhesion, or the intimidating power of the state in law enforcement. All of us participate in such contracts when we click "agree" online or sign long boilerplate forms that bind us to all sorts of things we barely understand like waivers of liability, non-disclosure and non-compete clauses, and mandatory arbitration of disputes.

In a broad perspective, the role of law in affecting individual behavior is shaped by what Sally Falk Moore called semi-autonomous social fields.[23] Individuals occupy social fields (cultures, organizations, etc.) with customs, rules, and incentives that influence individual behavior. Formal organizations—business corporations, governments, non-profits, and the like—are so ubiquitous, and have such a powerful influence on how laws operate in practice, that often "the bottom controls the top."[24]

6. Growth of legal policies over time

Legal history is a field virtually invented by Willard Hurst.[25] The relatively small number of legal historians prior to Hurst focused mainly on Supreme Court decisions. Hurst's wide-ranging interest on the growth of multiple legal institutions (federal and state legislatures, federal, state, and local courts, the executive branch, the Bar) and the relationship of law and the economy became a model for his many successors who greatly expanded the scope of the field. Equally influential was his meticulous empirical research method based on painstaking examination of original legal sources. Hurst's great interest was the relationship between law and the economy, specifically in the formative period of the nineteenth century. His first major work in this field was on the history of workers' compensation law that led to the Legal Process course (originally titled Law in

---

23 Moore, Sally Falk. "Law and Social Change: The Semi-Autonomous Social Field as an Appropriate Subject of Study," *Law and Society Review*, vol. 7, no. 4 (summer, 1973), 719-746. Cf. Niklas Luhmann's theory of autopoiesis in self-referential social systems where communications reproduce communications. https://www.zfog.bwl.uni-muenchen.de/files/mitarbeiter/paper2004_2.pdf.

24 Much of my research dealt with the implementation of government policies in organizations, school finance, and education policy, often published in social science and educational journals, books, book chapters, working papers, etc. Such venues can be problematic for social science researchers on law faculties, and for law schools, when productivity and reputation are measured by law review publications, ironically, a good example of law schools as semi-autonomous social fields.

25 Hurst published over three dozen books and articles, plus numerous book reviews. See https://law.wisc.edu/ils/works_by_hurst.html.

Society), coauthored with Dean Lloyd Garrison who had just hired him and encouraged him to do innovative work. Hurst considered the course to be a work of legal history as well as a trendsetter in legal process. He then wrote a history of the major American legal institutions called *The Growth of American Law.*[26] Two other major works were his magnum opus on the lumber industry[27] and the best-selling and highly influential *Law and the Conditions of Freedom in the Nineteenth Century.*[28] The lumber book remained his favorite because it so perfectly matched his goals for economic legal history, a meticulous study of the role of business and law in the beginnings and expansion of the lumber industry as it became the largest economic enterprise in Wisconsin, then completely disappeared having effectuated the complete destruction of the northern forest. A tension between capitalism and its limits can be seen in this work, no doubt discussed in Hurst's regular lunches with Aldo Leopold and later explored in *Conditions* (which both Dirk Hartog and Bob Gordon report as their first experience of being drawn to legal history).

Hurst's relevance to legal realism and instruction is perhaps best expressed in Dirk Hartog's comment in his interview with me that the law cannot be fully understood case by case and one doctrinal area after another (property, torts, contracts, etc.). Major legal developments usually occur in a coordinated fashion across multiple areas of law over a period of time. Or, as Hurst said in his oral history with typical understatement, sometimes it would be good if law students understood how we got here. Another close connection with legal realism was the overwhelming emphasis in his research on empirical facts about law and its impacts. After Hurst, the field of legal history became well established in many law schools, and research expanded greatly and evolved. As I learned from my interview with Dirk Hartog, Hurst's original focus on economic history declined as an interest of the field replaced by such topics as excluded groups, slavery, and immigration (but more recently has had a resurgence in the form of interest in colonialism and Atlantic studies).

7. Social needs, justice, and political progressivism

According to Horwitz,[29] social progressivism was an integral part of

---

26 Hurst, J.W., *The Growth of American Law: The Lawmakers* (Little Brown, 1950).

27 Hurst, J.W., *Law and Economic Growth. The Legal History of the Lumber Industry in Wisconsin, 1836-1915.* Madison: University of Wisconsin Press, 1984 (orig. pub. Cambridge, Mass.: Belknap Press of Harvard University Press, 1964).

28 Hurst, J.W., *Law and the Conditions of Freedom in the Nineteenth-Century United States.* Madison: University of Wisconsin Press, 1956.

29 Horwitz op. cit.

legal realism from the beginning, despite some academic squabbles.[30] One of the disputes concerned a distinction between legal realism as an empirical positivist description of what law does and normative legal realism as a moral and political critique. In fact, both perspectives are essential to progressivism because an empirically realistic description of law in action is the foundation of progressive thought. Law in action is factual; progressivism is counterfactual. With the success of progressivism, the counterfactual became the factual. Some scholars see Hurst's work on economic legal history as infused with a narrative of progressive problem-solving leading up to the New Deal.[31] Progressive research in legal history after Hurst, critical race and gender studies, for example, focused on new areas of law in action. Most generally, the very idea of critical theory rests on an understanding of how the institutional structures function to block social liberation.[32] That said, legal realism and law in action are not limited to Progressive movements. Lawyers in ordinary practice experience law in action every day; law and economics as a field of research can be thought of as a realm of law in action guided by considerations of efficiency.

Progressive elements in the four Wisconsin courses. The four innovative courses at Wisconsin are a combination of positivist and progressive legal realism (what is and what ought to be). A strong reformist element can be seen in every course.

---

30 One notable example was about who belonged in which school of thought (e.g., Llewellyn's realism or Pound's sociological jurisprudence). For Horwitz, the movement considered more broadly had various intertwined threads such as the critique of eighteenth-century common law reasoning as a formalist defense of property rights against redistribution, the work of progressive institutional economists who saw a role for government in relief of misery and regulation of corporations, and advocacy of the administrative state as an only institution with sufficient expertise and capacity to deal with problems of the industrial revolution and large corporations. Among the last group was Felix Frankfurter, a primary mentor of Willard Hurst. After Harvard Law School, where he took Frankfurter's seminar in administrative law, Hurst spent a year with Frankfurter working on lectures to be delivered by Frankfurter on the Commerce Clause.

31 Daniel Ernst, "Willard Hurst and the Administrative State: from Williams to Wisconsin," 18 *Law & Hist. Rev.* 1-36 (2000). Ernst reports that while in Harvard Law School, Hurst prescribed for himself a course of readings on the legal realists and was particularly impressed with Llewellyn's work on sales because it was close to economic reality. As note editor of the *Law Review*, Hurst worked with students, virtually as a coauthor, on administrative law topics that were of interest to Frankfurter.

32 Raymond Geuss, *The Idea of A Critical Theory: Habermas and the Frankfurt School* (Cambridge University Press, 1981) (a reflective theory, both descriptive and critical, which gives its agents a kind of knowledge productive of enlightenment and emancipation from often unsuspected forms of external and internal coercion).

Contracts. The Wisconsin contracts course deals with the problem of power in civil society, for example, contracts of adhesion imposed by large organizations on suppliers, customers, employees, and even hospital patients, under which one side knows that the other side has not read or fully understood the contract and has no power to change it. Consumer protection measures are sometimes enacted, e.g., on disclaimers of liability and pre-nuptial agreements, but just as often evaded by legal countermeasures, like compulsory arbitration before "kangaroo courts," or blunted by subsequent legislation obtained by lobbyists or by restrictive court interpretations.[33]

Criminal Justice Administration. Sensitivity to problems of justice pervades the course in Criminal Justice Administration, from the sweeping effort to identify and regulate unbridled discretion of the police to recommendation of less coercive methods for protecting public safety, such as problem-oriented and community policing. Police ride-alongs were an important source of data in the research leading up to the course. As a young social scientist,[34] Herman Goldstein was shocked at the rousting of gay people in bathrooms by police. Ride-alongs for students are part of the course to this very day. Today's course is refreshed with new problems of justice such as wrongful convictions and mass incarceration, and the current professors Klingele and Findley are active in many public service activities.

Legal History. Willard Hurst's research on economic legal history was built on a vision of the public interest and the state as its rightful guardian.[35] Hurst held any number of realist progressive positions, such as that since the state has granted corporations the charter to do business, it has unlimited power to regulate, and that interpretations of constitutional provisions like the dormant commerce clause should respond to practical necessities rather than relying on conceptual theories. He described his research and courses as dealing with development of public policy in the

---

33 "Nonetheless, looked at over time, in Galanter's words, 'the haves come out ahead.' Even if someone does obtain more favorable rules, 'frequently the well-organized can change the game back again.'" Macaulay & Whitford, op. cit., citing Marc Galanter, "Why the 'Haves' Come Out Ahead: Speculations on the Limits of Legal Change," 9 *Law & Society Rev.* 95 (1974).

34 "As an undergraduate at the University of Connecticut, Goldstein majored in political science and government. After graduating in 1953, he went on to earn a master's degree in governmental administration from the Wharton School at the University of Pennsylvania." Herman Goldstein, "How I Got Here," *The Gargoyle* (University of Wisconsin Law School, 2008), https://media.law.wisc.edu/m/zmjgx/gargoyle_33_2_5.pdf.

35 Daniel Ernst, op. cit.

dimension of time and maintained that administrative agencies often are the only institution with the competence to deal with complex economic problems. When he was hired at Wisconsin, he conceived of his most important mission as protecting the freedom of state regulation, such as the efforts of Elizabeth and Paul Raushenbush in workers' compensation.[36] Professors of legal history who followed Hurst at Wisconsin moved even more strongly in the direction of social critique and reform, for example, Robert Gordon and critical legal studies, Dirk Hartog and gender discrimination, and Mark Tushnet and the law of slavery.

Legal Process. The Legal Process course and book authored by Auerbach, Garrison, Hurst & Mermin embodies its own narrative of the evolution of justice well represented by a long excerpt reprinted in the book from an 1969 article by Carl Auerbach on law and social change in the United States.[37] In the spirit of Hurst,[38] Auerbach presents the role of law in the nineteenth and first half of the twentieth century as a gradual march toward a "combination of public and private rights ordering necessary to protect liberty and prosperity." Law in the nineteenth century encouraged industrialization through freedom of contract, protection of property, limits on discrimination by states against interstate commerce, generous grants of power to corporations, and sale of good government land in small pieces to encourage agriculture and business enterprises (note the realist reconceptualization of property as a state policy). This expansion diffusion of property, individual freedom and general prosperity were important achievements in their own right, but the social costs were also high. Social unrest, riots, strikes, and bitter elections led to legislative curbs on economic power, such as the Interstate Commerce and Sherman Antitrust Acts, which reduced the number of monopolies but left oligopolies in place.

---

36 https://workforcesecurity.doleta.gov/unemploy/pdf/Raushenbushes.pdf. Paul and Elizabeth Raushenbush were instrumental in the creation and adoption of the Groves Bill, which established the first unemployment compensation program in the nation. Elizabeth Brandeis Raushenbush was the daughter of Supreme Court Louis Brandeis (of Brandeis Brief fame). Willard Hurst was Brandeis' clerk, and Elizabeth recommended Hurst to UW Law School Dean Lloyd Garrison. Walter Brandeis Raushenbush was the son of Elizabeth and Paul and a faculty member of the law school until 1995.

37 Carl Auerbach, "Law and Social Change in the United States," 6 *UCLA L. Rev.* 516-532 (1959). The excerpt is in a section of the legal process book called "scope and objectives of legislative intervention and the public interest" introduced by a short reminder that while law is influenced by society it also has a social impact on behavior, the environment, and attitudes (citing school desegregation). This conception of law as both a dependent and independent variable is widely shared in the sociology of law.

38 E.g., *Law and the Conditions of Freedom*, op. cit.

In the twentieth century, Auerbach endorsed the full range of New Deal and post-New Deal reforms such as 1) Galbraith-like legislation that created centers of countervailing power, e.g., farmers' associations and co-ops, co-op grocery stores, and trade unions, 2) the Clayton Act regulating economic concentration, 3) social welfare legislation, such as minimum wages, maximum hours, public schools, child labor restrictions, public health measures, farm price supports, and unemployment insurance, 4) rights of citizenship like women's property and marriage rights and civil rights for African Americans, 5) consumer protections, e.g., in insurance and banking law and against false advertising, and 6) economic policy supporting full employment.

The result for Auerbach was that "a tolerable measure of social justice and individual freedom has been achieved in our society as a result not of the pursuit of a vision of an ideal economic system but of the political struggle which individuals and groups have waged, according to the rules of democracy, to satisfy their claims."[39] This enthusiastic defense of progressive legislation and democracy, taken from the Hurst Legal Process book, is a good example of the normative perspective on historical trends typical of legal realism in the tradition of Pound's sociological jurisprudence (which maintained that law should be reformed when it is out of step with social needs and justice).[40]

8. The importance of empirical research and social scientists on law school faculties or collaborating with law faculty members

Early realism. Social science research was important for the early legal realists in the 1920s and 30s.[41] Social surveys were part of a widespread progressive reform movement which held that if social problems were discovered, good government could correct them.[42] A survey of civil cases by Charles Clark and Robert Hutchinson discovered the largely administrative nature of state court proceedings, for example, uncontested divorces and foreclosures, settled auto claims, and simple debt collections. Clark, William O. Douglas, and Charles Samenow basically discovered modern criminal procedure (e.g., the fact that 70 percent of defendants plead guilty and only 1 percent went to trial). These studies, which were

39 Legal Process book, op cit., at 645, 652-56.

40 R. Pound, "The Scope and Purpose of Sociological Jurisprudence," 25 *Harvard Law Review* 489 (1912).

41 John Schlegel's book *American Legal Realism and Empirical Social Science* op. cit. is an excellent source generally and the source of the information mentioned here.

42 Schlegel, op cit., at 80-81.

staffed by professional social scientists who collaborated with the law professors, were funded by Yale Law School and grants from the Rockefeller Foundation and other agencies. As a young Dean, Hutchinson created an Institute for Human Relations at Yale to house the research. Douglas did a study of bankruptcy cases.

Another research institute that focused on the empirical effects of law was founded at Johns Hopkins (which then as now did not have a law school) by Herman Oliphant, Walter Cook, and Underhill Moore, after they resigned from Columbia Law School in 1928 in protest over the refusal of Columbia University's president to appoint Oliphant dean of the law school. The Hopkins Institute obtained funding from various sources and conducted a number of interesting studies but was discontinued in the early 1930s due to disagreements among its faculty and patrons about its mission and purpose. These early attempts to establish institutional homes for studies of law in action are interesting in light of such long-running enterprises as the Institute for Legal Studies at Wisconsin and the JSP program at Berkeley.[43] Similar influences can be seen in the development of the Wisconsin courses.

Willard Hurst. Besides being a world-class scholar, Willard Hurst was a leader in promoting research through fundraising, advocacy, and mentoring. Hurst returned to the faculty after WWII on funding from an SSRC/Rockefeller Grant.[44] He then was granted eight years half-time released from teaching from the Rockefeller Foundation on recommendation from SSRC (who were so impressed with him that they also put him on their own Board). During this long period of funding he wrote several of his early canonical books. The Rockefeller grant also provided him a full-time research assistant for the entire period of the grant. Hurst's research assistants included Lawrence Friedman who went on to write his own *History of American Law*[45] and collaborate with Stewart Macaulay on their book *Law and the Behavioral Sciences.* Within the law school and university, Hurst advocated relentlessly for the importance of research and research funding as necessary for the development of the faculty and the

43 Emeritus Professor David Trubek's role in creating the ISL is notable. This 1980 issue of the University of Wisconsin Law School magazine *The Gargoyle* features reports on the Institute and other law school centers and an interview with Willard Hurst on the importance of research and the Institute. http://gargoyle.law.wisc.edu/wp-uploads/2014/02/volume12issue1.pdf. Howard Erlanger served as director of ILS for 15 years and developed the Hurst Summer Institute, which provides an institutional home for Hurst's strong commitment to mentoring. Professor Mitra Sharafi is the current director. https://law.wisc.edu/ils/hurst_institute.html.

44 These facts from Hurst's oral history on file with UW Law School library.

45 Lawrence Friedman, *A History of American Law* (4th edition 2019, Oxford University Press).

reputation of the school. The research function, he believed, was too easily pushed aside for other priorities but was essential for keeping faculty refreshed and current in their teaching. In his view, faculty competence and reputation would decline in about five years without research support. In addition to this regular funding, Hurst obtained a long series of commissioned papers which led to the publication of other books and articles (among them from the Rosenthal Foundation at Northwestern Law School which led to his best-selling *Law and the Conditions of Freedom*).

Later in his career, in response to numerous offers from other schools, he was awarded the University's Vilas Professorship which allowed him to continue with half-time teaching and provided a budget for research assistance. Hurst's reputation nationally and within the university presaged the many university grants and awards held over the years by law school faculty up to the present time. Hurst himself did not have a degree in social sciences (nor did Bob Gordon), but today most professors of legal history have a PhD.

Remington and Goldstein. Frank Remington and Herman Goldstein and colleagues also had considerable success combining empirical and interdisciplinary research and external funding with law school instruction in the field of criminal justice, a field that Remington virtually invented (just as Hurst did for legal history). Remington started teaching at UW in 1949 and immediately became involved in rewriting the state's substantive criminal statutes, which led to his participation in revisions of the Model Penal Code, which then led to work with Wisconsin state judges on uniform jury instructions for offenses defined in the new Wisconsin code.[46] On the research side, he became the field research director of American Bar Foundation survey of the administration of criminal justice in the United States. The purpose of ABF study was collection of reliable data on the criminal law in action and recommending remedial measures in the four areas of police, prosecution, criminal courts, and sentencing, probation, and parole.[47] Herman Goldstein joined the ABF staff as a young social scientist gathering data in various cities and in 1964 was hired as a professor at Wisconsin, supported by grants from the ABF, the Ford Foundation, and the Russell Sage Foundation. Those grants also supported a series of summer seminars held at Wisconsin for law professors from around the country to study the findings of the ABF study (one of whom was Joe Goldstein of Yale). According to Herman Goldstein, the seminars

46 Edward L. Kimball & Frank J. Remington, *Contributions to Criminal Justice* (University of Wisconsin Law School and Board of Regents, 1994).

47 See http://www.americanbarfoundation.org/uploads/cms/documents/1955 - 1956 abf _annual report.pdf; https://scholarlycommons.law.northwestern.edu/cgi/viewcontent.cgi?article=4383&context=jclc.

and the report had a revolutionary impact on the thinking of law professors about criminal justice system because of findings such as the large number of citizens who experienced discretionary interventions by the police.

Social scientists on or working with the law faculty. The presence of social scientists on the law school faculty during this period was notable. On the criminal justice side were Herman Goldstein and Don Newman. Don Newman received his PhD in sociology from the University of Wisconsin and was professor of social work at Wisconsin, with a joint appointment to the law school. He was often identified as a criminologist. Newman occupied an office opposite Goldstein in the law school. He coauthored the first edition of the criminal justice administration course book and co-taught with Remington for several years. Remington drew him into analyzing the ABA survey's results on plea bargaining—and that became his specialty for several years. He wrote one of the several books coming out of the ABA study surfacing what was—up to then—the informal "plea bargaining" practice, resulting ultimately in legislation and court practices that introduced protections for the defendant.[48]

When Macaulay came to Wisconsin in 1957 as an assistant professor (in the same year as Gordon Baldwin), Henry Manne, a specialist in law and economics from the University of Chicago, came as a visiting assistant professor. Harry Ball was a sociologist on Frank Remington's projects and worked with Richard Schwartz and others to create the Law and Society Association. Friedman and sociologist Jack Ladinsky did a case study of the legal history of employer liability for industrial accidents. They used it to challenge the idea that the law necessarily lags behind the society and that legal change can be explained by the influence of great men.[49]

How Wisconsin Law School became a realist-friendly environment (and persisted over time)

Before concluding, it is informative to reflect on how the law school became an environment friendly to legal realism when almost all other schools were wedded to the traditional model. One link is the connection of legal realism with progressivism as a political movement. Legal realism had a strong progressive element reflected in advocacy for government intervention to mitigate harms flowing from the vast economic and social changes of the industrial revolution (e.g., the fight for workers' compensa-

48 Newman information from an email by Herman Goldstein to Clune.

49 Friedman & Ladinsky, "Social Change and the Law of Industrial Accidents," 67 *Columbia L. Rev.* 50 (1967).

tion). Wisconsin played a central role, serving as the laboratory of progressivism.[50] Influenced by its German immigrants, progressive reforms in Wisconsin included workers' compensation, regulation of railroads, progressive income taxation, direct election of senators, primary elections, and the legislative reference library or bureau (which helped expand legislative capacity to develop comprehensive social and regulatory programs, rather than only responding to constituents, in ways later admired by historian Willard Hurst). Almost all of these reforms were later adopted as amendments to the U.S. Constitution, expansion of capacity of the executive branch, or national legislation. Wisconsin professors were active in developing the reforms under what came to be known as The Wisconsin Idea, "the belief that efficient government should be controlled by voters rather than businesses and lobbyists, and that help from specialists in law, economics and the social and natural sciences would produce the most effective government possible." UW faculty helped draft laws and served as expert consultants.[51] A prime example was John R. Commons, who came to Wisconsin in 1904 to accept a position in labor economics at the University.[52]

> As part of the Wisconsin Idea, Commons worked closely with Robert M. La Follette to draft the Wisconsin Civil Service Law in 1905 and the Public Utilities Law in 1907. Commons researched and wrote policy for the regulation of workplace safety and for unemployment compensation. His students, Edwin Witte and Arthur Altmeyer, went on to create the Social Security program in the 1930s. Recognized for his scholarship in labor history and economics, Commons advocated collective bargaining and pragmatic compromise over rigid, uncompromising views."[53]

By the time Willard Hurst was hired by Dean Lloyd Garrison in 1937, the law school was full of New Dealers. Nathan Feinsinger joined the faculty at the University of Wisconsin School of Law in 1929. Feinsinger was appointed general counsel to the Wisconsin Labor Relations Board in 1937. In 1942, President Franklin D. Roosevelt appointed Feinsinger associate general counsel of the War Labor Board. He was promoted to Director of National Disputes in 1943, overseeing labor problems of a

---

50 https://www.wisconsinhistory.org/turningpoints/tp-036/ (books, articles, manuscripts on Progressivism and the Wisconsin Idea).

51 https://www.wisconsinhistory.org/Records/Article/CS417.

52 https://www.wisconsinhistory.org/Records/Article/CS507.

53 https://www.wisconsinhistory.org/turningpoints/search.asp?id=1003 (on the Wisconsin professors who authored the Social Security Act).

national nature, and became famous for his role in mediating a series of high profile labor disputes and strikes. Professor Jake Beuscher had spent time with Office of Price Administration during the war period, and after coming to the Wisconsin faculty in 1935, taught a course in land use regulation which, in its emphasis on natural resources and water quality, prefigured modern environmental law. From the 1930s, Beuscher worked with the Wisconsin legislature on practically every major development in environmental law over a period of decades.[54] Beuscher was instrumental in the creation of the internationally oriented Land Tenure Center at UW-Madison the activities of which drew in other Wisconsin law professors like Joseph Thome.[55] Hurst particularly admired Beuscher for his social activism and was disappointed when he was not appointed Dean to succeed Lloyd Garrison (Hurst oral history). Carl Auerbach, coauthor with Hurst of the Legal Process book, served as a government attorney in various government agencies, including the Office of Economic Stabilization and General Counsel of the Office of Price Administration. A second coauthor, Samuel Mermin, represented the Bituminous Coal Consumers' Counsel in extensive administrative hearings, briefs, and oral arguments under the 1937 Bituminous Coal Act. With the onset of World War II, Mermin spent five years in the Office of Price Administration's Enforcement Department and its successor agency, the Office of Temporary Controls. He served in various capacities, including chief of the Briefing Branch, special appellate attorney, and solicitor of the Litigation Division.[56]

Frank Remington was a student of Hurst's at the law school. Hurst functioned as a mentor of the next generation of empirical legal scholars like Lawrence Friedman and Stewart Macaulay. While Macaulay was a Bigelow Fellow at the University of Chicago Law School, he was mentored by Professor Malcolm Sharp, coauthor of the realist-oriented contracts casebook, *Kessler and Sharp*. Sharp encouraged him to undertake the empirical research that led to his pathbreaking article on non-contractual relations in business. The summer before he was hired at Wisconsin, Macaulay audited and taught a week of classes in a contracts class taught by Professor Nick Katzenbach using the *Kessler and Sharp* book. At

---

54 Statement of Arlen Christensen on nomination of Beuscher to the Wisconsin Conservation Hall of Fame. https://media.law.wisc.edu/m/jb4nz/gargoyle_25_3_5.pdf.

55 https://www.nelson.wisc.edu/ltc/ The Land Tenure Center was closed in 2003. https://news.wisc.edu/uw- madison-to-close-land-tenure-center/.

56 In this period (1943–1947), he prepared nineteen briefs of his own and presented nineteen oral arguments in appellate courts, both federal (including the US Supreme Court) and state; and he supervised the preparation of thirty-seven other briefs. https://media.law.wisc.edu/s/c_695/rdfgz/mermin.pdf.

Wisconsin, Macaulay adopted the *Kessler and Sharp* book when he became senior contracts professor and later named his own Hilldale Professorship after Sharp. He then partnered with Bill Whitford on their contracts course and book. Macaulay and Friedman coauthored the first version of their *Law and Behavioral Sciences* book while they were together at Stanford, an arrangement that continued when both returned to Wisconsin and after Friedman subsequently joined the Stanford faculty.[57] When Beth Mertz joined the faculty as a joint JD/PhD (anthropology), she became coeditor of the fourth and last edition of the book (and an active member of the law and society community).[58]

Walter Dickey was a student of Remington who went on to teach the criminal justice administration course after he was hired as a faculty member. Dickey also directed major related clinical programs (Legal Assistance to Inmates, Public Defender Project, and the Prosecution Project). At one point in his career, Dickey took leave from the faculty to become Director of the Wisconsin Department of Corrections. The introduction to the current version of the course includes an article by Dickey and professors Cecelia Klingele and Michael Scott, "Reimaging Criminal Justice."[59] Michael Scott, now a professor and director of the Center for Problem-Oriented Policing at Arizona State University, was a protégé of Herman Goldstein and longtime director of the POP Center at Wisconsin (also a former Madison police officer and graduate of Harvard Law School—see his article in this volume).[60]

Then arrived the next wave of socio-legally educated professors whose many outstanding accomplishments in teaching and research are beyond the scope of this paper.[61]

Conclusion

First, how should we assess a common opinion of scholars: that legal realism had some but modest lasting influence on legal instruction and

---

57 Friedman & Macaulay, *Law and the Behavioral Sciences* (Bobbs-Merrill Pub. Co., 1969).

58 Macaulay, Friedman & Mertz, *Law in Action: A Socio-Legal Reader* (Foundation Press, 2007).

59 Introduction to Criminal Procedure, 32-50.

60 https://publicservice.asu.edu/content/michael-scott.

61 A randomly selective list of just those arriving starting in 1971 would include myself, Tom Heller, Neil Komesar, Len Kaplan, Don Large (who taught the course on the new EPA), Mark Tushnet, Bob Gordon, Ted Schneyer, David Trubek, Howard Erlanger, Marc Galanter, and Joel Rogers. See Schlegel, 249-50: "By any account the Wisconsin program has been a success as well, whether one measures by looking at a list of the alumni of the program, the amount of research produced, or the continuance of work both in the Department of Sociology and the Law School that is identifiably law and social science."

research? The Langdellian case method is still the dominant method of instruction, it is said, and empirical research on law is rare, relative to library research on appellate cases and other legal texts. The first year curriculum has not changed substantially in fifty, or seventy-five, or one hundred years, it is argued, with some justification.[62] That would not be a fair conclusion looking at the four innovative courses at Wisconsin reviewed in this article, their national impact, and the many professors who have followed in the same tradition. But what about the broader impact? My sense is that the movement toward realism is broader both in this school and elsewhere in ways that permeate rather than replace traditional instruction and in non-traditional courses.

To be sure, the traditional case method and teaching of black letter law is still the prevalent if not dominant method of instruction especially in more traditional law schools (and bar exams). Textual interpretation remains the core of law and legal expertise. Law schools do not grant social science degrees or train social scientists. Contract, tort, and property, though morphed over time, are still the foundation of a liberal legal order along with regulation of the economy. Commercial transactions and informal decision-making must account for legal considerations even when no legal authority is invoked. Legislation and administrative rules must be drafted, and decisions are adjudicated in courts and administrative agencies. Rule skepticism (or sophistication) is more common than the naïve classical legal reasoning of Langdell and the Restatements of law, but interpretation still begins with legal texts.

Beyond the core, the influence of legal realism is more evident. Policy perspectives on appellate cases are at least as common as legal logic. Clinical instruction, strong at Wisconsin and virtually all other law schools, is in the spirit of legal realism, if not prominent among its original goals. Simulation courses abound. Law and economics, based on models of legal impact, has experienced explosive growth in the legal academy and is a common policy perspective on the law. Statutory and administrative law in areas advocated for by the realists now densely populate the second and third years of law school (recall that much research of the legal realists was done after the progressive movement and before the New Deal). Law professors with social science degrees dot the landscape, especially in elite law schools. Interdisciplinary degrees and collaborations have grown with the complexity of social problem-solving. Interdisciplinary research between law professors and professors in other departments abounds. Lawyers involved in policymaking inevitably interact with technical

62 "The contributions of Jerry Mashaw, William Eskridge and other Yale instructors to our understanding of the real world of law notwithstanding, the curriculum at Yale remains essentially what it was when I became its student 54 years ago—and long before that." Strauss, op. cit, at 185.

experts. Administrative rules proposed by regulated industries are the product of collaboration between legal and technical experts. Policies advancing environmental sustainability are invariably built on a combination of economic, technological, and legal expertise. Antitrust cannot be done without economics. Bioethics requires bioethical collaboration. Empirical research on legal policy has exploded outside law schools in social science departments and think tanks, and this research is readily available to interested law professors (e.g., in my own field of educational policy, the empirical research base is deep and informative). Lawsuits challenging gerrymandering like our own *Gill v. Whitford*[63] are an interesting example of the intertwining of law and social science. Not only are political scientists and mathematicians deeply involved in the litigation, statistical models and computer simulations helped create the legislative gerrymandering. Undergraduate courses in empirical legal studies and criminology have flourished.

To sum up with a metaphor, perhaps it is fair to say that the original design of the House of Law is recognizable, but the interior has been extensively remodeled, new wings have been added, and guest houses have been built on the same property.

Second, in schools that offer legal history, students can learn that long-run consequential trends in the law continue to the present time. The nineteenth century struggle between social welfare vs. business deregulation and resistance to income redistribution continues with new legal and political tools. Corporate monopolies that helped trigger the Progressive movement are once more a matter of heightened public concern. The power of organized labor—always a contentious subject—has dwindled under decades of attack but may be gaining new life. The 150-year-old struggle over voting rights continues amidst a high level of partisan activity, e.g., voter suppression, gerrymandering, money in politics, and a Supreme Court that has taken mixed positions. Disputes over immigration policy follow in a tradition at least 125 years old, not even counting slavery and its aftermath as the product of involuntary immigration. The movement for equal rights continues and has expanded beyond race and sex. Criminal justice across the full range of discretionary decisions has been with us for all of our history and has never been more important than with such issues as mass incarceration, police misconduct, and electronic surveillance. Environmental regulation, always contested, has acquired existential importance. The seemingly vaporous words "rule of law,"

63 *Gill v Whitford*, https://www.supremecourt.gov/opinions/17pdf/16-1161_dc8f.pdf; https://www.vox.com/2018/6/18/17474912/supreme-court-gerrymandering-gill-whitford-wisconsin. The Supreme Court subsequently ruled 5–4 in the *Rucho* case that partisan gerrymandering is a "political question" beyond the reach of federal courts. https://www.supremecourt.gov/opinions/18pdf/18-422_9ol1.pdf; https://www.scotus blog.com/2019/06/gerrymandering-symposium-supreme-court-confirms-that-it-will-not-save-our-maps-only-voters-can/.

referring to honest government and the constitutional order, have sprung suddenly vividly to life in real decisions leading to tangible and momentous consequences.

Acknowledgments

More than many papers, this was a collectively supported endeavor. Through the time of my blog on the New Legal Realism website to writing of this paper, I am grateful for the support of my local advisory group of Howard Erlanger, Stewart Macaulay, Elizabeth Mertz, and William Whitford. John Schlegel was helpful with the blog and its early framing of legal realism. Hendrik Hartog, in addition to his interview for the paper, in a series of emails basically coached me through thinking about the field of legal history. The colleagues who gave interviews provided essential information and insights were most helpful (Arlen Christenson, Keith Findley, Walter Dickey, Herman Goldstein, Hendrik Hartog, Cecelia Klingele, Stewart Macaulay, William Whitford). The usual disclaimer also applies with special force to an effort that tries to summarize the work of so many other people—the ideas in the paper are my own and not necessarily shared by those who provided such generous assistance.

Appendix: Methodology and Sources

For me, this project began with a blog written for the New Realism Project, "Law in Action, Law on the Books: A Primer" (June, 2013),[64] an essay that relied heavily on Macaulay's 1963 article on non-contractual relations,[65] Jack Schlegel's book on realism and empirical social science,[66] and a team of informal advisors (Howie Erlanger, Beth Mertz, Stewart Macaulay, Bill Whitford, and Jack Schlegel).

For this project honoring the four course innovators, again relying on informal advice from law school colleagues, I used these research methods:

1. Expanded readings on legal realism.
2. Reading and taking notes on the original books.

---

64 See http://newlegalrealism.org/2013/06/12/law-in-action-and-law-on-the-books-a-primer/.

65 Macaulay, S. (1963), "Non-Contractual Relations in Business: A Preliminary Study," *American Sociological Review,* volume 28, no. 1.

66 Schlegel, John H. (1995), *American Legal Realism and Empirical Social Science,* University of North Carolina Press, Chapel Hill & London.

3. Recording and transcribing six interviews:[67]
   a) for criminal law, 1) Professors Herman Goldstein, 2) Walter Dickey, 3) Cecelia Klingele and Keith Findley
   b) for legal history, 4) Professor Dirk Hartog
   c) for contracts, 5) Professors Stewart Macaulay and Bill Whitford
   d) regarding Jake Beuscher and environmentalism, 6) Professor Arlen Christenson.
4. For legal process, none of the authors is still alive for interview, but I found Peter Strauss's overview of the history of Langdellism and legal process extremely helpful.[68]
5. Reading additional sources in legal history including Hurst, Horwitz, and Hartog.
6. Reading the oral histories of Willard Hurst and Herman Goldstein on file with the University of Wisconsin Law Library.
7. Collecting data on when various courses were offered and who taught them from the UW Law Library. Many thanks to the whole staff and especially Kristopher Turner.

---

[67] I would like to make edited versions of the interviews available to the Law Library.

[68] Peter L. Strauss (2016), Review Essay: "Christopher Columbus Langdell and the Public Law Curriculum," *Journal of Legal Education,* vol. 66, no. 1, 157-185.

Reflections on Frank Remington, the ABF Survey, and the Wisconsin Law School[1]

Malcolm M. Feeley

Abstract

This paper is about the significance and impact of Frank Remington and Herman Goldstein's research on criminal justice administration flowing from the large American Bar Foundation project on the administration of national justice in the 1950s (funded by the Ford Foundation). The focus of the project was revolutionary for its time: a study of the discretion exercised by public officials at every stage of the criminal justice system: police, prosecutors, bail bondsmen, probation officers, lawyers, and judges. The goals of the project, to produce a new type of scholar of criminal law and to improve the administration of justice, were realized across a range of impacts on research, research institutions, and academic disciplines. Impacts on research included five large monographs written by the project staff, major law review articles written by professors who visited Madison and studied the project's findings, and Goldstein's pioneering work on problem-oriented policing. Impacts on academic disciplines included the Wisconsin Law School's Criminal Justice Administration course, Wisconsin's clinical law programs, the curriculum of the School of Criminology at Berkeley, and the expansion of the focus on criminal law in departments of sociology, criminology, and political science. Impacts on research institutions included the establishment of the School of Criminal Justice Administration at SUNY Albany, the Vera Foundation (later Institute) in New York City, the Police Foundation in Washington, DC, the Center for Court Innovation, and the President's Commission on Crime and Law Enforcement. The Wisconsin work is seen as in the tradition of Dewey's pragmatist philosophy in regarding the primary purpose of criminal justice system as providing institutions for solving concrete problems and achieving situational justice rather than as the interpretation of rules. In that tradition, the author calls for more research on problem-oriented prosecution and judging in addition to the existing research on policing.

---

[1] Originally prepared for the program "Law in Action in Wisconsin Law School Courses: 1950–1970," School of Law, University of Wisconsin, March 8, 2019.

Reflections on Frank Remington, the ABF Survey, and the Wisconsin Law School

In an earlier draft, I began by emphasizing how original Frank Remington was. And then I thought about it some more and concluded that he was not all that original. As an undergraduate and law student, he sang "On Wisconsin" and embraced the Wisconsin Idea. His great contribution was to march out to the barren field of criminal procedure and put that idea into practice, both within the state and then nationally. He was both an embodiment of the Wisconsin Idea and the Wisconsin tradition of legal realism, if these two ideas can even be separated. His great contribution was to apply this perspective to virgin territory: the criminal process. Remington's work built on a solid foundation that had been laid well before his student years. He launched his project on that foundation.

But there was a proximate cause as well, and like so many of the most important things in life, it appears to have been serendipitous. Following distinguished service in World War II, Frank returned to Wisconsin, took advantage of the GI Bill, and took an accelerated track for his B.A. and LL.B. degrees.

Frank graduated from the Law School in January 1949 and immediately was asked to join the faculty that fall. However, with a family to feed, Frank needed something to tide him over for six months. As he did for so many people, Willard Hurst came to the rescue. He arranged for Frank to work as a research assistant for Professor John Dawson at the University of Michigan. Dawson's specialty was contracts, and his current project was on unjust enrichment. He had a hunch and asked Frank track it down; Frank sat in Detroit's criminal court to see if prosecutors there used the threat of criminal prosecution to force unscrupulous businesspersons to make restitution to their poor victims. Frank found that this was so; prosecutors dropped the charges if they made restitution. This led to an epiphany: non-prosecution can have important social functions. More generally, prosecution and non-prosecution can serve a multitude of functions. For Remington, this was catnip. He was hooked.

He returned to Madison in the fall and started teaching criminal law with this epiphany in mind. Almost immediately, the Wisconsin Legislative Council asked him to undertake a revision of the Wisconsin Criminal Code. Drawing in two classmates who had graduated a year behind him, Margo Melli and Orrin Helstad, he worked tirelessly on this project for a good number of years, first producing a draft code, and then struggling to convince the legislature, lawyers, and judges to embrace it. Their point:

systematic codification was far superior to piecemeal court-made changes for developing a workable modern criminal process. After several years of lobbying, Remington, Melli, and Helstad succeeded in getting the legislature to adopt their code and to commit to continuous oversight and updates.

The project also drew the attention of Herbert Wechsler, who invited Frank to join the Model Penal Code Project through the American Law Institute (ALI), by then an important national institution, and one that has its origins in a collaboration between Wall Street and Wisconsin during the Progressive Era. One thing led to another, and in a few years—in 1953 or 1954—Frank became involved in a project that was to preoccupy him for the next sixteen years, studying the exercise of discretion in the criminal justice system—undertaking on a gigantic scale what he had done by himself in the winter of 1949 in Detroit for Professor Dawson. Not surprisingly, this project had many fathers: In a speech to the ABA in 1953, Justice Robert H. Jackson proposed that the ABA undertake a detailed national study of the administration of criminal Justice. Eventually, after a convoluted process, the idea was realized. It would be administered by the newly established American Bar Foundation, then associated with the University of Chicago; directed by Arthur Sherry, a professor of law at UC Berkeley; focus on real-world criminal justice administration; and use research methods pioneered in the University of Chicago's Department of Sociology in the 1930s, 40s and 50s. The project was weighted down with a glittering array of stars on its advisory committee (four Supreme Court justices or future justices, as well as an all-star cast of other legal luminaries and public officials). All this led to the project being well-funded by the Ford Foundation. From the outset, it also had a substantial staff to oversee and execute the study. Although Sherry was the nominal director of the project, it was Frank, based in Madison, who as Director of Field Research had the responsibility for administering the project and producing its work products. He had the good sense to draw in Lloyd Ohlin, a Chicago-trained sociologist, and Herman Goldstein, whose background was public administration, to help design and oversee the diffuse project.

From the outset, the project was hugely ambitious. It then both grew and shrunk. It was conceived as a national study of all fifty states, which was to be preceded by pilot research in three states. As the number of questions and issues grew, the staff concluded it was more useful to concentrate on in-depth work in the three pilot states rather than to expand nationwide, a choice that, in retrospect, avoided what surely would have been a catastrophe. Eventually this "pilot program'" consumed $1,000,000 of Ford's money, the equivalent of almost $10,000,000 today! Indeed, it is amazing that it did not topple from overweight at the top, but as the bigwigs turned their attention elsewhere, Frank, as "Director of Field Research," quietly continued to work on the project. Still, it is something of a miracle that it produced published results on the three sites on which it focused.

In many respects, it was a typical Wisconsin project and an example of the new legal realism before the term had been coined: it was collaborative research on the law in action with the aim of suggesting recommendations for improvements in the administration of criminal justice. Remington the lawyer, and Ohlin the social scientist, developed rudimentary protocols for field research, and recruited an army of researchers. After arranging to have them strategically placed with police, prosecutors, judges, and probation and parole officers, Frank and Lloyd gave them pats on the back and bus tickets and sent them on their ways to their sites in Wisconsin, Michigan, and Kansas. Their mission was to observe practices relating to crime detection, arrest, prosecution, conviction, sentencing, and parole; write up field notes; and send them back to Madison for analysis.

Frank had found his calling—to investigate the criminal process in action. He dug in and began overseeing the analysis of the excavated products. Although motivated in the same way as his mentor Will Hurst—to understand the law in action—his style was radically different. Will had his protégés and admirers and was a wonderful mentor—and as we saw, this included Frank Remington. However, Hurst was essentially a solo practitioner. In contrast, Frank was gregarious and capacious, the captain of a big, boisterous, and ever-changing team. He drew in students and colleagues with his infectious enthusiasm. Above all, he knew how to recruit talented young people, give them direction, immense responsibility, and plenty of freedom, then send them out on their own. I do not know how many of them sank, but a lot of them floated, and many soared. Furthermore, Frank was more of a doer than a writer. Over this career, he wrote a great deal, though much of it was coauthored reports to committees. In addition, in this immense project, he published very little, if anything. Repeatedly, he appears simply to have handed over vast chunks of the project for others to pursue and write up, though he could rightfully have claimed senior authorship of all of the five massive reports.

The ABF project was a reaction to an earlier set of crime surveys produced between about 1920 and 1940. One of those earlier reports still read today from time to time is Roscoe Pound and Felix Frankfurter's *Criminal Justice in Cleveland* (1922). However, their work—and the other early crime surveys—relied almost exclusively on published records: how many arrests, how many dismissals, how many guilty pleas, how many trials, and the like. These projects focused on case attrition and types of charging, but never interrogated the discretionary judgments that led to them. So the studies might report: one hundred arrests; fifty prosecutions; and only twenty convictions on original charges. The inference to be drawn: police made fifty bad arrests that did not allow prosecutors to prove charges; and in another thirty cases, prosecutors had over-charged—what went wrong?

The ABA-ABF-Ford-Wisconsin project asked decidedly different questions. Its animating concern was to understand the *discretionary* dynamics of the criminal process: It pursued answers to the journalists' standard questions: who, what, why, where, when, and how? Who made the important decisions?

Why were decisions made as they were? For what reasons? The focus was on *discretion*. Indeed, the project might very well have been labeled "Discretion in the Administration of Criminal Justice."

Discretion of the police. Discretion of the prosecutor. Discretion of the bail bondsman, discretion of the judge. Discretion of probation officers.

As I suggested earlier, Frank was in his element. He had a mandate—and near unlimited resources—to make sense of his bewildering experience in the Detroit criminal court in the winter of 1949. Frank's army of field researchers found discretionary decision-making everywhere, and at every stage of the criminal process. Reasons were not always as laudable as they had been in Detroit, but discretion ruled the day. Criminal laws and criminal procedures were not "applied," so much as they were used—invoked and ignored—selectively, in order to effect a host of ends never envisioned by their authors.

In retrospect, the findings reported by the project seem naïve and undisciplined. Indeed, they are. They were pioneering studies, the first—or near first—observational studies of police, prosecutors, judges, and probation and parole officers—to report on what had long been invisible in plain sight. At the time, they were revelatory, for not only law-in-the books law professors, but social scientists and historians as well. As one test of this: go to the library and pull out law review articles on the criminal process published in the 1940s and 1950s, and contrast them with articles published since the 1970s. Similarly, go to social science journals of the 1940s and 1950s, and then skip to the 1970s and 1980s. There are of course exceptions, notably my late colleague, Caleb Foote's study of bail administration in Philadelphia and New York City, the jury study project by Harry Kalven and Hans Zeisel at the University of Chicago, and the early empirical studies of criminal justice administration conducted by the Vera Institute. However, by the time these studies appeared in print, the ABF study was well underway.

Moreover, it is worth noting that all these other projects were also supported by the Ford Foundation under the same initiative.

Let me return to the administration of the project. Frank had an oddball strategy, based, I think, on his own affinity for discretion. After receiving marching orders by the advisory board and a blank check from the Ford Foundation, Frank took charge of the project in his own distinctive way. He hired talented advisors, Lloyd Ohlin and Herman Goldstein.

Ohlin give them a crash course in field research, and then he and Remington set them loose, armed them a long list of open-ended issues to look for. Accounts of some of their experiences are reminiscent of accounts of district officers in the Ottoman Empire sending periodic reports back to Istanbul, wondering what ever happened to them. Were they received? Opened? Ever read? Were they useful? In one instance, a frustrated researcher complained to the Ford Foundation program officer that the project's research strategy was random, and that it was a waste of time and money. The program officer gave a typical Ford Foundation response: "Don't worry, we are investing in people ... we are creating a new field."

For several summers in the late 1950s and early 1960s, field researchers would return to Madison, and along with other young scholars and graduate students, who Frank had invited, would take stock of the research to date. They waded through the boxes of field notes that had been filed during the year, identifying themes, coming to tentative conclusions, and tweaking the guidelines for further observation.

It simply cannot be the case, but it does appear to be so, that Frank and his advisory body did not give thought—or much thought—as to who would ultimately write up the reports that were based on this exponentially growing mountain of field notes. Researchers themselves, who assembled their notes and produced insightful analysis, wrote some of the articles. "Free riders"—young law and social science professors and graduate students invited to one or more of the summer institutes—wrote others.

Perhaps the two most well-known articles that flowed from the summer institutes were written by people who had among the least to do with the project, one-shot participants who dropped in for one of the summer institutes and returned home with a tenure article in hand. Joe Goldstein's *Police Discretion Not to Invoke the Criminal Process: Low-Visibility Decision in the Administration of Justice* (1960), and Sanford Kadish's *Legal Norms and Discretion in the Police and Sentencing Process* (1962), tenure articles both, are perhaps the most well-known publications flowing from the project. Ironically, these two articles came to diametrically opposite conclusions. Goldstein was suspicious of discretion and proposed to limit it. Kadish was much less wary of discretion. Such was Frank's generosity. Numerous other well-known articles developed in this way. (The list is long. See Ohlin and Remington, 1993.)

I don't know who was who, but after much delay, countless articles and five big books were eventually produced. However, the project did what the Ford Foundation program officer said he wanted: it created a new type of criminal law and procedure scholar and sent a great many of them out to revise the understanding of the nature of the criminal process. In particular, it created the careers of some of Frank's students, who no doubt were recruited to Wisconsin's LL.M. and S.J.D. programs with support from the project, and were given the opportunity to turn the jumble of field notes into books. Frank's graduate students were authors of at least three of the five monographs produced by the project: Robert O. Dawson (*Sentencing*); Frank W. Miller (*Prosecution*); and Wayne LaFave (*Arrest*). I am not sure about the trio of authors, Lawrence Tiffany, Donald M. McIntyre, Jr., and Daniel L. Rotenberg (*Detection of Crime: Stopping and Questioning Search and Seizure, Encouragement and Entrapment*). The author of the fifth volume was Donald Newman (*Conviction: The Determination of Guilt or Innocence without Trial*), who, at the time Frank drew him into the project, was an assistant professor in Wisconsin's School of Social Work. Certainly, the project enhanced their careers and the type of empirically based scholarship that defined their work.

Curiously, none of the three most important people on the project ever produced a substantial publication deriving directly from the project. Neither Frank, nor his two closest research advisors, Lloyd Ohlin and Herman Goldstein (this may be a warning for those of you attracted to big empirical research projects). Still, their importance was recognized. After a stint as Police Chief O.W. Wilson's administrative assistant in Chicago, Herman Goldstein returned to Madison to join the law faculty in the mid-1960s. Lloyd Ohlin went on to play an important role in the President's Crime Commission and receive an appointment at the Harvard Law School. In fact, most of those involved in the project came to occupy important positions on the President's Crime Commission, as researchers, advisors, and administrators. And all of them subsequently produced landmark scholarship which derived from their experience with the project. I will return to discuss the impact of the project on the work of the Crime Commission in a moment.

The ABF Survey of Criminal Justice Administration accomplished what the Ford Foundation most wanted: a transformation of the field of the study of criminal justice administration, and following that, a more informed form of administration of the criminal justice system. The project's influences were numerous and diverse. Indeed, it would be impossible even to begin to try to catalog them all. However, several of its most important effects are readily apparent and I discuss them briefly below.

Most obviously, the ABF survey—a research project—produced a library of research that illuminated the customs and manners of the police, prosecutors, defense, attorneys, judges, bail bondsmen, and the rest of the large cast of characters that shape the administration of the criminal process. It took some time for some of these results to be produced, but eventually five huge monographs saw the light of day. They set the standard for empirical research on the administration of criminal justice at the time, and this work led to a flood of even more sophisticated empirical research in the 1960s and onward.

In addition, the project:

–Led to the establishment of the School of Criminal Justice Administration at SUNY Albany, a school founded with the explicit mission to study the actual administration of criminal justice. Remington, Ohlin, Goldstein, and Newman all played important roles in the shaping of the mission and plans for the School, and in fact were asked en masse to become its founding faculty. Only Donald Newman accepted the offer, and eventually became its dean. (For an account of this development, see Ohlin and Remington, 1993.)

–Had, through the connection with Arthur Sherry, an influence on reshaping the curriculum at the School of Criminology at Berkeley and perhaps in the recruitment of Caleb Foote from the University of Pennsylvania.

–Challenged sociology, criminology, and even political science departments to expand their focus beyond the etiology of crime and official statistics reported by agencies to the empirical study of the administration of the complexity of the criminal process. I was one of those indirectly affected and drawn into the field.

–Changed the nature of teaching criminal law, and especially criminal procedure, by promoting "revolutionary" materials and casebooks, which forced the issue of "discretion" to be considered in all areas of the criminal process (including the publication of Remington and Melli's own materials and casebooks still used at Wisconsin). While some of us are disappointed that the project and later the findings reported by the President's Crime Commission did not have a greater impact on the way criminal law and procedure are taught in law schools, there is no question that vast differences took place between the 1950s and the 1970s. And it has made a substantial and permanent difference in criminal law and procedure course offerings at the University of Wisconsin.

–Encouraged the Ford Foundation to invest still more funds in "developing people" who could take a more realistic approach to the understanding of the administration of criminal justice, and who could make the process more transparent. Among them:

–Caleb Foote's pioneering studies of the administration of bail in Philadelphia and the allied project in New York City, which were supported by grants from the Ford Foundation.

–The Chicago jury study project, the single most expensive empirical study of the administration of justice (here the study of civil and criminal juries as compared to bench trials), at the University of Chicago, under the direction of Harry Kalven and Hans Zeisel.

–The establishment of the Vera Foundation (later Institute) in New York City, which began promoting bail reform and then pretrial diversion and has since launched a host of other innovations in New York City, across the United States, and even abroad. It has become the R&D unit of a criminal justice system with complex functions and management, but one which has no R&D capacity of its own. Incidentally, the founder of Vera, Herbert Sturz, was a graduate in Social Work from the University of Wisconsin at Madison. He clearly learned the Wisconsin Idea, and took it with him back to New York. He is one of my heroes, and for years when I was at the University in Madison, I unsuccessfully pressed for him to be awarded an honorary doctoral degree.

–The establishment of the Police Foundation in Washington, D.C., which decades later still continues to provide a forum for empirically grounded discussion of police practices and support for field research to test new police practices. The Foundation regularly encourages and works with both researchers and police departments to conduct randomized field experiments testing the efficacy of alternative policing practices and intervention programs.

–More recently, the establishment of the Center for Court Innovation, also initially supported by the Ford Foundation, which has pioneered in the development of problem-solving courts, an approach directly traceable to the work of the ABF survey and the work of its Associate Research Director Herman Goldstein and his pioneering book, *Problem-Oriented Policing*.

One contribution bears extended discussion, the project's impact in shaping the agenda of the President's Commission on Crime and Law Enforcement, which was created by President Lyndon Johnson in 1965, and supplying the commission with many of its advisors, key personnel, and research staff. When one looks though the list of those who played major roles on that commission and its various task forces, the names of those involved in Wisconsin-ABF project are all over the place. The project also was influential in the establishment of two related enterprises, the ABA's Minimum Standards of Justice Project, and Department of Justice's Standards and Goals Project. One only has to look at their missions, their structures, and the names involved in these various enterprises to see the handprints of the ABF's survey all over them.

Unfortunately, the importance of the publications of the ABF survey has been obscured by the work of the President's Crime Commission and developments that flowed from it: *The Report of the President's Crime Commission*; the Commission's various *Task Force Reports*; the establishment of the Law Enforcement Assistance Administration, and the founding of the National Institute of Justice. (See United States President's Commission on Law Enforcement and Administration of Justice, 1967.) Because the slow-paced publications of the ABF reports were overtaken by the mass of materials produced by the Crime Commission, the invaluable contribution of the former in shaping the latter is not so obvious.

Even a casual reading of the ABF reports demonstrates how important the approach pioneered by Remington and his colleagues and the people involved in both enterprises were in shaping the agenda of the Crime Commission. However, much of this has been lost in the chronology of the Crime Commission.

There is still another reason for the eclipse of the ABF project by the President's Crime Commission. The project emphasized that criminal justice posed an immense administrative and management challenge for officials, set about understanding the nature of the administrative mess, and offered reflection on how it might be better managed. Many of the most innovative features of the Crime Commission drew on this core insight and tried to point the way for still better understanding and management.

Unfortunately, however, the commission, and especially its influential Task for Report on Science and Technology, created a new nomenclature. To emphasize the need for clarity and management, Remington and the ABF named the project "The ABF's Survey of the *Administration* of Justice," perhaps unwittingly echoing the management and administrative concerns of the Wisconsin Progressives and the problem-solving approaches to management highlighted in the work of Chester Bernard, Philip Selznick, and John Dewey. However, by the time the President's Crime Commission was up and running, systems analysis was all the rage. In addition, owing to the interests of the Director of the Task Force on Science and Technology, Al Blumstein, an operations research expert on loan to the commission from the Institute of Defense Analysis, the term criminal justice *system* came to replace the term *administration* of criminal justice. (See Mayeux, 2018.) These changes both obscured the connection to the ABF project, and subtly shifted emphasis away from the focus on discretion, administration, and management in favor of a holistic rational systems approach.

Most readers have no doubt seen the famous funnel of justice that came to symbolize the commission's concern with the criminal justice *system* as a whole. There is no question that this picture was and is useful. But the operations research feature that drove the emphasis on systems analysis seemed to suggest the idea of a single synoptic perspective—the rational systems engineer—who could tweak the various conduits into and out of the funnel so that it could operate at optimal efficiency. The term "system" came to suggest something of a rational order whose different parts were working, or should work, in harmony, harnessed together to work towards the same objective. At least this view has been maintained both by the coiners of the term, as well the term's critics. Systems advocates maintain a quest for the well-oiled machine whose parts pull together. Critics maintain that this is both false in theory and false in fact. They maintain that the theory of adversarial process, which animates the criminal process, institutionalizes conflict, embraces conflicting values, amplifies differences of opinion, and indeed fosters antagonism and inefficiency is at the very heart of the system—all the time enabling vast discretionary judgment throughout the entire process. In addition, as the work of the ABF project makes so abundantly clear, so many other—noncriminal—objectives are bootlegged or superimposed on the criminal process that it is nonsense to conceive of it, even in ideal theory, as a well-oiled machine devoted exclusively to processing criminal charges.

In retrospect, it is unfortunate that the ABF's nomenclature was displaced. The ABF survey emphasized the need for the administration and management of highly discretionary decisions of low visibility made by line-staff. Even though the terms are allied, systems analysis conjures up a different set of challenges. Still, the ABF studies set in motion a revolution in the way we think about coping with the challenges of crime and its administration.

I should stop here, but want to go on to make three additional points:

First, I was warned not to say anything about the criminal law clinical programs at Wisconsin, but I cannot help myself. I must make one brief comment. My clinical colleagues and their students at Berkeley and elsewhere are always dreaming up ways to challenge the criminal justice authorities or probation officers for constitutional shortcomings. In Wisconsin, clinical faculty and students work in the offices with these officials, take an "administrative" approach, and ask, "How can *we* do things better?" The Wisconsin approach wins easily in my view. Just one illustration is the fact that two of Wisconsin Law's clinical faculty have served as commissioners of corrections in this state. This is just one of the many examples of the genius of Frank Remington's administration of justice approach.

Second, apart from his own wonderful contributions, one of Frank's great contributions was not only to recruit Herman Goldstein for the project, but also later onto the Wisconsin faculty. Herman is an influence without peer in the world of the police, not only in the United States, the UK, and Australia, but also throughout the world. When Herman's book, *Problem-Oriented Policing*, was reviewed by Lawrence Sherman, now the Director of the Institute of Criminology at University of Cambridge and himself a distinguished authority on the police, he wrote that it was the second-best book on the police ever written, the first being Patrick Colquhoun's 1796 book, *A Treatise on the Police of the Metropolis*. High praise indeed, except I think Larry got the order reversed. In Japan, the state designates a tiny handful of artists and scholars as "National Living Treasures." If Wisconsin had this practice, surely Herman would have been designated a Living Treasure. In addition, you had him among you for fifty years! All thanks to Frank Remington's foresight.

Finally, I want to say something about Remington's work and American legal realism, Wisconsin's tradition of law and society research and the new legal realism; and John Dewey's pragmatism. Frank represents all three traditions. I'll briefly touch on the first two because they are so easily recognizable to this audience, but then elaborate a bit on the third point that ties Remington to pragmatism.

Legal realism emphasized the indeterminacy of legal rules. Legal realists were rule skeptics: abstract rules cannot decide concrete cases. Now, and probably in the heyday of the Formalists, no one seriously denies that discretionary judgment is inevitably employed as a supplement when applying legal rules in all but the most cut and dry legal decisions. By now, we are all legal realists. Frank Remington certainly would have subscribed to this view. A minor but important tradition in legal realism emphasized fact skepticism. Legal decisions are indeterminate because facts are ambiguous. Here too Frank would agree. The new legal realism emphasizes law in context, and the value in shaping and sharpening discretion through informed empirical understanding of the law in action. To this end, it emphasizes collaborative research by social scientists and legal scholars in order to facilitate both the formulation of informed questions and in providing answers to them. One might say that Frank's entire career was testimony to these core principles of the new legal realism. Frank and his mentor, Hurst, also did more than reflect on the indeterminacy of rules.

Above all, however, Frank was a disciple of Hurst. Like Hurst, Remington was a major contributor to the law and society tradition, insisting on observing law in action, and uncovering its many nonobvious functions. This is seen in his own work, and the work of dozens of young scholars whose careers he helped to launch, and whose works he promoted. His influence was so widespread and varied, I could not even begin to develop a list here for fear of alienating the many people I would inadvertently omit.

There is one more feature of Frank's and Herman's work that to my knowledge has not been explored in any depth. Frank Remington's—and I should emphasize, Herman Goldstein's—perspective entails much more than supplementing the interpretation of legal rules with informed judgment. While their work certainly was informed by empirical research and legal realism, old and new, their approach was much more. They approach legal rules and legally relevant facts from a pragmatist's perspective. Law is not so much a system of rules to be interpreted, applied, and enforced (even as it is filtered through the indeterminacy of rules and facts). Rather, laws create offices, establish aims, and create arenas for solving concrete problems. They point to aims and set constraints and empower officials to invoke or not invoke the law in the process of addressing problems that are likely only to be roughly identified by legal definitions of offences. That is, the law establishes an arena in which problems are to be addressed. In this view, discretion is much more than an informed judgment or a psychological predisposition that is a necessary component for interpreting and applying rules. The law is an instrument—a resource—to be invoked or not invoked when addressing and trying to cope with concrete problems. What may be most important about the law is that it authorizes some people to exercise their discretion to invoke or not invoke a law in the process of solving concrete problems. This is something quite different from "applying" or "interpreting" a legal rule. It is administration in light of the aims of a regulatory regime.

In Frank's experience of the winter of 1949, he saw the prosecutor reaching out to invoke the threat of a criminal prosecution in what was ostensibly a civil matter in order to solve a problem: to render justice to those who had been defrauded. In Herman's pioneering work on the police, time and time again he watched the police "fail" to make an arrest because their intervention—just their presence—had already gone a long way to solve the problem at hand, or make an arrest not so much in anticipation of a charge and a conviction, but to diffuse an explosive situation. Alternatively, he watched them make arrests in questionable cases because their sense of justice led them to press for criminal sanctions. Although certainly discretionary and shaped by variable motives and senses of justice, these decisions are not so much a product of flexible interpretation due to ambiguous rules or uncertain facts as they are an effort at rendering situational justice. They reflect the realization that human experience is vastly more complicated than any set of rules laid down to try to govern it. John Dewey and the Pragmatist tradition recognizes this, and so understands law as a "tool" to be invoked or not invoked with discretion, not with the aim of interpreting and enforcing the law, but for the purpose of problem-solving.

This perspective is writ clear in the Vera Institute's monograph, *Felony Arrests*, which I think is the single best account of the administration of criminal courts ever written. That study finds that roughly fifty percent of all felony arrests are dropped by a prosecutor or dismissed by a judge. This is not because the police made bad arrests or prosecutors or judges were lazy or careless. It was in large part because about half of all arrests involve people who know each other—family members, friends, neighbors, coworkers, and the like. In such cases, police officers, prosecutors, defense attorneys, probation officers, judges—everyone—usually agrees that while all the elements of a crime are present, it is only a felony in a "technical" sense. It makes more sense to regard the incident as an interpersonal conflict that went too far. This means that unless there were severe injuries or damages, it makes little sense to press for conviction. Arrest was a reasonable situational response. It diffused the problem by separating the principals. After that, little is gained by pursuing criminal cases. At best, it is a social problem, not a crime, and best dealt within the family or neighborhood or by a social worker. What Remington and Goldstein found in their extensive first-hand experience with prosecutors and police is that this situation is not the exception but may be the rule. It is at the center of the administration of criminal justice, not the periphery. Their effort was to bring it to the fore, understand it, and help officials learn to solve problems they confront more effectively.

In this view, discretion and the exercise of discretion—and an administrative sensibility—is at the heart of an effective criminal justice system, which might best be understood as a poorly designed regulatory regime. It cannot be avoided, and rather than trying to banish it or reduce it to a bare minimum, Remington and Goldstein—like organizational theorists and students of administrative behavior—wanted to teach officials how to employ their discretion to the best advantage. Of course, they would acknowledge, discretion can be and is used in hateful and destructive ways. Indeed, study after study of police and racial minorities reveal this on a daily basis. So do studies of charging and sentencing. However, their response to these problems, following Dewey, is not to try to eradicate discretion (a fruitless task to begin with), but to devise administrative structures that provide meaningful oversight, and modes of recruitment and training that minimize the discrimination impulse to begin with. Of course, this is more easily said than done. But sixty years of trying to banish racial discrimination through efforts to restrict discretion have proven to be abject failures. Problem-oriented policing needs to be expanded to include problem-oriented prosecution and problem-oriented judging and sentencing as well. Since the ABF survey, this approach has continued slowly to gain adherents, but such an approach is still in its infancy.

Conclusion

The genius of Frank Remington was to conceive of the criminal process as an administrative process, and to try to design an administrative process suitable to the task at hand. To date, the most fully realized model of this is Herman Goldstein's model of problem-oriented policing. But the task is to expand this to all aspects of the criminal process, and most particularly the courts.

Not surprising is that this pioneering perspective emerged in Wisconsin. Wisconsin had the tradition of the Wisconsin Idea. It was the home of the Progressive movement. Wisconsin faculty helped shape and establish the American Law Institute (ALI). And, Wisconsin was among the first—perhaps the first—to embrace the modern administrative state. Frank Remington was a native son (who refused to leave the state when plied with attractive offers elsewhere) who imbibed this rich legacy and had the foresight to recruit Herman Goldstein to join him in the enterprise. The results included the ABF survey, a pioneering approach to teaching criminal justice administration, and ongoing collaboration with state and local criminal justice officials. All of these were long-established hallmarks of the new legal realism before the term was even coined.

Resources used in preparing this presentation

Recollections on many discussions with Frank Remington and Herman Goldstein during my time in Madison, 1977–1984, and occasional discussions with Erica Eisinger and Samuel Walker at various locations.

American Bar Foundation. (1955). "The Administration of Criminal Justice in the United States: Plan for a Survey." Chicago, IL: American Bar Foundation.

Armstrong, Walter P., Jr. (1968). "Administration of Criminal Justice: The American Bar Foundation Project." *American Bar Association Journal,* 54: 261-263.

Clune, William. (2019). "Legal Realist Innovation in the Wisconsin Law School Curriculum 1950–1970: Four Influential Introductory Courses," prepared for the program, "Law in Action in Wisconsin Law School Courses: 1950–1970, School of Law," University of Wisconsin, March 8, 2019, and adapted for publication in this volume.

Dawson, Robert O. (1969). Sentencing: The Decision as to Type, Length, and Conditions of Sentence. (Boston: Little, Brown).

Feeley, Malcolm M. (2018). "How to Think about Court Reform," *BU L. Rev.*, 98: 673.

Goldstein, Herman. (1990). *Problem-Oriented Policing* (Philadelphia: Temple University Press).

Goldstein, Herman. (1979). "Improving Policing: A Problem-Oriented Approach," *Crime and Delinquency,* 25 (109): 236-258.

Goldstein, Joseph. (1960). "Police Discretion Not to Invoke the Criminal Process: Low-Visibility Decision in the Administration of Justice," 69 *Yale L.J.*, 69: 543.

Kadish, Sanford. (1962). "Legal Norm and Discretion in the Police and Sentencing Process," *Harv. L. Rev.* 75: 904 (1962).

Kimball, Edward L. (1994). *Frank Remington: Contributions to Criminal Justice.* (Madison: Wisconsin Law School).

LaFave, Wayne R. (1970). *Arrest: The Decision to Take a Suspect into Custody* (Boston: Little Brown).

Mayeux, Sara. (2018). "The Idea of 'The Criminal Justice System,'" *American Journal of Criminal Law,* 45: 55.

Miller, Frank W. (1970). *Prosecution: The Decision to Charge a Suspect with a Crime* (Boston: Little Brown).

Pound, Roscoe, and Felix Frankfurter (eds.). (1922/1968). *Criminal Justice in Cleveland.* (Montclair, NJ: Patterson Smith).

Newman, Donald. (1966). *Conviction: The Determination of Guilt or Innocence without Trial* (Boson: Little Brown).

Ohlin, Lloyd, and Frank J. Remington (eds.). (1993). *Discretion in Criminal Justice: The Tension Between Individualization and Uniformity* (Albany: SUNY Press). (This volume contains an extensive, but far from an exhaustive, list of publications flowing from the ABF survey.)

Tiffany, Lawrence P., Donald M. McIntyre, Jr. and Daniel L. Rotenberg. (1967). *Detection of Crime: Stopping and Questioning, Search and Seizure, Encouragement and Entrapment.* (Boston: Little Brown).

Walker, Samuel J. (1992). "Origins of the Contemporary Criminal Justice Paradigm: The American Bar Foundation Survey, 1953-1969," *Justice Quarterly,* 9: 47.

United States President's Commission on Law Enforcement and Administration of Justice. (1967). "The Challenge of Crime in a Free Society: A Report." Washington, D.C.: U.S. Government Printing Office.

Vera Institute of Justice. (1974). *Felony Arrests: Their Prosecution and Disposition in New York City's Courts.* (Vera Institute of Justice, 1974; revised edition, New York: Longman, 1980).

Three Fragments on Doing Legal History, or Willard Hurst and Me

Hendrik Hartog

"legal history as a series of curiosities embedded in changing winds of historical practices" (Monica Huerta)

Abstract

This paper has three fragments or parts: first, an overview of what is it like to do legal history today; second, Willard Hurst's distinctive view of legal history, with its significant omissions and flaws; and, third, notwithstanding these flaws, reasons why Hurst's work is admired and relevant to this day. Hartog taught legal history at Wisconsin while Hurst was an emeritus professor, considers Hurst a mentor, and has regularly assigned readings from Hurst in his own courses.

Overview. Legal history involves a love of legal sources like archives and trial transcripts which require the historian to look beyond the law library. It is about but does not cause big major changes, such as feminism. As taught in law schools, it represents a kind of humanism, an understanding of past choices and lost alternatives, and a sense of modesty and normative restraint. It also brings a critical posture toward conventional legal histories, the histories within law, lawyers' histories, as well as toward conventional narratives of legal change, such as evolutionary or leftist determinism and originalism. But is legal history anything more than humanism and a critique of bad history within law? Willard Hurst certainly thought so.

Hurst and Legal History. The second part of the paper examines Hurst's views as illustrated in Hurst's book published in 1965, *Justice Holmes on Legal History*, as well as other works. Hurst agreed with Holmes on the importance of "will" as a creative force, which Hurst called individualism. Hurst's individualism, while a source of energy, was not idealized, as it contained strong elements of fallibility, greed, ambition, and waste. Hurst saw American legal history in terms of sequence and context, a contingent consequence of American democracy. He agreed with Holmes that law expressed the cumulative expression of deeply held values which led to the large and durable patterns we call institutions. For Hurst, these deeply held values were the middle-class point of view (individualism) and constitutionalism as both an enablement and a constraint on self-interest. The creative potential of individuals was released through laws such as property, contract, and business corporations. For Hurst, these embodied a faith in "manipulation and contrivance to increase yields from nature and social relations" (other people). Limits on these freedoms were created because of the abuse of power. "Constitutionalism" referred to representative democracy and the police power rather than constitutional law made by judges. Hurst was part of the *Lochner* generation in viewing the Supreme Court as an obstacle to benign social legislation (such as workers' compensation for accidents).

Hurst thus imagined a continuing community of politically competent Americans who made the policies and the laws and who constructed legislation in their image from the nineteenth century through the New Deal up to 1960, a view that seems to define American civilization yet leaves out much of American legal history. Omitted were the many groups who were excluded from democracy (women, African Americans, Native Americans), and those injured by law, for example, by the fugitive slave acts and legal violence of the federal government in expropriating Native American lands (such as by the rights sought by the Pike's Creek settlers featured in Hurst's widely read 1956 book, *Law and the Conditions of Freedom*). Hurst's view of history as a gradual evolution toward the national economy culminating in the New Deal paid little attention to political parties, race conflict, populist crises, waves of immigrants, Progressives, and labor movements. He saw constitutional rights as the enemy of benign social legislation rather than as a counter-majoritarian source of power which was the view that gained strength beginning in the 1960s, at the same time that he was writing. He showed no interest in the mobilization of subordinated classes and was dismissive of new left historians during the time that Hartog was at Wisconsin. His view of a homogenous American culture was shattered by the drastic cultural fragmentations that occurred toward the end of his career. A recurrent puzzle is Hurst's lack of historical periodization that other historians would recognize as distinctive phases of development (for example, ecological problems and policies other than Hurst's brilliant work on the destruction of Wisconsin's northern forests). A disturbing note is Hurst's citation in his Holmes book of *Buck v. Bell* as an example of how society should take steps improve health and technology, roughly the same rationale invoked by Justice Holmes in his opinion for the Court refusing to strike down the Virginia law requiring compulsory sterilization. Hartog does not believe Hurst was racist or a eugenicist, rather that he saw the law as a plausible exercise of the police power, which for Hurst also included public education, public health, roads, and social. But, written in 1965, it was another example of how Hurst had grown out of step with the times.

Hurst's relevance today. Despite the flaws, there remains much to admire and emulate in Hurst's work. First, Hurst's emphasis on the ideal of a middle class as a unifying force is validated by the long struggles of groups since the Civil War to become middle class as the only way to gain access to the legal benefits and rewards that America offered. Second, what excites Hartog about Hurst's portrayal of American law is his willingness to look at law as a human activity that takes shape across legal/doctrinal silos. All rights, Hurst wrote, were "limited by the neighborhood of principles of policy which are other than those on which the particular right as founded." His willingness to imagine legal fields as united by common problems and by a shared culture and common context stimulated a legal history that cross-challenged and transformed legal doctrine. Third, disdaining a search for origins (the notion that the past contained the germ of an answer to legal problems), his work is remembered for always starting in the middle of things. Legal and economic pasts were understood retrospectively and adapted. Fourth is his focus on contingency. Contexts would always bleed into new sequences. He said that "the life of the law represents no homeostatic functionality or self-adjusting process but the product of the qualities and defects of men's will and feeling." This meant, for him, the law was fundamentally legislative in character, and "the secret route from which law draws all the juices of life is consideration of what is expedient for the community concerned." In that sense one might say that, for Hurst, law was always politics, even if he seemed unconcerned with party politics, and that led him to a critique of what he called organic metaphors and evolutionary portraits of legal change. The middle class may have defined much of law in crucial moments of American history, but those middle-class manifestations of law were dependent on contingent and unpredictable decisions and relationships of many men and women and institutions who differed and fought about many things. He did not emphasize the explicit political struggles that underlay those decisions, but no reading of Hurst can escape a sense of the constant and continual underlying presence of the struggles. In that sense, his writings prefigure the strongest features of what would become critical legal studies.

Addendum/Afterword. In an addendum to his paper, Hartog urges thinking of legal history as an "accompaniment" rather than as a part of academic law, a perspective that he sees as compatible with Hurst. Hurst's work did not express an inside or outside view of law. Rather he saw law as ever an expression of culture, law as constitutive of society, and society constitutive of law (in this way prefiguring critical legal studies). Law is everywhere all the time. His great study of the lumber industry was meant to describe a particular set of legal and social practices but also to represent a fragment of the larger culture. Law/culture is fractal in that sense. When Hartog was still at Wisconsin, Hurst urged him to expand an essay on pig keepers in New York City in a way that would recognize larger patterns of judicial notice (thus avoiding the inference of a completely autonomous legal pluralism and counterculture). Deviant and resistant legal episodes always contain both hegemonic and oppositional cultures, for example, the modern tradition of constitutional rights as counter-majoritarian (as does the simple exercise of legal representation in criminal prosecutions). A constitutive view in legal history means that legal history cannot be seen as internal to the law or as an instrument of law reform. It is not only about law in action and the impact of law or only about law reform in the progressive mode. But it does fit the larger frame of law and social science as a study of both the inside and outside of the legal system, within a constitutive framework that ultimately dissolves that distinction.

Three Fragments on Doing Legal History, or Willard Hurst and Me

What does it mean to know law—to understand legal sources—as existing in historical time? That is the question, or rather, my question. Not how to mine a legal archive to make social or cultural or political or economic generalizations about a historical moment or an era. Not how to find the origins of, or an explanation for, a contemporary situation in longer legal time. Not what one can learn about the constraining power of a regulation, or about the failure of a regulation to constrain, or any number of other questions that historians and others today pose about law. Those are all ways of doing legal history that have concerned me at various times, and that may concern me again in the future. Here, though, my obsessions are defiantly (though awkwardly and inconsistently and naively) epistemological and jurisprudential. When I as a historian identify something as law, when I find myself seduced by a legal source—by a trial transcript, by a lawyer's brief, by a judicial opinion, by a passage in a treatise, or a letter or memoir of a litigant, by a justification for a statute or an interpretation of that statute—what is it that I am seduced by?

I'm not there yet, though. I have only glimmers of answers for the questions that consume me. But what you have here are three fragments that will possibly play a part in a longer work:

I begin with a sketch of what it is to do legal history today, in the wake of the enormous growth and development of the field of legal history in legal education, over the past forty years.

I continue with an extended examination of the answer Willard Hurst (one of the intellectual godfathers of the Law and Society Association and the founder of the modern discipline of legal history) gave more than fifty-five years ago to the question, "what does legal history do?"

Finally, in a fragment of a fragment, I spin off of Hurst to begin the work of suggesting an understanding of legal history less tied to legal thought and legal advocacy. How to practice a legal history that is something apart from legal scholarship.[1]

I should add that I wrote these fragments in part as an effort to situate legal history in tension with, and in conversation with, American legal education, with academic law as taught in American law schools. The genesis of this piece (or these pieces) intersects with my desire to under-

[1] In light of the evolution of my own thinking over the past year, since I presented this to the Davis Seminar, and in light of the cataclysmic events of the past year, I added a short addendum or postscript.

stand what it means that over the past forty years legal history, particularly American legal history, has become so thoroughly institutionalized within elite legal education. So that today a respectable law school is likely to have several faculty members who identify themselves as, and are probably professionally trained in, legal history.[2]

Fragment One

I have been a self-described legal historian for something like forty-five years. It has been good to me and for me. It has allowed me to have a profession and an identity and a certain amount of respect.

But what have I done, as a legal historian? That is harder to say. I have "educated" undergraduates and law students about the field of legal history. That is, I have introduced them to what other legal historians do. I have trained a number of graduate students, who have themselves "become" legal historians, often in law schools, sometimes in history departments. I have been part of, and in all immodesty I have played a part in, the construction of a community of legal historians that has flourished over the past forty-plus years. I have written books.

I have, it is important to add, also had the opportunity and the gift to have fallen in love with a number of primary sources—occasionally a whole archive—that I could explore and work with and write about. Being able to work with particular legal sources gave me immense and continuing pleasure. It is something close to an erotic charge to find a source that "does" what I want it to do, that can be played with in the ways that I as a historian play with my sources. Even when the source is "about" subjects—sexual violence, murder, abuse, slavery, oppression, any number of corrupt relationships, and so forth—that anyone not a historian would find immeasurably painful to deal with.[3] Historians know that finding the love object happens rarely. Like almost every historian, I have turned an enormous number of excruciatingly boring pages. And sometimes I have been compelled by the logic of what I meant to write and argue to attend to those excruciatingly boring pages. And yet . . .There is a six-volume set of published lower-court records, from the courts of early nineteenth century

[2] There is, on the other hand, an equally interesting question about the relationship of the legal history that I am writing about to the growing presence of studies of legal texts (particularly trials and cases) in several sectors of academic history, notably at Princeton University and of course, and in particular, at the Davis Seminar. That is a question I want to return to in the book-to-be that these fragments will probably attach to, but it remains to be worked out in the future. And there is a third question also to be confronted, also ignored here: about the forms of dialogue and conversation (the breaching of the silos) emergent and incipient (and wished for) between academic law and professional history.

[3] Thus, that wonderful conversation with other historians that usually begins: "What a cool source!"

New York City, that I have been using, better, exploring and playing with, since I was a graduate student. I still get a thrill every time I find a reason to open (today, go online to open) those records. Being able to read the testimony and the lawyers' arguments in any number of trials still feels like an undeserved treat. And there are other texts, including pamphlets and treatises and some canonical opinions and monuments of conventional (high) legal thought, that give me a similar sensation. As Willard Hurst once admitted to me, although said in his characteristically repressed Midwestern way, doing legal history can be a "hedonistic" treat (at least for some few of us).[4]

In one or two instances, my scholarship has been cited in judicial opinions. Seeing my work in those opinions has its satisfactions. And yet, it would be fatuous for me to claim that it is because of my scholarship that same-sex marriage was declared constitutional. I know, as any sentient adult would know, that my scholarship was, at most, legitimation for a conclusion arrived at by other means. Without my scholarship, nothing would have changed.

For the most part, my being as a legal historian has been indistinguishable from the being of many historians, full stop. I wrote books that relatively few people read. I have worked to make them accessible and readable for an imagined audience of history readers. But for the most part, they were read by other historians and by their students, if that. I taught students. I did the work that college professors do to help manage and administer the institutions we are a part of. I involved myself in a number of professional organizations that slightly widened the audience of those who might engage with me and with my work.

What does legal history do? Often that question becomes a question about why teach legal history and about how legal history has been taught. And that is a particularly complicated question, distinctively so, in the context of a law school.

When asked what was the good of the work that I did, when I taught in a law school, I often mouthed familiar language (more like clichés) about the humanistic goals of history (with legal history as nothing more than an instance of historical practice). I talked about learning about forgotten alternatives, about the widening of sympathy that history may offer, about the need to experience a wide range of normative moral and political judgments made in varying circumstances, about learning both about how different and about how similar the lives and the choices made by "others" in "other" times were. Good history (both good courses and good books) offers opportunities to imagine oneself confronting the dilemmas and choices and situations of those who lived in the past. And history, the

[4] By way of contrast, consider Sam Moyn's comment to the "Law and Legalities" class at Princeton in the spring of 2019, that legal history was boring.

study of the past, or of many pasts, allows the reader/student/writer to explore and argue over what were the beginnings, the middles, and the endings of stories. It is in that sense, unlike the study of the present, where endings are always unknowable. History involves many arguments about contingency and determinism. And more (of course there is much more): history involves a body of practices about record keeping and the construction and reconstruction and imagining of archives that become both the foundation for historical writing and, at the same time, a salient part of the record of human experience (and the foundation for future historical writing). Such archives may be of particular significance in a law school environment where the law library is treated by many to mark the whole of legal experience. Challenging that faith in the sufficiency of the law library is part, a salient part, of what a legal historian in a law school ought to be doing. Doing history is also centrally about critique and challenge: about the mobilization of reasons why prior interpretations were "wrong" or "right" or flawed. In their times as well as in other times. And history is also a philosophical or epistemological discipline, in which the question of the knowability (yes or no, but also more or less) of facts or events or experiences or interpretations is integral to the practice of doing history. Doing history (including learning history or arguing about history) "teaches" a kind of normative modesty or restraint, counters the relentless claims-making that is central to legal study and to political life. And this last, the insistence on modesty or restraint, may be the most important contribution history can make to legal understanding. At least, so it has been for me.

In so far as the work of legal history, that is teaching, is done in a law school, one may argue that all of these humanistic goods ought to be intrinsic to the training of lawyers who need to see the forgotten alternatives that once shaped law, whose sympathies and empathy could use widening, who should experience the range of normative judgments made in past situations. And who also ought to confront the immediate and ultimate unknowability—or the limited knowability —of legal pasts. It may be enough to say that history introduces some elements of humanistic inquiry into the law school curriculum. Doing legal history may affect consciousness and the moral imagination; sometimes. At least, doing and learning history may make lawyers into better lawyers.

Some will add that legal history has a core pedagogical mission, which is to socialize or assimilate students, who may soon become lawyers and judges and powerful legal actors, into the unbroken (or perhaps discontinuous and sometimes broken) narrative of the law across long history. What is a lawyer, at least in the Anglo-American world, but a participant in that long legal culture? And even if one disagrees, even if as a historian one regards the imagined continuing narrative of the law as a retrospective ideological construction, it may well be worth introducing the lawyer-in-training to the ideological foundations of that pervasive and still-present understanding.

And further, there is or was the (perhaps lost or forgotten) democratic promise of social history, opening up the question of who made law, beyond the elites, beyond the usual suspects of political and legal history (as well as constructing more complex human and humane portraits of otherwise stick-figure elites). What does it mean to reveal or to explore or to argue that many (all?) participated in the making of law, including any number of excluded or oppressed or subaltern peoples? What did historians think they were doing when they made those arguments? Were they opening up law for readers and students? Or were they reproducing a false consciousness?

But is being a humanistic voice in any of these varied modalities, along all of these dimensions, doing anything distinctively legal? I'm not making anything new. I'm not making something different. I am being a historian. Just a historian. And one part of doing legal history, at least for me, particularly in the years when I taught in a law school, rested on a kind of modesty or abnegation. I was not doing law. I was not offering legal answers. I was complicating legal answers, if anything. I was teaching a kind of reticence, even as I was also introducing students to the joys of discovery of the distinct worlds—and the love objects, the sources—that open up or become available through research into various legal pasts.

There is a somewhat different stance possible for the historian in a law school, one that deserves mentioning: To do legal history is to stand in a critical relationship (perhaps an aggressively critical relationship) to what I am going to call the conventional historicity within law. Better probably, the conventional historicities of the law. In this sense, legal history may stand apart, can be distinguished, as a practice, from other genres of history or historical practices, particularly those that explore the histories of professional or scientific formations or disciplines. I'm speculating here, but it strikes me as apparent that a critical stance about law (in legal history) usually means something different than a critical stance might mean in other arenas of historical writing and practice and education, because law is different than many other subjects or fields of historical inquiry. Unlike the history of science, for example, which begins with a confrontation with the denial or ignorance of historicity intrinsic to most of the natural sciences, legal history begins in critique and challenge, because law (at least law in the western world) always already has a history, is always located within a variety of political and economic and social historical assumptions and conclusions, many of which will find expression in legal texts. So, legal history often begins with a challenge to the conventional wisdoms (or imagined conventional wisdoms) of the histories (in U.S. legal culture often called lawyers' histories) that shape and define doctrinal law, private and public, in judicial opinions and treatise writing, in law review writing of all sorts, and in statutory debates.

Inescapably, legal history confronts a slew of narratives and spoken and unspoken historicized understandings about legal change, about temporal continuities and periodizations, about durées longues (and short), that are pervasive in law and in legal scholarship. These are the conventional histories within the law. A listing of those conventional histories will always be incomplete, because there are so many of them. And I won't try to provide one here. In the contemporary US-centric academic legal world, here are a few obvious candidates: evolutionary functionalism is still one, as is originalism in several forms. Claims to continuity offer another (law and economics, wealth maximization, or the very long common law tradition). Lefty or feminist or critical race theory skepticism is a third (whatever you think is happening, however hopeful it seems, in the end it all ends up structurally in the reproduction of hierarchy, or hierarchies). Legal process studies almost always reveal or demonstrate how a variety of regulatory initiatives or cultures are constrained (successfully or unsuccessfully, unhappily or happily) by administrative law. Any common law case, any of the chestnuts of the first year law school casebook, when examined closely, will require accounting for a history that has been forgotten or skipped over. To look at such a case, to free it from the bonds of the class casebook, as much superb recent legal historical scholarship does, will almost inevitably invite historical thinking.

Bob Gordon's writings remain an essential repository of how historians (and lawyers who identified with or participated in professionalized legal history in American law schools) have confronted the historicities of the law, although Kunal Parker and others have been complicating and developing Gordon's portrait. I could stop to engage with Gordon's brilliant and canonical mappings of the many varieties of history in law. But I won't, because my goals are different.[5]

Let me note that I read Gordon and others who trail in his wake as implicitly claiming that to do legal history within a law school is to do legal scholarship as it ought to be done. Or to put it less confidently: if there is always history in law, does that mean that doing legal history, even when it is done by professional historians who identify with history rather than with academic law (although they teach in a law school), is just a modality of doing law (probably with a critical edge)? I suspect Gordon might say yes (reluctantly, and only if forced to do so). If that is the case, though, if doing legal history is just doing law, then is the point of legal history

5 Robert Gordon, *Taming the Past* (New York: Cambridge University Press, 2018); Kunal M. Parker, *Common Law, History, and Democracy in America, 1790–1900: Legal Thought Before Modernism*, Cambridge Historical Studies in American Law and Society (New York: Cambridge University Press, 2011).

simply to do academic law or legal scholarship better, to offer a more self-aware or critical account of that inevitable historicity? Is the fundamental goal of work in our field, of what we do, to challenge bad history (the kind conventionally found in legal texts—cases, treatises, the justifications for statutes and regulations)?

Is that enough? Is doing legal history anything more, anything different than doing "law," or correcting the bad history in often "bad" law?

Willard Hurst certainly thought that it was more than that.

Fragment Two

Bill Clune called. He is a friend, a former colleague from Wisconsin Law School, and a distinguished student of legal implementation. Once, early on in his career, he coauthored a famous article about school finance reform, an article that could be said to have launched a generation of litigation and, to some extent, a reformulation of how public education would be financed in many states across the county. His scholarship did something, changed the legal landscape in several important ways.[6]

Today he is a member of a small community of mostly older legal scholars who are working to create a new movement in legal scholarship, one they have called "the new legal realism." He has begun writing about the Wisconsin Law School as a site of pedagogical experimentation, about what it was (in the period 1950 to 1970) to do and to know and to participate in what was then called "law in action." He regards Willard Hurst's legal history as one element in the construction of a body of useful knowledge for the law; a body of useful knowledge he is working to reclaim. He is particularly focused on how Hurst taught legal history to generations of law students at Wisconsin. He believes . . . I'm actually not completely sure what he believes about legal history. But I am confident that he believes legal history does something. And his reading of Hurst's legal history convinces him that Hurst caught something important about the relationship between American law and American capitalism that illuminates and explains . . . something.

We have a much longer conversation, about Hurst and about my relationship with Hurst. I have already promised to participate in a lecture event in the winter about Hurst and Wisconsin. I had expected that I was expected to do the usual hagiographic happy talk about Hurst as a mentor and about the transformative effect reading him had on my life (all of which is true). But this longer conversation led me back to reading Hurst.

And what I found is the subject of this second fragment.

---

[6] John E. Coons, William H. Clune III, and Stephen D. Sugarman, *Private Wealth and Public Education* (Cambridge, MA: Harvard University Press, 1970).

Most historians know Bob Darnton's advice (drawn from his study of the great cat massacre in eighteenth-century Paris). When you don't get what someone was doing, when something you read or examine, a joke or a practice or a text, makes no sense, that is the moment when historical work properly begins. "By picking a document where it is most opaque, we may be able to unravel an alien system of meaning." To offer historical understanding means to take on and to decipher texts, passages, jokes, actions, and images that seem, that are, how to put it, just wrong or stupid. The historian's task is not to make the joke funny, nor is it exactly to explain the joke. It is certainly not to show how a joke then is like or connects to or offers a point of origin for what we find funny today. It is, rather, to situate that joke in its times, perhaps to come to understand how it seemed funny when it was spoken. The goal is not to obliterate distance or time, to make the past accessible or to bring it closer to us. Instead, it is to distance or separate oneself, while allowing the reader some insight into the varieties of human experience, beyond the immediate and the close at hand.[7]

Here I treat one work of Willard Hurst's, his late book of lectures, *Justice Holmes on Legal History*, as if it were a great cat massacre. Obviously, that may seem a weird, perhaps perverse, goal, particularly for those who know me. I always thought of Willard as a mentor. Actually, a dearly beloved mentor. His work has been my lodestar for close to half a century. My students—law students, undergraduate students, and graduate students—have had Hurst imposed on them yearly, for the forty-three years that I have been teaching. I would possibly not be a legal historian, but for having come upon the work of Hurst when I was in law school.[8]

And, to go farther, Hurst did not live in some distant past, when cat massacres occurred. He was roughly the same age as my father. I knew him well during the years I taught at Wisconsin. He was an emeritus faculty member by then, but active and intellectually forceful. He and his wife Francis were very kind to Nancy and to me. He was, when I first met him, only a bit older than the age I am now.[9]

---

7 Robert Darnton, The Great Cat Massacre and Other Episodes in French Cultural History (New York: Basic Books, 1984).

8 Hendrik Hartog, "Snakes in Ireland: A Conversation with Willard Hurst," *Law and History Review* 12, no. 2 (Autumn 1994): 370–90.

9 I might add that in our many conversations Willard and I never talked much about the teaching of legal history, as such. I don't think he cared very much about law teaching, and he was uninterested in educational experiments. He cared about his legislation course, and he

In preparation for this talk, I opened up *Justice Holmes on Legal History,* a work I had bought on remainder sale in Boston when I was a graduate student, but that I had never read carefully. I now realize that it can fairly be characterized as summarizing what American legal history meant for Willard Hurst, as of 1964, shortly after he published his masterwork, *Law and Economic Growth*, at the end of nearly two decades of work. In its pages, I found a mysterious work that bore little relation to the legal history that I have practiced or taught for the past forty years. It is a book shaped by values that were already archaic in 1965, when it was published.[10]

Let me not overstate my distance from Hurst's understanding. There remains much to draw from the Hurst corpus for a present-day understanding of what I aspire to as a legal historian. Or, as I will explain in the third "fragment," I continue to draw from it. Hurst remains good to think with and through, even when much of one's thinking is against.

In the lectures that became *Justice Holmes on Legal History*, Hurst used quotations from Holmes's judicial opinions and occasional writings. (He did not quote from Holmes's earlier explicitly historical writing, writing that became the canonical but largely unreadable work, *The Common Law*). These quotations (often aphoristic) allowed Hurst to reflect on what legal history was as a useful practice. By practice (not a word either Holmes or Hurst used), I mean to mark Holmes's and Hurst's notion that thinking through what they understood to be American legal history allowed access to a broader and deeper understanding both about the nature of law in America and of American history, full stop. What Hurst sought was something like the philosophical understanding that Holmes in the last two pages of his famous essay/lecture "The Path of the Law" declared just out of reach of those who merely practiced law. Hurst was not interested in making legal history useful for legal practice, as such. Hurst meant to articulate the meaning of "American law." And for him,

believed strongly that law schools ought to focus on legislation rather than the judiciary. He liked that a course he had co-created a generation earlier, that focused on the evolution of workmen's compensation law, was called "law in society." And he liked assigning and teaching a variety of set pieces in American political and constitutional thought (for example, the debate between Jefferson and Hamilton over the constitutionality of the Bank of the United States, almost everything that Hamilton wrote about economic policy, the Dartmouth College and the Charles River Bridge Cases, some Holmes, and a few other chestnuts that focused on law or legislation and the economy). But teaching legal history to law students didn't really interest him.

[10] James Willard Hurst, *Law and Economic Growth: The Legal History of the Lumber Industry in Wisconsin, 1836–1915* (Cambridge, MA.: Belknap Press of Harvard University Press, 1964).

perhaps not for Holmes, that came close to articulating the meaning of "America."

I don't mean to suggest that Holmes and Hurst thought alike. And they certainly didn't write alike. As Hurst regularly acknowledged throughout the text, Holmes was hostile to the "middle-class culture" that lay at the heart of Hurst's understanding. Holmes also did not, according to Hurst, reflect hard about legislation. His focus always rested on the judiciary. And Holmes was bored by the social science of his day, even as he acknowledged the emerging power of science and economics. By contrast, Hurst identified with the social science of his time, and he was immersed in the functionalisms characteristic of postwar sociology. While Holmes emphasized the centrality of "will" and the "martial spirit" (Hurst was not entirely immune to that as well), Hurst gave more weight to the inevitable fallibility and the failures that marked the lives and ambitions of willful men (this he would later acknowledge he drew primarily from his reading of Reinhold Niebuhr). He regularly pointed to the wastefulness that had long characterized American life (this was of course the core of his massive study of the legal destruction of the forests of northern Wisconsin across the nineteenth century, published around the same time as the lectures that became *Justice Holmes on Legal History*).[11]

And yet, Hurst channeled Holmes for several purposes. He too focused on "will," although often translated into the language of "individualism." And they shared much. Both were committed to understanding law as "experience," (which provided something like the organizing understanding for Hurst's whole book), to legal positivism (that is, to understanding law as an expression of and an embodiment of the monopoly of legitimate violence in a society), and third, to what I might call a romantic anti-romanticism. That is, both made a fetish of being tough and hard headed.

Mostly, though, Hurst read Holmes for his own purposes, to make his own arguments. And one should not read *Justice Holmes on Legal History* for insight into the thought of Holmes. It is Hurst's book.

Hurst's point of view, his understanding of the experience of "American legal history," began with two dyads. First of all, his approach required the need to take seriously both "sequence" and "context," although he realized that they were often difficult to distinguish from one another. I'm going to write more about his sequencing than about his contextualizations, although I will eventually return to the latter. For the moment, suffice it to say that his contexts are mostly cultural and economic generalizations, not legal categories. Second, the substance of his understanding of both the sequential and the contextual in American legal history relied on two categories: "middle-class culture" and "constitutionalism," or the

---

[11] For the influence of Neibuhr, see Hartog, "Snakes in Ireland: A Conversation with Willard Hurst."

constitutional ideal. Together these two dyads, sequence and context and middle-classness and constitutionalism, produced or organized the continuing content of American law.

American law was, he thought, recognizably and continuously and distinctively American law across the two centuries of American nationhood. That was his relevant "sequence." The law that concerned him was not part of a still longer Anglo-American or common law or even longer "Western" sequence or tradition. Nor did he ever think outside of the national context, not to imperial or colonial or post-colonial or "globalized" law or legal life. Nor was he interested in legal comparisons or transplants or in the transnational movement of legal ideas. It was always American law that concerned him. In part because he minimized the juridical and emphasized the legislative, his legal history was the contingent consequence of American democracy. He did not care about the long history of a juridical culture of elite and non-elite professionals, of lawyers. He was derisively dismissive of questions of origins, and the contexts for his sequence were produced by white male nationals, by voters, by those he regarded as relevant American citizens.

Lawyers and other juridical actors were important to the sequence only insofar as they gave legal content to what "we" made of the law. He wrote constantly about what "we" made in and of the law. And his "we," which I will return to, always imagined a participatory community of American "men" who both made and were subject to the law that they had made. The content of the legislative (context) was produced through a striving and individualistic and exploitative middle-class culture, as it interacted with the conservatism of a constitutional (mostly judicial) culture that required law to serve "public" purposes.

The content of the sequence, that is, the content of what remained continuous over the course of American history, was "the strong producer orientation and the weak consumer interest" in public policy. And that he thought resulted from a preoccupation with "opening up a raw new continent." Indians, native peoples, were not surprisingly absent from this distinctively Turnerian vision of western expansion.[12]

A focus on sequence led him momentarily towards reflections on what were the core texts—we might say, the archive—of legal history. Commitments found in a variety of legal documents (he mentions the Declaration of Independence, the Federal Constitution, the Louisiana Purchase, and Lincoln's call for volunteers), put "life" into a sequence that could not be

[12] James Willard Hurst, *Justice Holmes on Legal History* (New York: Macmillan, 1964), 13. Tala Khanmalek, who read an early version of this talk, emphasized to me the extent to which such an absence is really a presence ignored. I think that is a crucial insight. Also, Bill Clune, in reading an earlier draft, wondered about the absence of attention to consumption and the interests of consumers.

stopped. And one might say that is all, or nearly all, of what those documents did. There is not a glimmer throughout the book on the ways a constitution or phrases from constitutional documents might constitute aspirations or produce a democratic culture, or might challenge the dominant culture. And the political salience of grand constitutional decisions (let alone the work of the U.S. Supreme Court) was also not attended to. Hurst's focus on the sequence that becomes American legal history mostly relied on attention to what Holmes called "little decisions." To which Hurst would add the course of routine legislation voted on by majorities of white American men. How those documents and decisions, large and small, achieved an order or a manifest sequence of American law is mysterious and only partly articulated in the book. Much of the time, he seems to be arguing that laws merely reproduced what existed elsewhere. (Here he comes close to his protégé Lawrence Friedman's line from his *A History of American Law*, about the ways law is always merely reflective of everything else in the society). Hurst's own framing of the issue: "Law has poignant human significance because it has given formal embodiment to hard-bought, shared perceptions about the relations of men to each other." And that frame is complemented by Holmes's aphorism that law is the "witness and external deposit of our moral life." A couple of pages later he quoted Holmes for the notion that "Cumulative experience works its greatest effects on men's lives by (1) developing the content of their most deeply held, least questioned, values and attitudes and (2) developing the structure and processes of the large and durable patterns we call institutions." One can only conclude therefore that an archive of legal texts is no more than suggestive or reflective of the substantive content of American law.[13]

Hurst believed, as Holmes did, that a full understanding of the meaning of history (or to put it differently, as each of them might have, that which lay behind or beneath the law) was ultimately beyond our human capacities (here the influence of Niebuhr on Hurst seems manifest). Still, striving to do legal history "bends effort toward realizing the creative potential that resides in individuals and their society. . . [S]uch explorations in time offers more than instrumental values; it feeds hungers which are part of our being." He then quoted Holmes in Holmes's most warlike voice, from a speech to Harvard undergraduates. While their scope for achievement was narrowing, Holmes hoped they, the Harvard students, still had "the barbaric thirst for conquest, and there is still something left to conquer." To do legal history was a little like making war.[14]

---

[13] James Willard Hurst, *Justice Holmes on Legal History*, 22–24.

[14] James Willard Hurst, *Justice Holmes on Legal History*, 17.

Hurst did not disagree with Holmes on this, but his lectures moved in a different and a perhaps less violent direction, by identifying two "time-rooted" patterns of values and attitudes. One was the middle-class point of view. The other was constitutionalism.

For him, constitutionalism was only understandable as constraint and limit. Properly understood, constitutionalism disciplined the middle-class attitude by requiring the articulation of public reasons for actions by self-interested individuals (members of the middle class), who were the primary makers of [American] law. He acknowledged regretfully that constitutionalism sometimes became a "fighting faith," particularly when it emphasized "zeal" for group more than individual interests. Individualism became "blunted" because "men" worked to realize their aspirations more and more through group action: as farmers, or as urban voters, or as "white Southerners." He acknowledged the abolition of slavery as an exception, as an instance when the constitutional ideal protected "individuality." But for the most part mobilizations of the constitutional ideal expressed unattractive group interests.[15]

One should note that footnote four in the *Carolene Products* case did not exist for him (to talk American constitutional law in its familiar code, for just a moment). That is, he never acknowledged the existence or the presence of "discrete and insular minorities" that needed and deserved protection from the "middle-class" inclinations of legislatures. That significant portions of the American population could not participate as voters or as legislators in his "we" was not something he acknowledged. And the fear of *Lochner*, that is, of constitutional claims that would defeat reformist legislation, remained strong for him, even more than a half century after the *Lochner* case was first decided. One might almost say *Lochner* (as filtered through the New Deal constitutional transformation) remained constitutive of his framework. "[S]hrewd men could warp individualist symbols of the constitutional ideal to sanction unchecked organized power." Implicitly he was arguing, as Progressives had a generation earlier, that corporations had made constitutionalism into a tool that interfered with the legislative goals that "we" wanted and needed. As a result, "we delayed realistic handling of problems posed by the modern economy." "We" had to learn that the "individuality which the constitutional ideal exalted could have valuable substance only in a humane social context; this was the solid meaning in the growth of social legislation. So at least a man of historical perspective must see the matter."

[15] James Willard Hurst, *Justice Holmes on Legal History*, 38. I imagine that behind this, though mostly not articulated, also lay a Cold War understanding that constitutionalism, understood as the rule of law, distinguished U.S. history from authoritarian and totalitarian regimes. It is remarkable, though, that this anti-totalitarian perspective on constitutionalism played no public role in his argument.

Here he referenced Holmes's dissent in *Lochner*, evidently without rereading it (for Holmes, unlike Hurst, made it clear that he had little faith in social legislation).[16]

For the most part, though, it was the "middle-class point of view" that predominated across the two centuries of American history. And articulating dimensions of the middle class point of view was his core goal. The "constitutional ideal" succeeded mostly as a force that occasionally moderated and shaped that point of view. "Save for the tragedy of the Civil War, we contained the tensions of a mighty growth within the political process. The dynamic of this achievement was largely in our subscription to the constitutional ideal," which reduced protest to legalism (except of course for the Civil War). But what he meant by the constitutional ideal was not at all the liberatory or emancipatory impulses that others would draw out of the Thirteenth and Fourteenth Amendments, as shaped by Lincoln's words and a reconfiguration of the Declaration of Independence. Hurst quoted without comment and with implicit approval several of Holmes's many dismissive comments about the Fourteenth Amendment.[17]

What was the middle-class point of view (we might say, "middle-class culture")? He emphasized its moral ambiguity or multiplicity, even as he embraced it as an organizing understanding. "The legal historian needs the term . . . precisely because it connotes diverse qualities and defects . . ." What did it "connote"? "[I]ndependence of mind and will, and creative energy," as well as "capacity for waste and wrong." At its core was individualism and will(fulness). He quoted Holmes: "The joy of life is to put out one's power in some natural and useful or harmless way. There is no other way. And the real misery is not to do this . . . More important to act than to vainly attempt to love one's neighbor as one's self . . . Life is action, the use of one's powers. As to use them to their height is our joy and duty, so it is the one end that justifies itself." And that led Hurst to expound on what he earlier (in his 1956 *Law and the Conditions of Freedom*) called the release of (creative) energy, and he tied that to scientific revolution, to "discov-

[16] James Willard Hurst, *Justice Holmes on Legal History*, 39.

[17] James Willard Hurst, *Justice Holmes on Legal History*, 39, 95, 96, 110. I want to add a paragraph here about the ways Hurst still is incorporating a typically Progressive critique of the Constitution (Beardian), as well as of the judiciary that was articulating or giving power to notions of constitutional rights. His mentor, Felix Frankfurter, once marked the Fourteenth Amendment as one of the less important parts of the document. When asked what were his formative moments in his "becoming" a legal historian, in my interview with him in 1994, Hurst remembered a close reading of Charles Beard's reductive account of the making of the Constitution in a tutorial at Williams College. This was, he remembered, his first experience of thinking seriously about American history. Hartog, "Snakes in Ireland: A Conversation with Willard Hurst."

ery," and to enlarging markets. (In 1964, he also identified the release of energy with Schumpeter's notion of "creative destruction.").[18]

Hurst's description of the middle-class point of view then becomes a paean to who "we" are and were. Soon I will return to the protean but constrained dimensions of this "we." First, though, let me sink into a few of the dimensions of what middle-classness meant. "We had faith in the creative potential of individual men and women (this is, by the way, one of the only mentions of women), if they were given a chance to show what they could do." Who the "we" there were is not clear. Not the individual men and women, but someone else—policy makers? "[W]e appreciated that man (here women disappear) was a self-centered and passionate creature who could not be trusted with unlimited scope for his will." So, how to deal with that? "We extended the suffrage and generously endowed the legislative power (and, in the national government, the executive branch). On the other hand, we put government under constitutions, emphasized the separation of powers, created a federal rather than a unitary legal order, accepted the development of judicial review, and developed the informal checks and balances of party politics. So, too, in providing a legal framework for private activity we mingled encouragement and surveillance." As in his earlier book of lectures, *Law and the Conditions of Freedom*, he emphasized the law of property and contract, of franchises. Delegations of power and dispersions of power were "natural to the individualism, the activist bias, and the rational skepticism of the middle-class view of life." Although there would be some movement (that is to say, "we groped") towards public controls of private power, for the most part law was used to promote "expansion" rather than to limit "expressions of private energies of will." "We" counted on market processes rather than politics. (Party politics is remarkably absent from his litany of the features of middle-classness.)[19]

"We," he continued, "pursued our faith in manipulation and contrivance to increase yields from nature and from social relations." In other words, "we" exploited both the environment and one another (and other human beings). In particular that meant that "men" were free to "experiment with the structure and uses of the business corporation." Corporations and corporate law served him as a recurrent example.[20] Gradually, "[w]e became uneasily conscious" that such unrestrained experimentation

---

18 James Willard Hurst, *Justice Holmes on Legal History*, 27; James Willard Hurst, *Law and the Conditions of Freedom in the Nineteenth Century United States* (Madison, WI: University of Wisconsin Press, 1956).

19 James Willard Hurst, *Justice Holmes on Legal History*, 41–49.

20 Note that five years later, he published a book composed of lectures on the history of the corporation.

left us dependent on large-scale private organizations. After some floundering ("in the Romantic period of nineteenth-century politics"), the twentieth century saw "a return to the realism of the founding fathers." That is, "we" came to the realization that "what the powerful want is more power." And that return to realism meant a renewed understanding that "law existed to serve men, and not men to serve law." Or, as he put it in what seems to me a core sentence: "So we fused our middle-class disposition to use law as a tool and our constitutional faith that law might properly and safely be used so, because it was our law and our government and its justification was in serving our life." And then he offered a variety of conventional illustrations of the fruits of that fusion, including the subsidization of public education and the building of road systems.

"Middle-class men were striving men," who directed their striving within the realm of "present experience." (In our published 1994 interview/conversation, he and I had argued about whether that focus on "present experience" meant necessarily selling out the future in the pursuit of short term advantage, which is how I read his history of the clear-cutting of the trees of northern Wisconsin.) Holmes, using the materialistic categories of the late nineteenth century, had evaluated "men" on "the total of human energy which they embody—counting everything, with due allowance for quality, from Nansen's power to digest blubber or to resist cold, up to his courage or to Wordsworth's power to express the unutterable, or to Kant's speculative reach." As always for Holmes, "The final test of this energy is battle in some form —actual war—the crush of Arctic ice—the fight for mastery in the market or the court." Hurst, by way of slight contrast, gave more weight to what he identified as the middle-class expectation that "will should be disciplined and moderated by reasoned calculation and by cautious sense of man's limitations." But more importantly, his middle-class culture was defined by the deeply individualistic and self-centered "we" that he mobilized. It was not a product of some kind of collective agreement.[21]

I have come to think of Hurst's "we," which has yearly been a subject of ridicule among my graduate students (who have discovered it while required reading of his earlier *Law and the Conditions of Freedom*), as more than a rhetorical quirk. Obviously, his "we" excluded many, most, of the American population. It ("we") was white men, one might say, those he recognized as striving individuals and consumers of law and voters. No native peoples; no women; no one who could not participate fully in nineteenth or early twentieth-century political society. It is hard to know if he would have included Catholics or those who worked with their hands or those who did domestic work or care work.

[21] James Willard Hurst, *Justice Holmes on Legal History*, 28.

For us, living in the twenty-first century, what leaps out with his "we" are the absences. All the "others" who constituted America at any moment in its history. The consequences of those exclusions was a radically narrowed understanding of what the subjects of legal history are and were: corporate charters, but not the enforcement of the fugitive slave acts, not the expropriation of native lands, not domestic violence laws, not apprenticeships, and not indentured labor. The household and the family he imagined was for the most part a non-legal domain.

(All this may seem obvious. But I have to add that his absences retain a certain paradoxical quality for me, because of what "Hurst" and Wisconsin legal history long stood for, in my mind and in the minds of many legal historians. For me, "Hurstian" meant the widening of legal history to incorporate the whole of social experience. In my late 60s way, I wanted to imagine "everyone" in the law, and I hoped to uncover ways that "everyone" participated in the law. Did I, did legal historians of my generation, just misread him for all of these years?)

What strikes me now, even more than the seeming exclusions, is how chaotic and mysterious his "we" was. His "we" were the makers of laws, that is, preeminently voters and legislators. But his "we" were also the political movements and the persons (including corporations) that elected legislators and produced the initiative for legislative products and projects. His "we" were also clients and consumers of laws, those who used facilitative laws to constitute and to sustain relationships and were regulated or disciplined (reluctantly or resistantly) by some laws. Sometimes his "we" became social scientists and historians. For example, early in his chapter on "context," he cautioned "us" to avoid fallacious metaphors as explanatory devices, and not to over-organize explanations by focusing on a multiplicity of explanations. Doing so might tempt "us towards unreality." His "we" were not for the most part lawyers, certainly not creative lawyers, finding novel or integrative tools to represent the previously unrepresented. Lawyers perhaps reproduced or translated the individualistic wants of his collective "we." But not much else. Much of the time his "we" was or is a god-like presence (a very Unitarian god I suspect, or an invisible hand) that directs the society ("us") in its undirectable way towards an expression of individual freedom.[22]

It is possible, perhaps, to rationalize or order the mystery of the "we" as something like a distillation of how a republican self-governing people have made and have experienced the realm of law. His "we" imagined a continuing community of politically competent Americans, who made the policies and the laws, and who constructed legislation in their image. If I had time, or the inclination, I might try to produce such a political theoretical reconstruction of what he was doing or trying to do. One might end up

22 James Willard Hurst, *Justice Holmes on Legal History*, 60.

with something like a version of the "Imagined Community" that Benedict Anderson and his successors have mobilized in global studies of the rise of nationalisms. It certainly resembled a 1950s reading of Tocqueville's *Democracy in America*.

But I am more struck by the way his "we" floats across generations and periods. There is really no periodization within his sequencing. There is an implicit movement as the economy grows in scale (though global markets remain out of view), a gradual evolution from what Robert Wiebe once called "island communities" towards the nationalized economy Hurst and others identified with the New Deal. But the "we" remains continuous and unchanged. No parties, no race conflict, no populist crisis, no waves of immigrants, almost no Progressives, and no labor movements. In this, his writing is quite similar to what was being produced as "American Studies" at the time he wrote, a field in part defined by its similar (but more explicit or self-conscious) rejection of the conventional periodizations of American political history. When he wrote about "sequence," his goal was to argue for an unchanging (or little changing) continuity across the whole of American history (from the American Revolution to the 1960s). Implicitly, he assumed an American exceptionalism that worked to find an American nature, sometimes called a "civilization," across the centuries.

I once lived within the faith that Hurst and the Wisconsin Law School in which he was a leading intellectual presence embodied a heroic heterodox alternative against the stultifying orthodoxies of postwar American legalism. Certainly, that is how I understood it during the years (basically the 1980s) when I lived and worked in Madison. It was a place unlike other law schools, where serious and critical inquiry about law was possible. A shining light marked by its difference, its distinctive identity, within the constellation of American law schools. And the reason why it was different or distinctive for me lay in part, in very large part, because of Willard Hurst.

And yet, now (today) I want to emphasize a few of the ways that the Willard Hurst of *Justice Holmes on Legal History* was a man of his time, of a piece with other elite white law professors of his time. Or to put it more directly: in significant ways his thought belongs to a generation of elite lawyers—legalists—now gone.

Let me start with what is striking, shocking even, about reading *Justice Holmes on Legal History*. Here was a summation of his understanding of American legal history, published in 1965, produced (spoken in lectures at Iowa; then written up and published by a major commercial publisher of the time, Macmillan) in the midst, the heyday, of the civil rights movement. And yet this was a summation without anything about the history of race in America. Nothing about slavery. Nothing about freedom struggles. Abolitionists and women's rights do not appear. Nor do any of the core constitutional actors we identify with the civil rights movement. Likewise, there is nothing about native peoples or borderlands. Nor anything about immigration restriction or exclusions (even as the Hart-Celler Act would be enacted at exactly this same time). There is one bland mention of white Southerners as an organized interest group. The challenges that *Brown v. Board of Education* raised for conventional constitutional thinking, a challenge that was ubiquitous and a matter of constant discussion at that moment throughout the legal academy, does not appear. The only attention given to the Fourteenth Amendment draws on Holmes's dyspeptic thoughts about its general insignificance. The Thirteenth Amendment never appears.

It is conventional to identify Hurst with Wisconsin. Doing so might be said to excuse him and his exclusions and omissions, by identifying him with the state and with the predominately white northern Midwest. He was, one might suggest, just writing about what he knew. But that is nonsensical, and radically inconsistent with the knowing and sophisticated and cosmopolitan person he was. And it is also inconsistent with his ambitions, which were to make Wisconsin exemplify national tendencies and values. (It is, as well, totally wrongheaded about the history of the state.) He knew, and he excluded, intentionally, knowingly, one might even say, brutally. Just as one cannot read his brilliant evocation of the Pike's Creek settlers of the 1830s and their claims to constitutional rights (at the beginning of his 1956 *Law and the Conditions of Freedom*) without knowing that the rights they claimed were intended to mobilize the violence of the federal government to expropriate the native peoples on whose lands those settlers had settled illegally, so it must have been with civil rights in 1965. His contexts bleached out conflicts that he must have known of, but that he chose not to discuss, that he regarded as irrelevant or parenthetical to the themes that concerned him. His writing tacitly condoned immeasurable violence. Race—struggles against Jim Crow as well as the expropriation of Indian lands—messed up the analysis. If he had taken those seriously, he would have had to reconstruct his frame, his structure, radically.[23]

---

23 Farah Peterson, in reading an earlier draft, commented that my language still softens what was really "murder." For a suggestive and illuminating portrait of how early expropriation of native lands—using credit, mortgages, and foreclosures—was conducted while using private law, see the writings of K-Sue Park. K-Sue Park, "Money, Mortgages, and the Conquest of America," *Law and Social Inquiry* 41 (2016): 1006–35. One might add that Park, in her insistence on a long continuity between seventeenth-century foreclosures and the mortgage crisis of the twenty-first century, offers what seems to me to be something of a Hurstian analysis of exactly what Hurst avoided.

A second, related point, smaller but equally shocking: Hurst worked to characterize the overarching policies that shaped law. He claimed that one could reduce law's "concerns" to three functional domains: natural resources, human nature, and society. With regard to the first of these, he introduced the history of the environment in the following way. He began in classic Turnerian fashion, as always, ignoring the presence of native peoples. Because "we" were "on a naturally rich, long underpopulated and unexploited continent," "we" learned to be concerned with what he called "the physical and biological bases." And that led to giving "land title" a prominent place in legal development. But it also led to a desire for population increase (for that European white population), which meant for him easy immigration, favoring the family farm, and supporting urban growth (a fairly banal and inexplicit list). But, he continued, "we" only pushed for activities that promised quick and easy gains. There was little attention to long-run productivity. (Here, one assumes he was waving at his just-published book on the lumber industry and the destruction of the Wisconsin forests.) Eventually, he continued, "we" would learn to protect the environment. That was genuine progress from his perspective. And for him that included reforms that provided for the health, safety, and the "self-respect of men and women" (a phrase that is not defined or described), and even "the genetic soundness of the human population." This passage then concluded with a footnote that blandly cited to Holmes's infamous opinion in *Buck v. Bell*, where Holmes had defended eugenic sterilizations. This was, of course, the opinion that included the odious phrase, "three generations of idiots are enough."[24]

Sixty pages and one chapter/lecture later, Hurst returned to the theme. He agreed with Holmes that one could not do much to change "the lot of the mass of men by rearranging legal institutions of property." Holmes had called the notion that it was possible to use property law to produce "an economic paradise"[25] "twaddle." For both of them, apparently, "the true sources of material improvement lay in more rational control of population increase, and in applying men's organizing genius to the means made available by science and technology." It would be a better legislative strategy, Hurst wrote, "to improve the quality than to increase the quantity of the population." Again, the passage concluded with a footnote to *Buck v. Bell.*[26]

---

24 James Willard Hurst, *Justice Holmes on Legal History*, 69.

25 Harry N. Scheiber, "At the Borderland of Law and Economic History: The Contributions of Willard Hurst," *American Historical Review* 75, no. 3 (February 1970): 744–56.

26 James Willard Hurst, *Justice Holmes on Legal History*, 121–23.

I don't believe that Hurst was a racial eugenicist.[27] His implicit point was, rather, that *Buck v. Bell* was an ordinary police power decision, founded on plausible (rationally defensible) legislative grounds. Hurst did not have to like forced sterilization. It wasn't his business to challenge or critique, so long as (to use his frame of reference) legislation—here understood as the mobilization of the violence of the positive state—was founded on the overarching policies that properly shaped American law. No more than Holmes agreed with many of the legislative policies he approved judicially, that he regarded as constitutional. In that sense Hurst's thinking remained rooted in a typical legal Progressive mindset that saw constitutional rights as constraints (mostly the possession of corporations that managed to constrain reform legislation) and that placed hope for the future on an unleashed police power, on legislative freedom to innovate and institutionalize, freed from those constraints.[28]

It goes without saying that Hurst was very different from the legal process scholars who were the dominant intellectual forces in the mainstream American law schools in the 1950s and 1960s. He had little interest in formal processes, in the separation of powers. He did not obsess about administrative discretion in the post-New Deal state, and he was not interested in the problem of the judicial role, in the functions and place of "the least dangerous branch" in a democracy, or in formulating the judiciary as a "counter-majoritarian" institution, as the legal process scholars were. It might be said that he continued the reformist "legal realist" project of the 1920s and 1930s, as it was being abandoned or qualified by legal process scholars. He fundamentally rejected the obsession of legal process scholars with fine-grained readings of Supreme Court opinions. He was ever the anti-doctrinalist.[29]

---

27 Again, Farah Peterson suggests that I might be muting or avoiding a harsher reality.

28 One might speculate farther that there was at that time, in the 1960s, for men like Hurst, an apparent relationship between the environmentalism that did shape Hurst's understanding and that led to *Law and Economic Growth* (originally inspired by listening to Aldo Leopold as a young faculty member at the law school) and population control understandings. Garrett Hardin's "Tragedy of the Commons," one of the founding texts of modern environmentalism, published just three years after Hurst's book, began as an explanation by a population biologist of the inescapability and the tragic consequences of the "population bomb." One can read Hardin and Hurst as sharing something like a liberal eugenicist perspective.

29 It occurs to me late that one could characterize him as an odd combination of a legal realist and a 1950s functionalist sociologist. That is, he understood law, as Hale and Hohfeld and Llewellyn did, law as fundamentally constitutive of relationships and structures in the society. (Here, he ironically presages much that can be drawn out of Gordon's "Critical Legal Histories.") That is the reason why studying law reveals (he would say, modestly, law offers insight into) America. At the same time, he draws from the same cultural matrix that Riesman and Bell and Merton and Parsons and others of his contemporary social scientists drew from. (Tocqueville first of all.) He imagined American culture (by which he meant middle-classness)

And yet, he remained marked, like the legal process scholars were marked, both by the inheritance of progressive legal thought and, I would suspect, by the Cold War. How to think about rights, when rights were understood fundamentally as the possession of alien corporate interests or as ways of constraining or limiting reform? More, how to think about rights when the New Deal and World War II had transformed the relationship between rights and reform? All of them, legal process scholars and Hurst alike, continued to view those questions through a lens that posed constitutional rights as the enemy of democratic processes (majoritarianism). Unlike Hurst, legal process scholars could not escape worrying about *Brown*, about the introduction of a new and different way of imagining rights and the discourses of rights, and about judicial activism. But that was because they regarded the work of the Supreme Court as their core subject, unlike Hurst who wanted to write about "America."

Like other elite lawyers of his generation, he didn't attend to the significance of race, and the Cold War was a continuing (implicit or semi-conscious?) presence. The Cold War had shaped him, leaving him reluctant to embrace collective solutions, anxious to mark himself as not a radical. He was afraid of or cool to socialism or social reform, even as he supported many of the social reforms that were celebrated in a Progressive Wisconsin. He was not interested in the ways that rights would be marked and shaped by the language and the activities and the mobilizations of subordinated classes. (One of the striking moments in my 1994 interview/conversation with him occurred early on, when I noted that his course had become a mandatory one for the many "new left" history graduate students who then populated the history department at the University of Wisconsin. He was dismissive of their interests and their interest in law. And he made it clear that their education was not a matter of much concern to him.)

And I suspect that his unperiodized sequencing of America drew on many of the same understandings that made it possible for the legal process scholars and their contemporaries in the humanities and the social sciences, for the academic men of that generation, to look at America "as a civilization."

By 1965, that understanding was already under challenge. Not only by the civil rights movement, but also by Black Power (and soon, Indian power, and the women's movement), by the student-led free speech movement, by the New Left, and by the emergent practices of the disci-

---

in terms of "individualism." The state was mostly facilitative of individual freedom. His individualism was rooted in property and contract and the corporate form (both in its commercial and industrial variations and in its creation of voluntary associations). For him, individualism drew on the particular notions of bourgeois freedom that attached to legal rights and transactions and state-created institutions.

pline of history, particularly of social and later cultural history. Consensus history fragmented. The idea of America as a civilization became an archaic artifact. Such understandings fell apart because of the fragility of their own premises, as well as by contemporary events.

One might conclude that by 1965 Hurst was already slightly out of date, particularly in his commitment to a Progressive vision of legislative power as well as his reconstruction of what we might call a "consensus" history. I imagine that his "we" must have already been heard as odd to his audience when he delivered the talks to the University of Iowa Law School faculty or lectured to Wisconsin law students. Or at least so I imagine.

Fragment Three: From Hurst to an Erotics of Legal History

What is left of Hurst's legal history?

Actually, a lot. I want to hold on to his notion of the collective power of the middle-class point of view. In the face of the apparent fracturing of notions of a common or a hegemonic culture,[30] and in opposition to the ubiquitous pluralisms and postmodernisms of contemporary intellectual legal life, it seems important to work towards finding ways to describe the dimensions of a common culture (and the roles that law may have played in the construction of and the sustenance of that common culture). Can it be done without the celebratory American exceptionalism that accompanied it? Not so sure. But I hold to a faith in the effort to articulate what may or may not have been, at least some of the time, a common legal culture.

It is not so difficult to reframe Hurst's middle-class perspective as describing the longstanding hegemonic power of a particular—lumpy, incompletely articulated—but clearly exclusive and powerful understanding of law as it was experienced by a diverse and multitudinous range of Americans. That perspective is not that different from what Barbara Welke provided in her *Law and the Borders of Belonging*. There was, she would say, to reframe her slightly, a powerful "we" that ruled American law. It did so, in large part, by excluding others, knowingly so. Law set the ground rules for who belonged and who did not belong in the society. It produced, coercively, a middle-class society dominated by the apparently productive white men.[31]

One might add that much of American constitutional history, certainly the constitutional history of post-Civil War America, has been defined by the struggles of those excluded, of those who did not "belong," to find a kind of belonging, including citizenship and the capacity to mobilize

30 Daniel Rodgers, *The Age of Fracture* (Cambridge, MA: Harvard University Press, 2012).

31 Barbara Welke, *Law and the Borders of Belonging* (New York: Cambridge University Press, 2010).

rights. It is a mark of the continuing power of that culture that those who did not immediately belong to the dominant class, to what might (inadequately) be called the middle class, knew that they had to find ways to reveal or perform or produce identities that might properly be called middle class, to become "middle class" in core ways. There was no other way to gain access to the legal benefits or the legal rewards that America offered.

Since the 1960s, legal historians have produced wider and deeper portraits of how constitutional claims worked (occasionally and intermittently) to challenge middle-class culture.[32] Any fair understanding of the coercive cultural power of American law as a historical phenomenon would have to add much on the incompleteness of that hegemonic power, its susceptibility to challenges. The cracks and fissures in the legal culture, its inability to impose uniformity or clarity, are at least as important as its singularity as a continuing historical presence. And we (legal historians) have learned much from historical works that mobilized the Gramscian notion that law necessarily allowed even the subordinated and the relatively powerless a sense of "membership," if only a thin one.

It is always a little bit of this and a little bit of the other. The glass half full or half empty. (I have argued elsewhere that reading legal texts in history ought to lead to a recognition of the muddle that history reveals in the law). Gay marriage as mostly merely reproducing heterosexual marriage, a paradigmatically middle-class institution. But transformations in adoption law and in custody law, halting movements towards approval (or an ending to disapproval) to polygamous and polyamorous relationships and of the ways of the queer and of the transgendered, plus the general removal of constraints on sexual behavior "outside" of marriage, all suggest that what is understood as the law that governs "private" households has changed, has moved far from the older and still coercive "middle class" point of view. Or, to take a second obvious example, consider the multiple and changing complexities of birthright citizenship and the uncertainties of who is a "person" entitled to the protections of the Fourteenth Amendment. We have those complexities and uncertainties to thank for an occasional fracturing or undoing of executive and legislative

---

32 Hendrik Hartog, "The Constitution of Aspiration and 'The Rights That Belong to Us All,'" *Journal of American History* 74, no. 3 (December 1987): 1013–34. We might usefully borrow from a brilliant recent essay by Ken Mack, about the legal strategies of subordinated groups around university admissions: to serve their clients, lawyers for those groups learned that they needed to work in at least two registers. On the one hand, they had to convince courts and institutions that their clients wanted to become as if "at one" with middle-classness. Often this came under the guise of "assimilation." At the same time, they always retained, and sometimes articulated, a more critical aspiration (mostly hidden, but appearing suddenly at particular historical moments), which was to transform—sometimes to destroy—middle-classness and the institutions to which they wanted access for their clients. Kenneth W. Mack, "Second Mode Inclusion Claims in the Law Schools," *Fordham Law Review* 87 (2018): 1005–31.

efforts to mobilize middle-class prejudices. The thin sense of constitutionalism that required law to serve public ends (as emphasized by Hurst), "that all public or private decision makers be accountable by some criteria outside of themselves," sometimes has become a momentarily stronger constraint, imagined by way of creative lawyering to require an undoing of established policies. Certainly more so than Hurst ever imagined (or conceded) in 1965.

What strikes me as of enduring significance in Hurst's portrayal of American law, what excited me when I came upon it in the early 1970s, and what excites me still, is, first of all, his willingness to look at law as a human activity that takes its form across doctrinal silos. His work fundamentally challenged the conventional wisdoms and the categories of doctrinal law teaching and of legal thought. I particularly liked his phrasing at one point, when he referenced what happened when nineteenth-century statutes interfered with either the Commerce Clause or the Contracts Clause of the U.S. Constitution. All rights, he wrote, were "limited by the neighborhood of principles of policy which are other than those on which the particular right is founded." In some ways, he continued, the notion of the police power, as it was elaborated over the course of the long nineteenth century, was in its nature a challenge to doctrinal silos (or to singular constitutional mandates).[33]

Legal doctrine was probably more important than Hurst acknowledged. He was such a good lawyer himself, so quick at conventional legal analysis, that he deprecated it as a skill and a frame for historical analysis.[34] But his willingness to imagine legal fields as united by common problems and by a shared culture, by a common context (often, in the 1950s and 1960s identified with what Hurst and his colleagues called the "law in action"), stimulated a kind of work, a legal history that crossed and re-crossed and challenged and transformed legal doctrine.[35]

One might almost say that to do Hurstian legal history—or, rather, legal history as I want it to be—is to imagine the intersections of diverse doctrinal streams and legal cultural streams at particular historical moments, as they became manifested and helped produce and reproduce the formations and structures in our legal histories. Inevitably there is a

---

33 James Willard Hurst, *Justice Holmes on Legal History*, 67.

34 As a result, the emergence of a field of study and inquiry dedicated to the history of legal thought did not interest him in the slightest.

35 See, for example, much of the recent literature on the law of slavery. Or Risa Goluboff, *Vagrant Nation: Police Power, Constitutional Change, and the Making of the 1960s* (New York: Oxford University Press, 2016). And I would add, as the late Betsy Clark once said in a panel in the early 1990s on Hurst's scholarship in the early 1990s, Hurst was himself a historian of ideas, an intellectual historian.

muddle at the point of those intersections, a certain chaotic or complex incoherence. But a conscientious historian—better, the historian I would like to be or become—ought to avoid resolving the muddle, by picking one theme out, because it is presumptively "important," (often, for presentist or legally salient reasons) while the rest is noise, to be dismissed or diminished or ignored. Instead, the legal historian confronts a conceptual and a writing and a jurisprudential problem: how to characterize and present the law that was there, in that situation. How to tell all of it, or at least as much of it as is necessary to produce a feel for the situation as a whole.[36]

Secondly, Hurst practiced a legal history that avoided questions of origins. Indeed, Hurst was deeply impatient with and dismissive of origins and origin narratives. (Here Hurst stands in opposition to main and continuing tendencies in the "discipline" of legal history, and I believe he is usually right, and the discipline is often wrong.) The reader is and was thrust into a legal event or problem or situation that occurred at a particular time. Like Holmes (at least the Holmes of "The Path of the Law,"; the Holmes who authored *The Common Law* twenty years before "The Path" had a different orientation, a commitment to the search for origins), Hurst disdained the notion that a deeper past contained the germ of an answer to the legal problems that women and men confronted in their own present tense. His legal history never situated a legal event or problem or situation within a singular long legal history, because he did not believe in the explanatory power of such singular legal histories. The work he is remembered for, the work I remember him for, always started in the middle of things.[37] Strands of longstanding doctrinal understandings or long-term economic commitments are understood and explored. The contingencies of the laws that come into view, as they combined and interacted, the relationships produced, may require looks back at various themes. But the multiple pasts that constituted the present moment or problem that he is exploring are understood only retrospectively. His selection of contexts (partial and incomplete as they were) always bled into sequences. Many pasts that could plausibly play a part in what it was—the law, the relevant

---

36 I am reminded of Sally Falk Moore's appreciative invocation in her essay on "semi-autonomous social fields," of a line from Malinowski where he asserted a desire to explore "all the rules" within a particular social field. Sally Falk Moore, *Law as Process an Anthropological Approach* (London: Routledge & K. Paul, 1978). For myself, I would be content with an ambition to explore "more" of the rules.

37 Nor was he concerned to describe "it" as the foundation for a present-day world (or situation). His legal problems or events, while important and constitutive of our world or exemplary of an American culture, were never framed as "the transformations" that produced "us." I should add that Hurst knew how to write a history focused on origins. Early on, while serving in the military during World War II, he wrote a history of treason for the Department of War.

law—that needed to be explained and understood. How to arrange, how to describe or to characterize those contextual sequences or sequential contexts, raised difficult writing issues, ones that helped produce some of the oddities and the awkwardnesses of Hurst's own writings. (As a writer, he was fundamentally a clunk, and he never resolved the writing problems he confronted.) But his subjects always remained "the law" as it was in its historical moment.

It is important to add that Hurst is of little help once one reaches the point of imagining a historically situated legal text or case or archive or problem as a contingent intersection of diverse doctrinal and historical and economic streams. I am struck by the absence of any awareness of periodization in Hurst's contextualizations, even as his work thrusts the reader into particularized historical moments. How could he continue to write as if the situations he was describing lived in an unperiodized "America"?[38] How could he not have known that things happened at a particular time and not at any other, given his own work? How could he escape a notion of the distinctiveness and particularity of the past (of the past as a foreign country)? What was his signal accomplishment, his study of the legal destruction of the Wisconsin forests, his scholarly monument and still a chilling ecological classic, but a precise (and a precisely dated or periodized) historical portrait? (All that law, all that legislation, all those many little decisions and continuing relationships, from varying doctrinal and legislative sources, mobilized across the middle years of the nineteenth century, to cut down all those trees in northern Wisconsin at the least cost. All that "law" could never have been mobilized earlier, during the late eighteenth and early nineteenth centuries. And most of us look with shock at the results, at the denuded landscape, today, as Progressives did already by the early twentieth century. It could only have happened when it did, and not at another time.) Yet, not for Willard Hurst. It is something of a mystery to me how Hurst so deeply understood the power of contexts that cut across legal fields, while not understanding those contexts as knowable only historically—that is, by making their histories as specific and precise as possible—that is, by periodizing.

But thirdly I would celebrate—and work to emulate—his focus on contingency. "The life of the law represents no homeostatic, functionally self-adjusting process, but the product of the qualities and defects of men's will, imagination, and feeling." That meant for him that all law is and was fundamentally "legislative" in character. By which he meant that "the secret root from which the law draws all the juices of life . . . [is] considerations of what is expedient for the community concerned." In that sense, one might say (he would definitely not have said), it was all and always

---

38 In conversation, Dan Rodgers suggests that he allowed sociological functionalism to do the work that historical periodizing should have done.

politics, all the way down (even if he seemed unconcerned with party politics). And that led him to a critique of what he called "organic" metaphors, of evolutionary portraits of legal change. Middle-classness may have defined all or much of the law at many crucial moments in American history. But what those middle-class manifestations of law were or would be depended on the contingent acts and decisions and relationships of many men and (women and) institutions, who differed and fought about many things. Not on any imagined evolutionary necessity. He did not emphasize the explicit political struggles that underlay those acts and decisions. (Holmes did, at least in the middle pages of the "Path of the Law.") But no reading of the Hurstian corpus can escape a sense of the constant and continual underlying presence of those struggles. And in that sense, his writings prefigure the strongest features of what became critical legal studies (even if he wrote in a different, a more Protestant or Unitarian and often functionalist, register). Implicit in his practices lay a kind of historicist faith that demonstrating the contingencies of the past may reveal the freedom to break with apparently fixed categorical or legal understandings.[39]

All this leads me towards a perhaps peculiar interest in exploring the legal (or jurisprudential) natures of the historically situated events, texts, and problems that are our subjects. It is of course a feature of the present moment that historians today know legal sources and archives as interesting sites, as something more than merely a window on to the important things to study. But historians (and also law professors) continue to attend less to the jurisprudential status, to the formal and informal features, that make such sources and archives knowable as law. The law-ness of the legal sources is perhaps taken for granted.[40]

It is only lately that I have realized that some of my love for such sources is also rooted in their identity as legal objects. They are not merely occasions for storytelling, though they are certainly that. They are trials or texts about trials produced to illuminate legal possibilities and conclusions. They are statutory commissions or constitutional conventions, produced by legal or constitutional mandates, whose language is constrained and empowered by those mandates. Our sources may be drawn from correspondence between lawyers and lawyers or between lawyers and clients (real or imagined), about debts or duties or obligations or risks

---

39 James Willard Hurst, *Justice Holmes on Legal History*, 62. For the conventional understanding, one that I shared, of Hurst as a contrast case to critical legal studies, see Robert W. Gordon, "Critical Legal Histories," *Stanford Law Review* 36 (1984): 57–125.

40 Why else is there a Davis Seminar devoted to "law and legalities"? It is also striking that in the Davis seminar presentations of 2018–2019, there was, with the exception of Lena Salamayah's and Tatiana Borisova's presentations/papers, relatively little interest in (or attention to) the qualities of sources—archives—as law.

seen on a variety of legal (as well as commercial) horizons. The legal objects we (or I) care about may embody streams of lawmaking and law interpreting and legal relationships located in and across multiple and conflicting jurisdictions.[41] Wherever they are found, however they are found, whatever they "are," such sources generate stories that are fundamentally "legal" stories. At least they do so for me.

Of course it is also true that such texts and archives are more than "merely" legal objects. They evoke and express a culture (and cultures) and a political economy and ecologies and social norms and racisms and male rage and desires to exterminate or expropriate and imperial ambitions and greed and cosmopolitanism and impulses characterized by compassion and love and respect for human dignity. And more. Almost always, at least among the objects I find myself most attracted to, there will be several (certainly more than one) set of norms and streams of passions. Even if one didn't feel love for those sources as legal objects, even if one looked at them "merely" as embodying or evoking features of their times, as articulating forms of social life, or cultural forms, they would remain worth looking at (without concern for their relationship to whatever it is that "really" draws our attention).

And yet, the jurisprudential issues always also remain, at least for me. What does it mean that some such set of documents are called "law"? What does it mean that documents are recognized as "legal"—sometimes as legally binding, as creating obligations (that some of our subjects will happily or unhappily breach or violate)? What do we mean when we apply the legal label? When we imagine these documents—this archive—as something other than the detritus of a political or cultural or a commercial or an imperial moment? When we become aware of documents as rooted in and expressing a legal temporality, one that necessarily implicates analytic questions about "law" and what might be called juristic authority? Debates about positivism and about the relationship of these objects to "politics" and political authority, about what Hart might call primary and secondary legal fields, and about the ways in which juristic work and practices become recognizable and reproducible as "legal" (or not) at and in a historical moment or situation, all that becomes part of what we do as legal historians (what I do as a legal historian). Of course the law is not merely or solely state power. But to do legal history is also to do something that takes seriously the contingent and unsettled history of the instantiations of "law," as law, of the mobilizations of the expressions of legal violence, across cultures and regimes.[42]

---

[41] I have lately found myself particularly caught up with the doctrinal fields variously known as the conflicts of laws or "choice of law" or sometimes "private international law."

[42] Aldo Schiavone, *The Invention of Law in the West*, trans. Jeremy Carden and Antony Shugaar

To know law as "law" is not to deny that such sources are also composed of a muddle of themes and streams, legal and non-legal. Indeed, a serious effort to think "legally" about the legal objects that historians cherish (or at least that this legal historian cherishes) requires a recognition of the complexities and the contradictions and the multiplicities that those objects contain. That is, after all, where the fun begins. And it is also why these objects are worth attending to, why they may even justify our "love." At least for someone who wants to be a legal historian. Or at least for this someone who claims to be a legal historian.

References

Coons, John E., William H. Clune III, and Stephen D. Sugarman. *Private Wealth and Public Education.* Cambridge, MA: Harvard University Press, 1970.

Darnton, Robert. *The Great Cat Massacre and Other Episodes in French Cultural History.* New York: Basic Books, 1984.

Goluboff, Risa. *Vagrant Nation: Police Power, Constitutional Change, and the Making of the 1960s.* New York: Oxford University Press, 2016.

Gordon, Robert W. "Critical Legal Histories." *Stanford Law Review* 36 (1984): 57–125.

Gordon, Robert W. *Taming the Past.* New York: Cambridge University Press, 2018.

Greengrass, Jessie. *Sight.* New York: Hogarth, 2018.

Hartog, Hendrik. "The Constitution of Aspiration and 'The Rights That Belong to Us All.'" *Journal of American History* 74, no. 3 (December 1987): 1013–34.

------. "Snakes in Ireland: A Conversation with Willard Hurst." *Law and History Review* 12, no. 2 (Autumn 1994): 370–90.

Hurst, James Willard. *Law and the Conditions of Freedom in the Nineteenth Century United States.* Madison, WI: University of Wisconsin Press, 1956.

Hurst, James Willard. *Justice Holmes on Legal History.* New York: Macmillan, 1964.

------. *Law and Economic Growth: The Legal History of the Lumber Industry in Wisconsin, 1836–1915.* Cambridge, MA: Belknap Press of Harvard University Press, 1964.

Mack, Kenneth W. "Second Mode Inclusion Claims in the Law Schools." *Fordham Law Review* 87 (2018): 1005–31.

Moore, Sally Falk. *Law as Process an Anthropological Approach.* London: Routledge & K. Paul, 1978.

(Cambridge, MA: Belknap Press of Harvard University Press, 2012).

Park, K-Sue. "Money, Mortgages, and the Conquest of America." *Law and Social Inquiry* 41 (2016): 1006–35.

Parker, Kunal M. *Common Law, History, and Democracy in America, 1790–1900: Legal Thought Before Modernism*. Cambridge Historical Studies in American Law and Society. New York: Cambridge University Press, 2011.

Rodgers, Daniel. *The Age of Fracture*. Cambridge, MA: Harvard University Press, 2012.

Scheiber, Harry N. "At the Borderland of Law and Economic History: The Contributions of Willard Hurst." *American Historical Review* 75, no. 3 (February 1970): 744–56.

Schiavone, Aldo. *The Invention of Law in the West*. Translated by Jeremy Carden and Antony Shugaar. Cambridge, MA: Belknap Press of Harvard University Press, 2012.

Welke, Barbara. *Law and the Borders of Belonging*. New York: Cambridge University Press, 2010.

A 2020 Afterword: Towards an Understanding of Legal History as Accompaniment

Hendrik Hartog

1. As a preliminary, generated by the times in which we live: Did the flu epidemic of 1918 affect James Willard Hurst and his family? Did it leave him with a skepticism about the capacity of law to change things or to control the times in which he lived? An awareness, of the kind that has recently confronted all of us, of how forces or phenomena beyond merely human law can upend all expectations about normal life. In the past, I identified Hurst's downbeat skepticism about the power of law with his reading of Reinhold Niebuhr (leaving it unclear whether Niebuhr was simply a way to identify or label his own dyspeptic sensibility, or if he was actually changed by reading Niebuhr). But now I wonder: did the flu epidemic of 1918 affect him and his family?[1]

2. On rereading, it is apparent to me that last year I obscured what I wanted to suggest in the last pages of the third "fragment" where I wrote about the need for legal history to return to a consideration of jurisprudence.

I don't pretend that I have now resolved the ambiguities with which I littered that last section. But here are some further thoughts, perhaps clarifications.

A. Legal history—the primarily American legal history that I and Hurst and Lawrence Friedman and Morton Horwitz and Robert Gordon produced over the past generations (call it something of a mainstream in the writing of American legal history) seems to me today, even more than last year, defined by its institutional settings (and perhaps by the fact that we are all privileged white men). All of us were, at least for much of our careers, legal academics who wrote for an imagined audience of other legal academics. In that institutional setting, it is and was taken for granted that law has a more or less clear inside and outside. Many years ago in an early canonical article about Hurst, Bob Gordon fixed that image, using the metaphor of a box. His point then was to mark Hurst's originality within the world of legal scholarship. Most legal scholarship, he explained,

[1] Allan Gurganus, "The Wish for a Good Young Country Doctor," *The New Yorker*, May 4, 2020. It is worth noting that Hurst came from a part of the Midwest not far from the farms that Gurganus describes.

occurred inside the box of the law. By contrast, Hurst found explanations for and perspectives on law outside the box.[2]

A recent helpful essay by Charles Barzun points out that whether one works on the inside or the outside of the box, commitment to the existence of an inside and an outside conforms to a core and conventional understanding, one that is identified in modern Anglo-American jurisprudence with H.L.A. Hart's *The Concept of Law*.[3]

It occurs to me today that Hurst, at least in the lectures that became *Justice Holmes on Legal History*, was edging towards a somewhat different understanding of law, one that denied the salience of a clear inside and outside. In part, his alternative understanding emerged because he believed that legislation was the centerpiece of whatever law was in America. And he imagined legislation as an expression of a democratic culture, although one modestly restrained by "constitutionalism." In any event, in those lectures he suggested a perspective that made the central problem to be solved how law (in whatever institutional form it appears) expresses culture. (Perhaps that put him closer to a position that Barzun identifies with Henry Hart, as opposed to H.L.A. Hart.) And I suspect he would have rejected an image of law as defined by a box.

B. If I had had the right words last year, I might have said something about how the work of legal history may provide an alternative to the unitary notion of law that I identified with Hurst. And that would have led me towards an understanding of legal history as "accompanying" plural and multiple understandings of law.[4] Without denying its violence and coercion (themes that Holmes certainly highlighted), law when understood through historical practices and techniques may also offer portraits and evocations of localized and particularized and plural understandings and ways of being, for spaces and practices that are apart from what lawyers or legislators will ordinarily recognize as "law." Here I mean to pose a stronger challenge than I was able to last year, both to Hurst and to much recent legal historical writing (including much of my own work as a legal historian). In different ways, in so much of mainstream legal history, law is regarded as constitutive. And by law, we mostly mean state law (or

---

2 Robert W. Gordon, "J. Willard Hurst and the Common Law Tradition in American Legal Historiography," *Law and Society Review* 10 (Fall 1975): 9–44; William Forbath, Hendrik Hartog, and Martha Minow, "Introduction: Legal Histories from Below," *Wisconsin Law Review* 1985 (1985): 759–66.

3 Charles Barzun, "The Tale of Two Harts; A Schlegelian Dialectic," University of Virginia Legal Theory, Public Law and Legal Theory Paper Series (Charlottesville, VA, 2020).

4 Staughton Lynd, *Accompanying: Pathways to Social Change* (Oakland, CA: PM Press, 2012); Barbara Tomlinson and George Lipsitz, *Insubordinate Spaces: Improvisation and Accompaniment for Social Justice* (Philadelphia, PA: Temple University Press, 2019).

the phrases and language games that we identify with state law). For Gordon and those (like myself at times) who build from his "Critical Legal Histories," this means that law is everywhere and all the time. For Hurst, the point was that the particular or the local is worth exploring only because it embodies larger patterns, never as a distinctive or plural or separate understanding.[5]

Consider how Hurst used the story of the Pike's Creek settlers at the beginning of *Law and the Conditions of Freedom,* or the significance he assigned to his study of the Wisconsin lumber industry. For him, one studies the temporally and geographically local and apparently particular in order to find the general and the national and the continuing. And he did so without much actual interest in the local or the particular or the distinctively separate. In the lumber book, commercial lumbering in Wisconsin stood in for the economic life and practices, the commerce, of the larger nation. It is, as a result, not at all surprising that his masterwork, *Law and Economic Growth,* begins with a review of the history of the Commerce Clause, before diving into the minutia of Wisconsin decisions that helped to produce the denuding of the northern Wisconsin pine forest. It is the Commerce Clause that sets the scene and that makes the local possible.

I might note that a significant part of what once drew me and other historians to Hurst's work, back a generation and more ago, was the intuition that Hurst was providing something like a Braudelian histoire totale by way of law. I think this is what Harry Scheiber pointed to in an important essay that first brought Hurst to the attention of a larger community of historians.[6] Everything was "in" law. In this sense, as I suggested in my third fragment, Hurst prefigured critical legal studies, and offered another version of a constitutive theory of law. He offered a legal history in which everything connected together, in the law.

The end of that sense of a potentially seamless history, an American legal histoire totale, is part of the history of history in the late twentieth and early twenty-first centuries. We live today in an "age of fracture," to use Dan Rodgers's wonderful phrase. I have played a small part in the coming of "fracture," I fear, at least for legal history. And I can only acknowledge my responsibility with at best ambivalence.

All this leads to a memory: When in 1985, I published an essay, "Pigs and Positivism," about the possibility of a distinctive and alternative understanding of pig keeping in early nineteenth-century New York City,

---

5 See, for a modest challenge, Laura F. Edwards, *The People and Their Peace: Legal Culture and the Transformation of Inequality in the Post-Revolutionary South* (Chapel Hill: University of North Carolina Press, 2009). But see as well, Jessica Lowe, review essay, "Law and Social Inquiry."

6 Harry N. Scheiber, "At the Borderland of Law and Economic History: The Contributions of Willard Hurst," *American Historical Review* 75, no. 3 (February 1970): 744–56.

Hurst wrote me a long memo about how I ought to expand the project suggested by the essay. He said he liked what I had done. But he suggested (strongly) that I use this story to tell a broader one about judicial notice and the forms and the history of judicial notice. By "judicial notice" he meant the restricted practice by which judges are permitted to account for forms of (possibly distinctive) local knowledge. Which was an interesting idea, and it would have been a way to make a national doctrinal legal story out of my story about a case that tested the right to keep pigs in one early modern city. But it was definitely not what I wanted to do then, although I was not certain then why I was not interested in following the path he sketched out for me. I think I finally understand why I did not do what he so kindly suggested I do, and also what concerned him. What he suggested was a way to make the story of my pigs part of a seamless (or a less particularized or localized) understanding of what it might mean that pig-keepers had their own legal consciousness. He wanted me to situate New York's pig-keepers in a national and recognizably legal story of how the law made space for local knowledge, while colonizing and partly incorporating that knowledge. And he wanted me to write it as if most of it happened inside formal state law (the space of judicial decisions). He was not interested in the ways that the pig-keepers' lawyers (as well as members of the New York City Common Council) were using law as a kind of accompaniment that allowed a distinctive understanding of law and legal culture to continue to survive.[7]

There is obviously much more to say about the alternative portrait of law that some recent legal history poses, a theme I plan to return to soon. For the moment, let me mark two features of legal accompaniment that some of the best legal history implicitly attends to. First of all, I would focus on the ways lawyering may accompany particularities, pluralities, and distinctive ways of legal being. Oddly, here Holmes's notion of the "bad man of the law" from his lecture/essay "The Path of the Law," becomes helpful.[8] Holmes had no interest in distinctive collective identities, or what we today would call legal pluralism. But his notion of how a lawyer acts on the basis of an understanding of a client as a "bad man," who cannot escape the coercion and the violence of state-centered law ("that

7 To give his suggestion its due: I imagine that Hurst was concerned with the "who cares?" question. How to choose the right particularity or distinctive sensibility or practice. How to distinguish significant particularities from mere noise. One answer is that some particularities, like Hurst's Pike's Creek settlers or his lumber industry, embody the general or the national. But is it enough, in the alternative, to celebrate the particular or the strange or the different or the deviant? Sometimes, perhaps. But we all know from our own reading that the aesthetic and moral burdens of justifying distinctiveness are great. And there is no handy shortcut.

8 In addition to Holmes's essay, I would point to the voluminous writings of Staughton Lynd about work in Youngstown, Ohio.

which is more powerful than we are"), but who can rely on lawyers (who accompany and advise) to mitigate the effects of that power and, occasionally, to allow spaces where alternative or plural understandings to survive (for a time) or even flourish, reveals how lawyering becomes a kind of accompaniment. That is to say, lawyering or effective legal counsel may make it possible for "bad men of the law" (which may be all of us) to live their lives and life plans as they please, or less unhappily than they would do so otherwise, even though they don't care at all about forms or the substance of "the law" (which is why they are "bad men"). Secondly, if Hurst had had a more generous view of constitutionalism, one less tied to early twentieth-century understandings (call it the fear of *Lochner*), he might have understood constitutionalism as occasionally offering space for deviant rights consciousnesses. Constitutionalism, as we understand it today, necessarily incorporates the contradictions and multiple possibilities that lawyers have drawn out of the constitutional text. It allows notions of federalism and state sovereignty and personhood (under the Fourteenth Amendment) to be used for many purposes. It puts in question notions of apparently settled understandings, like the plenary power. It can even make space for protests, including those that harm some private properties.

I don't, on the other hand, want to go too far down the legal pluralism road. In the end, the task for legal history (for what legal history should "do") should be, I suspect, to find a balance between law as universalizing and hegemonic and law as a space for conflict and as an arena for disparate and distinctive worldviews and understandings. I don't want to deny the former while finding space for the latter. As the legal anthropologist Paul Dresch put it in a particularly helpful survey of a multitude of studies of legal systems in many times and places, textual and formal law offers something close to a general public morality. In studying particularities and contradictions and diversions, in emphasizing "legalities," one does not want to lose the capacity to explore the history of that (changing and contingent) general public morality that state law (written law) may express. As well as the coercions and violence of state law.[9]

3. One final addendum: In the original essay, I did not clarify part of what drove me to ask the question, "what does legal history do?" Behind the question lay a desire (a wish) to describe legal history as a practice that is neither academic law nor conventional history as practiced in history departments. Today, I would want to make that wish somewhat more strongly, almost as a claim: that legal history accompanies both academic

---

9 Paul Dresch, "Introduction. Legalism, Anthropology, and History: A View from Part of Anthropology," in *Legalism: Anthropology and History*, in *Legalism: Anthropology and History*, ed. Paul Dresch and Hannah Skoda (Oxford, U.K.: Oxford University Press, 2012), 1–39.

law and legal thought, on the one hand, and law reform and policy, on the other. And it is also not the same as the work that non-legal historians do in using legal sources for their own purposes.

To be a legal historian is to participate in a discipline and in distinctive conversations. Legal history has its own understanding of law and of the work involved in coming to an understanding of law. What do I mean by accompaniment here? Eventually, I hope to write a book on the theme. But for the moment, let me point to two conventional understandings, neither of which fully captures the possibilities I am seeking. Legal history is like the instruments and performers that accompany the soloist or singer in any of a number of genres of music. It provides color, thickening, enriching, a bass line. What else are the reasons for contextualizations and periodizations and critique, the characteristic modalities of legal history when confronting legal doctrine? But legal history also "accompanies" in the sense of traveling with conventional modalities of law. Without legal history as a travel companion, as company, law is empty and even more exposed than it will be.[10]

In emphasizing a notion of legal history as an accompaniment to law, I am also marking legal history's separation from law (academic law). It is a travel companion, not a unity or a merged identity. For the past generation, much of the best legal history (particularly in its law-school-based identities) has been shaped by a desire to change law and to critique law, by way of doing legal history. As I wrote in my first "fragment," that writing typically understands legal history as legal writing done right. Without denying that way of doing legal history, or its small successes, I would want to insist on legal history as an accompaniment and as, in some ways, a distinct conversational community.

Or, to put it differently, perhaps legal history does not need to justify itself in terms of its utility for law. It is a humanistic practice that does several things, including accompanying law. It also accompanies and "travels with" other modalities of historical writing. The uses that legal writers make of legal history may be what they do, but does not itself define what legal history is, or (the entirety of) what it does.

That is, of course, a claim that moves legal history quite far from notions of "law in action." But I am not certain that legal history can withstand scrutiny as a tool or technique in a "law in action" toolbox.

References

Barzun, Charles. "The Tale of Two Harts; A Schlegelian Dialectic." University of Virginia Legal Theory, Public Law and Legal Theory Paper Series. Charlottesville, VA, 2020.

[10] Here I follow in the footsteps of Tomlinson and Lipsitz.

Dresch, Paul. "Introduction. Legalism, Anthropology, and History: A View from Part of Anthropology." In *Legalism: Anthropology and History*. In *Legalism: Anthropology and History*, edited by Paul Dresch and Hannah Skoda, 1–39. Oxford, U.K.: Oxford University Press, 2012.

Edwards, Laura F. *The People and Their Peace: Legal Culture and the Transformation of Inequality in the Post-Revolutionary South*. Chapel Hill: University of North Carolina Press, 2009.

Forbath, William, Hendrik Hartog, and Martha Minow. "Introduction: Legal Histories from Below." *Wisconsin Law Review* 1985 (1985): 759–66.

Gordon, Robert W. "J. Willard Hurst and the Common Law Tradition in American Legal Historiography." *Law and Society Review* 10 (Fall 1975): 9–44.

Gurganus, Allan. "The Wish for a Good Young Country Doctor." *The New Yorker*, May 4, 2020.

Lynd, Staughton. *Accompanying: Pathways to Social Change*. Oakland, CA: PM Press, 2012.

Scheiber, Harry N. "At the Borderland of Law and Economic History: The Contributions of Willard Hurst." *American Historical Review* 75, no. 3 (February 1970): 744–56.

Tomlinson, Barbara, and George Lipsitz. *Insubordinate Spaces: Improvisation and Accompaniment for Social Justice*. Philadelphia, PA: Temple University Press, 2019.

Herman Goldstein's Impact on Society, Law, Police, and Me

Michael S. Scott

Abstract

This paper traces the influence of Herman Goldstein on Professor Michael Scott personally and on the law, the police, and society. Scott began his contacts with Goldstein while writing an undergraduate thesis at University of Wisconsin-Madison and subsequently taught Goldstein's courses at UW Law School. Scott's exceptional career includes service as an officer in the Madison Police Department, Harvard Law School, service as police chief and administrator in several large cities, and presently the Director of the Center for Problem-Oriented Policing, a research center that produces and disseminates information about how police can effectively and fairly address specific public-safety problems. The center has published guidebooks on seventy-five different problems, each with its own analysis of references, situational criminology, and suggested problem-solving.[1]

Regarding impact on the police, the goal of problem-oriented policing (POP) is to improve the police institution by making the police more effective and fair without over-reliance on law enforcement and the exercise of coercive authority. Success depends on leveraging a perpetual

[1] https://popcenter.asu.edu/all-problems. The listed problem guides are: abandoned building and lots, abandoned vehicles, acquaintance rape of college students, aggressive driving, animal cruelty, assaults in and around bars, bank robbery, bicycle theft, bomb threats in schools, bullying in schools, burglary at construction sites, at retail establishments, and at single-family homes, check and card fraud, child abuse and neglect, child pornography on the internet, chronic public inebriation, clandestine meth labs, crimes against tourists, cruising, disorder at budget motels, disorder at day-labor sites, disorderly youth in public places, domestic violence, drive-by shootings, drug dealing in open-air markets, drug dealing in privately owned apartments, drug-impaired driving, drunk driving, exploitation of trafficked women, export of stolen vehicles, false burglar alarms, financial crimes against the elderly, gasoline drive offs, graffiti, gun violence among serious young offenders, hate crimes, home invasion robbery, homeless encampments, identify theft, illicit sexual activity in public places, juvenile runaways, loud car stereos, missing persons, misuse and abuse of 911, panhandling, pedestrian injuries and fatalities, people with emotional illness, physical and emotional abuse of the elderly, prescription drug fraud and misuse, rave parties, retaliatory violent disputes, robbery at ATMs, at convenience stores, at pharmacies, and of taxi drivers, school vandalism and break-ins, sexual assault of women by strangers, shoplifting, spectator violence in stadiums, speeding in residential areas, stalking, stolen goods markets, street prostitution, street racing, street robbery, student party riots, thefts of customers' personal property in cafes and bars, of scrap metal, of cars in parking facilities, and of cars in residential streets and on driveways, traffic congestion around schools, underage drinking, and witness intimidation.

frustration of the police—not feeling as though their knowledge and expertise is tapped by policy makers. In response to the crack cocaine epidemic and the 9/11 terrorist attacks, policing took a turn toward a militarized approach for both drugs and terrorism. But in 2020, problem-oriented policing stands ready to help the police move ahead, especially in relationships with minority communities, waiting only for political forces to urge them in that direction.

In terms of legal education, the courses taught at UW Law School by Goldstein and Scott recognized that police treated formal law (on the books) as a tool used to achieve particular goals of policing. Students need to know the nature of police business, the various goals and objectives of police, and the multitude of incentives and disincentives that push and pull police officers toward some actions and away from others. Only one of the original Goldstein courses is now taught at UW Law School, but Professors Findley and Klingele are keeping the Goldstein tradition alive through their required first-year course, Introduction to Criminal Procedure, which, for example, requires that students take police ride-alongs. See their interview in this volume.

In terms of impact on society, especially in these days of Black Lives Matter, Goldstein well-understood that fair treatment of all people was fundamental to policing and that citizens' quality of life depended on it. In *Policing a Free Society*, he noted the numerous ways in which police commonly mistreated members of minority communities, such as campaigns of harassment; stopping and questioning on flimsy legal grounds; selective enforcement of laws on the basis of race; remaining ignorant of or disinterested in the customs, cultures, and norms of minority communities; refusing to hire minority applicants until ordered to do so by courts; and mistreatment of minority officers once hired. He said that unfair and biased policing is inherently bad policing and advocated hiring people with good values as police officers and developing them for leadership roles. Problem-oriented policing itself is a valuable approach to police reform, for example, as it encourages police to seek and out and listen to the concerns of minority communities and think of responses beyond conventional criminal law enforcement, such as informal conflict resolution, conveying information to discourage problem behavior, issuing warnings, reinforcing informal social control, altering the physical environment, bringing in needed social services and other community resources, and protecting high-risk victims. In this, it draws heavily from the criminological field of situational crime prevention.

Herman Goldstein's Impact on Society, Law, Police, and Me

Michael S. Scott

I have titled this chapter to signal readers of my aim to reflect on what Herman Goldstein and his ideas have meant to society, law, police, and me: ordering them from most to least important, at least in the large scheme of things. However, I will take them up in precisely reverse order because that's the order in the long process by which I came to understand his significance.

Me

My now-forty-year career is bookended by Herman Goldstein: my introducing myself to him at its outset in 1980 and eulogizing him in 2020, nearer to its end. And the University of Wisconsin, including the Law School, features prominently in my career arc.

I was first introduced to Herman—"Professor Goldstein" to me then—in 1980 when, as a University of Wisconsin undergraduate majoring in Behavioral Science and the Law (now known as the Legal Studies Program) and focusing on the police, my thesis advisor, then-sociology professor, Howard Erlanger advised me to go over to the law school and introduce myself to Professor Goldstein and, in turn, solicit his advice on a proper reading list to inform my thesis. I chose to write my thesis on the occupational perspectives of police officers: how they understood the world in which they worked, and why. Professor Goldstein was more than generous to me, providing me an extensive and carefully considered reading list. It contained the works of the leading policing scholars of the time: Michael Banton, Egon Bittner, Robert Fogelson, George Kelling, Wayne La Fave, Peter Manning, William Ker Muir, Arthur Niederhoffer, Albert Reiss, Jonathan Rubenstein, Jerome Skolnick, John Van Maanen, William Westley, James Q. Wilson, and, of course, Herman Goldstein. It was a comparatively small canon to that found in many other fields but comprised much of the extant research on the police, and plenty for an undergraduate to digest.

At least five significant things came to me out of this introduction: 1) a referral to an innovative UW summer internship as a uniformed police intern in the Middleton, Wisconsin, Police Department that deepened my understanding of policing and police culture; 2) special permission to enroll in Professor Goldstein's Law School course, The Role of the Police in a Free Society, that enabled me to learn in person what I had read in his book, *Policing a Free Society*, and more; 3) most important to me at the time, an A on my thesis and completion of my major requirements; 4) after my graduation and while applying to become a real police officer, an offer to work with Professor Goldstein as a research assistant on his first test of the problem-oriented approach to policing that examined, in collaboration with the Madison Police Department, the problems of drinking drivers and repeat sex offenders; and 5) a passion for and commitment to improving policing as a career.

Since that fateful first meeting with Herman in 1980, he was—and remains posthumously—one of the most important people in my career and life, advising me, recommending me to others, and, ultimately, collaborating with me. From being one of his research assistants, I became a Madison police officer (to this day, the most fulfilling job I've ever had); a Harvard Law student (during which time I spent one summer at the Police Executive Research Forum [PERF] in Washington, DC, working for another of Herman's protégés, UW Law alumnus Gary Hayes, interviewing leading police chiefs and publishing a guidebook for new police chiefs, and the second half of another summer—after confirming for myself during the first half of that summer that corporate law was not my true vocation—rejoining Herman as a research assistant on what became his second book, *Problem-Oriented Policing*); the legal assistant to the New York City police commissioner (working largely on advancing a community problem-solving approach to policing); a researcher at PERF; the director of administration for the Fort Pierce, Florida, Police Department; the special assistant to the St. Louis police chief (brought in to lead a transition to problem-oriented policing); the first chief of a new police agency in Lauderhill, Florida; a visiting fellow with the U.S. Department of Justice Office of Community Oriented Policing Services (during which time I collaborated with Herman and others in establishing the Problem-Oriented Guides for Police and the Center for Problem-Oriented Policing); a clinical professor at the University of Wisconsin Law School (more on this later); and currently a clinical professor at Arizona State University's School of Criminology and Criminal Justice. Herman's understanding of and approach to policing has profoundly influenced my work in every one of these positions. Whatever influence I might have had on the police field is due largely to what I learned from Herman.

Police

When I made the transition from studying the police to becoming the police, one of the early insights I came to was that not all police officers viewed Herman Goldstein through the same lens I did. I joined a police department that was about a decade into a major transformation—from a conventional police agency that understood its purpose to be one of law enforcement and disorder suppression to which ends the exercise of coercive authority was deemed quintessential, to one of public service and order maintenance to which ends the exercise of coercive authority was deemed a last resort. The department's officers had self-divided their loyalties into two camps—the "A team" and the "B team"—the former being those sympathetic to the police chief's reforms and the latter being those vehemently opposed. Broadly speaking, the reforms were to: diversify the police ranks by gender, race, and ethnicity; elevate the educational level of the ranks; emphasize verbal persuasion over physical coercion in officers' dealings with the public; significantly restrict and reduce the degree of force, particularly deadly force used by officers; promote officers' respect for and protection of the public's civil liberties, especially those guaranteed by the First, Fourth, Fifth, and Sixth Amendments to the U.S. Constitution; and encourage officers to embrace the service dimensions of policing and not just its law enforcement dimensions (see Couper, 2012). This might all seem rather tame, uncontroversial fare today, but it decidedly was not then. By virtue of his close and public association with the police chief, Herman Goldstein was viewed as being anti-police by B-teamers. New officers, such as I, were probed and pressured to join one team or the other. Although the political dynamics of American police agencies vary substantially across agencies and over time, in nearly all places and at all times there exists some form of this basic A team/B team dichotomy between which police officers must align themselves.

As Herman's scholarship evolved from its focus on police *administration* and the basic arrangements for policing society (reflected in his first book, *Policing a Free Society* [Goldstein, 1977]) to police *operations* and the manner in which police should address their substantive business (reflected in his second book, *Problem-Oriented Policing* [Goldstein, 1990]), his ideas began to connect with and change the day-to-day work of police *officers*, not just police *administrators*. After the early experimentation with problem-oriented policing in Madison, the approach was brought closer to the line levels in such places as Baltimore County, Maryland; Newport News, Virginia; San Diego; Philadelphia; Tulsa; Atlanta; Tampa; New York City; Los Angeles; and Chicago. Published reports, police conferences, and police training programs helped spread Herman's problem-oriented approach first to dozens and then hundreds more jurisdictions throughout the country and to the United Kingdom, Canada, and beyond. In a not entirely foreseen twist, the problem-oriented approach was beginning to hold as much appeal to some line-level police officers as it did to some police administrators. To be sure, the approach probably was never deeply embraced by more than perhaps five percent of an agency's officers, but it is generally the case that the surest path to police reform is through the hearts and minds of the right five percent of officers in any agency.

Influencing the hearts and minds of police officers, though, is no simple task. Herman learned early in his career that many well-intended police reforms proposed from outside police agencies, or even from within, by police administrators foundered when they clashed with the norms of the police subculture or police union opposition. To the degree that problem-oriented policing has been embraced by rank-and-file police officers, this has largely been due to its tapping into one of their eternal frustrations—not feeling as though their knowledge and expertise is tapped by policy makers, whether inside or outside the police agency. Herman explicitly called for tapping into just this knowledge and expertise, directly involving line-level officers and detectives in identifying and analyzing problems, and developing and implementing new responses to them. Herman developed a respect for the challenges faced by line-level officers and empathized with the often unrealistic expectations placed upon them by society, and at times by their own bosses. Problem-oriented policing was designed in large part to close the gap between idealized notions of policing and its realities.

This is not to say that police officers or their unions have uniformly embraced problem-oriented policing: many officers still find greater comfort in a more routinized approach to policing in which performance standards are easier to meet and to count, such as the number of arrests made, citations issued, buildings checked, calls handled, cases cleared, and so forth. Problem-oriented policing draws police out of those comfort zones into the often messy realm of critical analysis, innovation, and reconciliation of competing interests and expectations among multiple stakeholders. Problem-oriented policing might be enormously satisfying when success is realized, but it tends to be harder work than much of routine policing. In its best form, problem-oriented policing has great potential to narrow two critical gaps in policing: that between the public and the police, and that between the police rank-and-file and police administrators. It does so largely by concentrating everyone's attention on addressing the substantive problems of policing—the behaviors and conditions in communities that compromise citizens' quality of life. In the traditional policing approach, far too much of both these relationships focus on the divergence of interests rather than on the commonality of them.

Largely by virtue of Herman's involvement in the early Harvard Kennedy School of Government's executive sessions on community policing in the mid- to late-1980s, problem-oriented policing was increasingly integrated into notions of community policing, thereby giving a rather amorphous idea greater precision and a process for effective police action. The approach was given a further boost when President Bill Clinton's hitherto campaign promise to add 100,000 more police officers to the country's police forces was operationalized through the creation of the US Department of Justice's Office of Community Oriented Policing Services which provided funding to police agencies committed to training and assigning those new officers to engage in community problem-solving, a mashup of community policing and Herman's problem-oriented policing.

By most accounts, and consistent with my own experiences working in New York City, St. Louis, and South Florida, the citizens with whom police were now collaborating to address local crime and disorder problems seemed to appreciate and value this policing style. This seemed especially true in the minority communities to which many community police officers were assigned, as it represented a dramatic departure from the historical policing styles that alternated between over-policing and under-policing minority communities. And the police officers, in turn, seemed to appreciate and value the newfound respect, trust, and cooperation they were getting from the public.

In retrospect, the 1980s through 2000 seem an apex of police reform as it relates directly to the manner in which police officers engage and collaborate with the community to promote public safety and security. Asserting so does not deny the very real and seemingly parallel militarization of the American police, largely as a response to the crack cocaine crisis of that era (see Kraska, 2007; ACLU, 2014), but neither trend wholly negates the effects of the other. It might be fair to say that important lessons came out of that era as to both what police did right and wrong in terms of creating a policing style well suited for an open and democratic society.

In response to 9/11 terrorist attacks on New York City and Washington, D.C., American policing took yet another historical turn, this time away from community problem-solving and even more strongly toward a militarized approach to addressing both terrorism and drug-market concerns. And the economic collapse of 2008 put another dagger in the heart of community policing, as it was deemed a luxury that local governments could not afford. Yet, perhaps paradoxically, it was during the 2000–2010 period when problem-oriented policing realized its greatest advances through the federal support that led to the creation of the Problem-Oriented Guides for Police and then to the Center for Problem-Oriented Policing. This body of work has come closer than anything prior to realizing Herman's vision for a well-organized, readily accessible, practitioner-oriented, research-based body of policing knowledge. Indeed, Herman and I discussed this vision many times, decades before it came to fruition. Also, during this period, the academic community put several stamps of approval on problem-oriented policing, deeming it an effective approach to crime control (see National Research Council, 2004: 243-246; Weisburd et al., 2010). These endorsements were supplemented in the following decade with Herman's being awarded the Stockholm Prize in Criminology in 2018, largely for his work on problem-oriented policing and by a follow-up meta-analysis of the effectiveness of problem-oriented policing by the Campbell Collaboration (Hinkle et al., 2020).

In 2020 in the United States, it feels like problem-oriented policing stands ready to help American police move ahead in terms of both their effectiveness and their relationship with minority communities, waiting only for the political forces to urge them in that direction. The political and professional trends in the United Kingdom and New Zealand have returned police to problem-oriented policing as their preferred policing style.

Law

Herman Goldstein had, to say the least, an unconventional connection to law and legal education, especially so for a member of a law faculty. His formal education and training was in public administration. He may still be the only University of Wisconsin Law School faculty member who was not formally trained in law. This means that he was not trained to do the very thing that most law schools train their students to do: to think like a lawyer. Yet he shared responsibility with his law school colleagues for the professional education and development of prospective lawyers, at least within the general field of criminal law and criminal justice. At the time he was hired to the UW Law School faculty, notwithstanding his unconventional training, he was a good fit. Willard Hurst's promotion of legal realism, embodied in the work of colleagues like Stewart Macaulay and Frank Remington, meshed well with Herman's view that the law only partially, and sometimes indirectly, either prescribed or proscribed what the police did. The police whom Herman observed in action often treated the formal law as a guide, suggesting their actions, or as a tool, used to achieve a particular police goal. Accordingly, Herman recognized that teaching students the formal law would not get them far in their understanding of how the police—and other criminal justice systems actors—operated. To develop that deeper understanding, students needed to know the nature of police business, the various goals and objectives police have, and the multitude of incentives and disincentives that push and pull police officers toward some actions and away from others. Contrary to conventional views that policing was relatively straightforward and simple—find law violations and gather the evidence necessary to support a prosecution thereof—it was really quite complex, and all the more so because its practitioners for most of police history were not especially well educated or trained. In essence, as Herman's work on the American Bar Foundation's Survey of Criminal Justice taught him, police officers were routinely confronting rather complex social problems and often improvising short-term responses to them.

Beyond helping his colleagues redesign the teaching of criminal justice at the University of Wisconsin Law School—primarily to teach students how the criminal justice system is actually administered in addition to the formalities of substantive and procedural criminal law—Herman also developed two additional courses on the police in particular: one was entitled The Role of the Police in a Free Society; the other, Selected Problems in Policing. The former course—and the one I took as an undergraduate—explored the nature of the police function, police discretion, political accountability of the police, police misconduct, and the police relationship to the criminal justice system. The latter course homed in on specific types of policing problems—street prostitution, drug dealing, street robbery, chronic public inebriation, organized crime, etc.—enabling students to develop a nuanced understanding of the unique challenges posed by each problem type and the need for careful analysis of each problem toward shaping an effective and appropriate response to it, one that might or might not prominently feature police action and/or the invocation of the formal criminal process. Just as Herman sought to wean police off their reliance on the criminal justice system as the preferred response to all policing problems, in these law school courses he likewise sought to wean law students off their preconceived notions that all policing problems can be resolved by resort to the formal invocation of the law.

Herman knew well that only a few of his law students would enter the policing field after graduation; that the majority of them would become something else, interacting with the police in various capacities, some directly such as prosecutors, defense attorneys, or judges; and some indirectly as legislators, government executives, police board members, non-government attorneys, and the like. In this way, Herman aspired not only to teach those students who planned to work in the criminal law field how to interact with the police, but he aspired to teach all his students about the unique role and authority of police in a free and open society. Whether his students emerged from his course with greater or lesser respect for the police than when they started was less important to Herman than that they emerged with a changed understanding of police, one far more informed and sophisticated than the one they might have formed from a steady diet of police procedural television shows and films.

I was recruited to the UW Law School faculty in 2003 by Professor Emeritus Walter Dickey, one of Herman's closest faculty colleagues. Herman had retired from UW in 1994 and the above-described courses were no longer being taught. Walter wanted Herman's legacy preserved in part by offering those courses once again. So I taught them for ten years, building on Herman's syllabi. I found ways to get the students who enrolled in those courses to meet, observe, and work with police officers as much as possible, continuing Herman's tradition of bringing the police into the classroom and the students onto the streets. I was able, with the close collaboration of Clinical Professor Emeritus Ben Kempinen, to establish a paid internship that had selected students work jointly with a police department and its prosecutor's office studying a real-world crime or disorder problem using a problem-oriented approach, and helping them develop a more effective response to it. Students worked on problems such as homelessness, home-invasion robbery, drug overdoses, domestic violence, child sex trafficking, theft of scrap metal, and acquaintance rape.

Just as interest and engagement in problem-oriented policing among police has waxed and waned over the decades, so too has interest and engagement in legal realism among law school administrators. When law school applications and admissions plummeted nationally and at UW, and the UW Law School felt compelled to conserve resources, my position and the police-prosecution internships were cut. The Role of the Police in a Free Society course appears to still be taught, at least on an intermittent basis, but the Selected Problems in Policing course appears to have been dropped altogether. It troubled Herman greatly when his courses were allowed to lapse after his retirement, and troubled yet more when this happened again. It was always remarkable that the UW Law School taught its students about the police in the way that Frank Remington and Herman Goldstein, and later, I, did. Not many law schools go beyond criminal procedure and Fourth, Fifth and Sixth Amendment law in their treatment of police and policing. But, with obvious personal bias, it seems equally remarkable that it has stopped doing so. Perhaps it will come back yet again. Presently, Professors Keith Findley and Cecelia Klingele are keeping the Remington/ Goldstein tradition alive through their required first-year course, Introduction to Criminal Procedure. For more about this course see their interview in this volume. Professor Klingele also teaches the Goldstein course, The Role of Police in a Free Society, when possible.

Society

This leaves me, lastly, to reflect on the significance of Herman Goldstein's ideas for society at large. The most obvious significance is that the police serve and protect society; thus, what and how well police function necessarily affects its clientele—the public. As Herman asserted in his first book: The strength of a democracy and the quality of life enjoyed by its citizens are determined in large measure by the ability of police to discharge their duties (Goldstein, 1977: 1).

In 2020, the American police once again find themselves the object of strict and harsh public scrutiny, with the death of George Floyd at the hands of police being the straw that broke the camel's back, a back that has been long burdened by other unnecessary deaths, particularly of minority citizens, and by a long, long history of poor police treatment of minority citizens and their communities. This historical moment feels to many to be unique—and while it might turn out to be if transformative change actually occurs—it is also but the latest of many episodic moments in American history when the fairness or the effectiveness of the police has been called into profound question (see Walker, 1985; Scott, 2008). But the question has been called again and it invites consideration of Herman's understanding of and approach to policing, especially as it might or might not relate to the present-day movement to reform policing in the United States.

The current moment in history is often characterized by two slogans: "Black lives matter" and "abolish (or defund) the police." To my understanding, they are linked one to the other. Both slogans emerged out of the tragedies of the deaths of Black men at the hands of police. Accordingly, "Black lives matter" is implicitly directed at the police, who are believed by many to care little for the preservation of the lives of Black people, especially young Black men and boys. "Abolish (or defund) the police" implies that society—or at least its disenfranchised members—would, on the whole, be better off if police did not exist. This further implies that society is capable of policing itself without need for organized police forces.

In that Herman is not alive to speak his own mind about the current critique of American policing, it must be gleaned from his past words and actions. It can fairly be said that the entirety of Herman's career and published works was centrally about police reform, or as Herman preferred to put it—improving policing. And, as Herman asserted, improving policing improves society. How, precisely, does it do so?

In *Policing a Free Society*, Herman noted throughout the book the numerous ways in which police commonly mistreated members of minority communities, from campaigns of harassment through stopping and questioning them on the flimsiest of legal grounds; to selective enforcement of laws on the basis of race; to tolerating criminal offending in minority communities by those who bribe police to do so; to remaining either ignorant of or disinterested in the customs, cultures, and norms of minority communities; to refusing to hire minority applicants until ordered to do so by courts; to the mistreatment of minority officers once hired. And he makes clear that all of these practices, and others, must end in the interest of improving policing. It is now widely understood that police mistreatment of minority citizens compromises public trust in police, which in turn makes it harder for police to enlist minority citizens' cooperation in criminal investigations and other matters. Moreover, it fuels resentment which can translate into verbal abuse and assaults of police officers. But these are instrumental reasons for police to improve their treatment of minority citizens: helping officers solve crimes and keeping them safer. Herman understood well that police needed to improve their treatment of minority citizens and communities not solely out of self-interest, but because it was the fair and just thing to do in its own right, that fair and impartial treatment of all people was fundamental to policing, and that the very quality of life of the citizenry depended heavily upon it. Unfair and biased policing is inherently bad policing, irrespective of any other consideration. To this end, Herman strongly advocated recruiting and hiring people with the right principles, values and character to be police officers; and also developing the best of them purposefully for leadership roles in policing to ensure that the policies and practices of police agencies were aligned toward fundamentally fair policing.

What then of Herman's problem-oriented policing approach? How, if at all, does it speak to the larger issues of fair and impartial policing? It doesn't do so directly in the manner that reforms such as implicit bias training for police or federal court-ordered consent decrees to end unconstitutional and racially biased policing practices do. In fact, if one attended a training course on problem-oriented policing—including one taught by me—it wouldn't be obvious how problem-oriented policing addresses at all the concerns of the Black Lives Matter, and similar other, social justice movements. Yet, I would argue—and know that Herman did as well—that it very much does.

Problem-oriented policing comprises several core elements that speak to fair and impartial policing. One is that the police need to listen to and take seriously the public-safety and security concerns of all communities, especially those communities who lack substantial political power to ensure that their voices are heard. Giving disaffected people a voice in what police pay attention to in itself helps build trust.

Another core element is the careful exploration of the various interests at stake in policing problems. This exploration often reveals the hidden interests of third parties (that is, those other than the principal offender and the principal victim) which facilitate the problematic behavior or conditions. For example, some open-air drug markets operating in and around privately owned apartment complexes thrive because the complex owners and managers implicitly or explicitly tolerate or facilitate it through their property-management practices, all in the interests of maximizing short-term profits. As a consequence, a police response to the drug market limited to arresting and prosecuting drug sellers might not only be ineffective (sellers are easily replaced), but also be unfair in holding accountable only one set of actors in the problem, ignoring the culpability of others who are profiting from the illegal market.

Yet another core element of problem-oriented policing is the deliberate and broad search for alternative responses to the problem. This part of the problem-solving process explicitly encourages police to think of responses beyond conventional criminal law enforcement, such as informal conflict resolution, conveying information to discourage problem behavior, issuing warnings, reinforcing informal social control, altering the physical environment, bringing in needed social services and other community resources, protecting high-risk victims, etc. It draws heavily from the criminological field of situational crime prevention. Two possible equity benefits can emerge from this broad search for alternatives. One is the benefit of soliciting input and support from the affected communities for the desired response. When people have a voice in what police do, they tend to support that action. The second is that employing alternatives to criminal arrest and prosecution helps reduce the often-disparate impact that enforcement has on minority communities. As a general proposition, the less coercive authority police use, the greater support and trust they enjoy in affected communities. At a minimum, deliberating with the affected communities before police act helps reduce the likelihood of unintended negative perceptions about biased treatment of minority citizens.

Through some of these same core elements, problem-oriented policing also addresses demands to "defund the police." Although few legislators are likely to seriously entertain the demand to abolish the police altogether, many will consider shifting resources from police to other government sectors. In this regard, Herman Goldstein's ideas, which he described as "shifting and sharing responsibility for public safety," are most relevant. The careful analysis of local problems, along with the broad search for alternative responses, quite often lead police and the public to recognize that many problems left to police to handle can, in whole or in part, be better or as well-handled by entities other than police. Problem-oriented policing builds this consideration—who does or should "own" this problem—into the problem-solving process (see Scott and Goldstein, 2005). Within the context of this careful consideration, shifting some resources along with responsibility from the police to others might well be warranted. It is in this context that "community policing" can come to mean more than just what more the police can do for the community, but what the community can do for itself that would obviate the need to invoke the riskiest and most coercive aspects of policing.

Conclusion

Herman Goldstein meant a lot to me personally and to my career, as he has meant to so many other individuals who had the privilege of knowing and learning from him. He and his ideas have also meant a great deal to the entire police profession. His is one of the best-known names in a field that hasn't historically paid much heed to academia. Especially well known is his problem-oriented policing concept, familiar to police around the world, principally in developed, English-speaking nations, but increasingly also in developing, non-English-speaking ones. Herman has also influenced the legal academy through the manner in which he sought to broaden traditional legal education. His many students, especially those who have become legal scholars and teachers themselves, cannot help but have been influenced by his unique approach and brilliant teaching skills. And although most people in the world will never have heard of Herman Goldstein, his ideas, scholarship, passion, and genuine human kindness and decency has raised, however marginally, their hopes for safety and security, and a better quality of life.

References

American Civil Liberties Union. 2014. *War Comes Home: The Excessive Militarization of American Policing.* New York: American Civil Liberties Union.

Couper, David C. 2012. *Arrested Development: A Veteran Police Chief Sounds About Protest, Racism, Corruption and the Seven Steps Necessary to Improve Our Nation's Police.* San Bernardino, CA: CreateSpace Independent Publishing Platform.

Hinkle, J., D. Weisburd, C. Telep, and K. Petersen. 2020. "Problem-Oriented Policing for Reducing Crime and Disorder: An Updated Systematic Review and Meta-analysis." Campbell Systematic Reviews. https://doi.org/10.1002/cl2.1089.

Goldstein, Herman. 1977. *Policing a Free Society.* Cambridge, MA: Ballinger Publishing Co.

Goldstein, Herman. 1990. *Problem-Oriented Policing.* New York: McGraw-Hill.

Kraska, P. 2007. "Militarization and Policing—Its Relevance to 21st Century Police." *Policing* 1(4): 501-513.

National Research Council. 2004. *Fairness and Effectiveness in Policing: The Evidence.* Committee to Review Research on Police Policy and Practices. Wesley Skogan and Kathleen Frydl, editors. Committee on Law and Justice, Division of Behavioral and Social Sciences and Education. Washington, D.C.: The National Academies Press.

Scott, M. 2008. "Progress in American Policing? Reviewing the National Reviews." *Law & Social Inquiry* 34(1): 171-185.

Scott, M., and H. Goldstein. 2005. *Shifting and Sharing Responsibility for Public-Safety Problems.* Problem-Oriented Guides for Police. Response Guide No. 3. Washington, D.C.: U.S. Department of Justice, Office of Community Oriented Policing Services.

Walker, S. 1985. "Setting the Standards: The Efforts and Impact of Blue-Ribbon Commissions on the Police." In *Police Leadership in America: Crisis and Opportunity*, ed. William A. Geller, 354–70. Chicago: American Bar Foundation and Praeger Publishers.

Weisburd, D., C. Telep, J. Hinkle, and J. Eck. 2010. "Is Problem-Oriented Policing Effective in Reducing Crime and Disorder?" *Criminology & Public Policy* 9(1): 139-172.

Interview of Dirk Hartog by Bill Clune

Abstract

Legal history has changed a lot since Hurst. A large secondary literature has appeared within and outside law schools, and many more legal historians have been appointed. The field has also moved in new directions such as gender and sexuality, race and the significance of the Civil War, borderland citizenship, and viewing legal history through the lens of imperialism, colonialism, and Atlantic World studies. Over the last thirty years, Hurst's interest in the history of capitalism and economic growth diminished, but in the last ten years it has become central again through the lens of slavery studies, particularly the debate over whether slavery and slave law were capitalist or anti-capitalist. A debate has developed about the origins of anti-slavery conventions from older sources or modern human rights conventions. Another shift that has occurred away from Hurst's focus on statutes toward storytelling from trial transcripts and finding the voices of subaltern populations. On the other hand, an interesting rebirth of Hurst's focus is that some of Professor Hartog's Indian students see his work as relevant to post-colonial history in India.

In retrospect, Hurst's work had strengths and weaknesses. In framing the history of capitalism, he largely ignored oppressed and unrepresented groups, but he did recognize the ruthless greed of the communal "we" that plundered the northern forest. His brilliance came in framing lawmaking as an exercise of improvised social construction cutting across doctrinal areas guided by an underlying consensus of economic liberty and constraints (constitutionalism).

Law students can learn important lessons from a legal history course. One is the historicity of law viewed from the outside as influenced by context and from the inside as having its own sense of history and context. Reflecting a "living law" perspective, Chief Justice Warren in the *Brown* case said that we can't know what the drafters of the Fourteenth Amendment intended, but we must decide what it means today. Justice Scalia adopted the more conservative approach of originalism, but adherence to the text of the amendment is what preserves birthright citizenship. Courts generally reflected societal views on same-sex marriages as they changed drastically over twenty years. Professor Hartog wrote a book on slavery and freedom in New Jersey which highlighted the concern of legislators that freed slaves might end up on tax-supported poor-relief rolls, especially given high rates of interstate mobility. The book follows Hurst in tracing legal change to multiple influences that cut across doctrinal categories (e.g., taxation, not just emancipation) but departs from Hurst on the importance of migration. Law and economics, sometimes viewed as the rival of legal history, reflects the historical influence of economic forces on law and judges' awareness of such considerations. As for acceptance of legal history among law students, Professor Hartog experienced a great deal of skepticism at Indiana when he taught legal history as a required course but very little when he arrived at Wisconsin, undoubtedly because of Hurst's legacy.

Periodization in history offers an interesting perspective on Hurst. Hurst saw a long period of consensus and conflict around economic liberty and regulation continuing perhaps to the present day and was not interested in conventional periods dated by presidential terms or conventional labels (e.g., the Gilded Age). Historians since Hurst might emphasize longer and wider periods such as the international slave trade. Immigration and race is another recent example of interest to historians dating from the Chinese Exclusion Act. The idea of an underlying broad consensus is something that may have been lost in recent historical studies.

Bill Clune: What are the main subjects and authors that you consider important to includein the legal history course including but not limited to Hurst, and why did you make this choice?

Dirk Hartog: Some of this is just time passes. I just made a list of what would be the core subjects. I'm not going to list all the authors, because one of the big changes just over the past forty years is that a huge secondary literature has appeared in lots of different fields. Some of this is about those little weird legitimations of legal history where Willard was a core figure of the Wisconsin faculty, but a marginal figure within legal education and within legal doctrine in other ways. Legal history has become respectable.

Bill Clune: Right.

Dirk Hartog: Also, that has happened in different ways both in history and in law. To give you an example: someone asked the dean of a leading law school how many legal historians can you afford to have, and the dean said, "We can have as many as we find interesting because we regard legal history as one of three core methodologies." The others were law and economics and normative political philosophy, that are just central to the practice of legal scholarship. I've heard something similar from the Northwestern team. I can no more imagine that forty years ago than anything else.

The other side is that for different reasons, legal history has become a fashionable form of scholarship for lots of historians. There's a lot more production than there was in, let's say, 1980 when Willard stopped teaching.

Bill Clune: He began a field which then became legitimated and expanded.

Dirk Hartog: Yes. I'm trying to write something. Your phone call and the emails came at an odd time because I have to write a response to a conference in Israel about legal history, and so I've been thinking about this stuff in weird ways. There's a kind of odd conjuncture.

That's the first answer. The second is that the field has moved in directions which are mostly away, though I think they return to the themes that were central to Willard's work. Just to take three obvious ones, which I think you flagged already, one is gender and sexuality. A second is slavery, race and the significance of the Civil War. That now is moving towards borderlands and citizenship questions.

Dirk Hartog: Then the third, which intersects with the borderland citizenship questions would be generally thinking about American legal history through the lens of imperialism, colonialism, and in a small sense about international human rights.

Bill Clune: I get that.

Dirk Hartog: Now for probably most of the last thirty years, the history of capitalism, which I suppose one could say was Willard's subject, or the history of economic growth and modernization were off the table or less significant. In the last five to ten years, oddly in part through the lens of slavery studies, the history of capitalism has come back and it has suddenly become quite central again. That's on the subject. All of those produce literature, and I don't think it's worth giving you lots and lots of names of people.

There's actually a furious debate we're going on right now. I actually find it relatively uninteresting, and I think it's about whether to understand slave law and the slave regime as fundamentally a market-capitalist institution or as an anti-capitalist institution. Right now, the pro-capitalist side is winning, though I actually think it actually needs more legal history. That also connects, like how the slavery side intersects with what's history is typically today called Atlantic World Studies, which inevitably turned slavery into a problem of colonialism and imperialism.

Bill Clune: Right.

Dirk Hartog: Then there's the intersection with whether modern conventions against slavery and whether it's older conventions or older histories are relevant to the modern international human rights conventions about slave law. All of these produce both a historical literature and a legal scholarly literature in the last generation, in which some people are in both of them but a lot of people are either one or the other.

Another shift that occurred was away from Willard's emphasis on legislation and statutes. I think, again, to mark, I don't know if this is marking me, or if it's marking the generation, if there's a standard alternative to the appellate case in recent work, it is the trial or the trial transcript. That has to do as much with the growth of cultural history in the last forty years as anything else. Also, I think a desire for the subaltern voices for the voices of those who are caught up. Also, what Willard was not good at, but which became central I think both to the fashion for legal history in the law schools and for legal history more broadly, which is the return of storytelling.

Trials are inherently easier to tell stories with. I do think when you ask what are the main subjects that you consider important to include in a legal history course, a lot of what I do today and what I think a lot of people do is have a lot of individual trials and transcripts, which are about storytelling. That may be about my sensibility as much as anything else. It's about how I learned history.

Bill Clune: Far from appellate cases.

Dirk Hartog: Yes. Sometimes they come out of appellate cases, so I will tell the story that lies behind the appellate case, but actually your questions made me think that it's interesting that for Willard, the answer was read the statutes. I have one graduate student, one or a couple, who spent their lives reading statutes. One of them is writing a history of the Field Code.

Bill Clune: You've noted in the past that Willard largely ignored the history of oppressed and underrepresented groups, but he did understand the ruthless quality of greed as a component of economic growth. The communal "we" that he identifies as responsible for stripping the northern forest was also responsible for oppressing and stealing from Native Americans.

Dirk Hartog: Yeah. He was aware, as I mentioned. I read this really odd book of his, which I'd never read. I owned, but I'd never read, called *Justice Holmes on Legal History*, in which he's actually more explicit both about the dark side, but also about the ways in which this expresses what he there calls a "middle-class sensibility," which I actually think is a very useful frame for what was all through his work.

Bill Clune: Absolutely. I don't want to interrupt you, but I think a thing that's just stunning about *The Growth of American Law* is that it is a story of the creation and development of just all of our main legal institutions in real time. As you said in some of your emails, you're thrown right in the middle of it as though it's rising up before you as a process of social construction.

Dirk Hartog: Yeah. I still think that's Willard's brilliance. I think it's what caught me originally. It's what gets other people into his work, is that sense of how do you describe this world that's all around you and in which you may have had a year of law school, but you can't separate covenants from titles from contracts from torts. It's all happening. It's all systematically working together. Just a quick parenthesis on this. One of the things that's, it's not wrong with legal history, but one of the things that legal history sometimes gets identified as about, which I think is wrong, is that it gets framed as a search for origins. I actually think from the beginning Willard was a kind of contrary . . . countered that. I don't think he was self-conscious about that, but he wasn't particularly interested in where did the law come from or where did a particular doctrine. He was interested in why all the trees got cut down.

Bill Clune: I mean he did say in *Growth*, for example, that our courts tend to be modeled on England, and we had bicameral legislatures because England had it, and there wasn't much thought given to it, and it doesn't really seem like a good idea. He kind of talks about origins and critiques them at the same time.

Dirk Hartog: That's right. He could do origins, and there's this odd book that he wrote when he was in the military during World War II about the law of treason. Even today when treason prosecutions occur in this country, there's always a citation to Willard's memos on the law of treason, which are very old-fashioned, carries you back to medieval origins of treason law. He could do the originalist thing if he wanted to.

Bill Clune: Perhaps we could turn to the purpose of teaching legal history to law students.

Dirk Hartog: I think what I want students to get is some sense of the historicity of law itself. I'm not sure that's what Hurst would have said.

Dirk Hartog: I think he would have said something about the usefulness of history or the functions of history. By the historicity, I think I would mean both what's obvious is that there's history in law constantly and that people are always thinking that lawyers are always thinking historically. When I teach, I use very conventional examples of that. I use *Brown vs. Board of Education* and the arguments in Warren's opinion about the meaning of the Fourteenth Amendment and also about the fact that at the time, that all the judges at the time of *Brown* believed in a living Fourteenth Amendment. They were not originalists.

They all assumed that it doesn't matter. They actually say, or Warren says quite explicitly, "We don't know what the drafters if the Fourteenth Amendment intended, so it doesn't matter, and we have to decide in the present moment what the Fourteenth Amendment means."

Bill Clune: They had a different sense of the role of history.

Dirk Hartog: Yeah. Some sense of just the historicity of interpretive stances, because then I'll probably . . . if I were teaching it, I would mention Scalia thinks differently about what's the business of fixing a text, of determining what a constitutional text is about. Because of my own work, I might use same-sex marriage and the fact that twenty years before the court talks about same-sex relationships as inherently criminal, and by 2015, they can talk about it as a legitimate choice. These historical assumptions are built into the transitions that are going on.

I think one of the changes, which I think CLS and both Kennedy and Horwitz are part of that transition, is that I would assume that one can see these assumptions in the doctrinal cases just as much as you can see them by going outside of the doctrinal cases.

Bill Clune: Yeah. It's a window that's high in the skyscraper, but it is a window.

Dirk Hartog: Insofar as, in that sense a legal history course can drive the student towards different sources, but it also can drive them to different reading practices.

Bill Clune: Oh that's very good.

Dirk Hartog: To go to your second question, what can a law student learn about law and legal institutions that can't be known exclusively from appellate cases, this may be my own take, but a lot of it is just that doctrinal categories are just artificial fragments of the history of legal education, which don't have to do with the problems that lawyers actually confront in their lives. If you want to cut down the trees of Northern Wisconsin, you're going to move seamlessly from property contract torts, from doctrinal category to doctrinal category, and the problem doesn't get captured by the doctrine.

Bill Clune: Can you say a little bit more about that?

Dirk Hartog: Okay.

Bill Clune: I haven't read the lumber book, by the way.

Dirk Hartog: The number of people who have actually read the lumber book is small, but it is brilliant.

It is really amazing. I wrote a very small book just now about gradual emancipation in New Jersey, and slavery and gradual emancipation. One of the things, and in an odd way, though it's 150 pages long, rather than 1,100 pages.

Bill Clune: Yeah, I love that.

Dirk Hartog: 200 pages with footnotes, but 150 pages of text, rather than 800 pages of text, is that to write about slavery and freedom on New Jersey, I spent an enormous amount of time writing about poor relief, because in fact, the central problem for the legislatures in New Jersey is they didn't want slaves dumped on the poor-relief rolls.

Bill Clune: Oh yeah.

Dirk Hartog: If I treated it just as a problem of freedom, I would not have seen the relationship to welfare policy. For the legislator, it's a very Hurstian point, the basic things that New Jersey legislators were driven by was not to increase the tax rolls. You're not going to see this if you're simply caught within particular doctrinal categories.

Bill Clune: Right. That's very interesting. If you were teaching law from a problem-oriented perspective, you might have cases on both of those things grouped together, but you wouldn't discover that by going down one doctrinal silo or looking at one case.

Dirk Hartog: The things that Willard didn't do, which I think people, I guess like me, do today is we assume mobility and the migration of peoples across jurisdictional line and would not treat Wisconsin as a closed jurisdiction.

Bill Clune: Yeah, there's a wonderful vibe to his work of reasonable white people in Wisconsin and Midwest.

Dirk Hartog: Yeah. First of all, even those reasonable white people were moving across jurisdictions constantly. To understand their problems, you actually can't stick with Wisconsin. Again, to take my own work, in this gradual emancipation study, I have to spend a lot of time in New York City because both enslaved people and a lot of masters are moving constantly between New York and New Jersey.

Bill Clune: Makes sense.

Dirk Hartog: Part of the migration of people, once there's a steamboat, it's incredibly easy for an enslaved person to catch a ferry and disappear into the free Black community in New York City. That creates a whole series of separate legal problems. Part of legal history is, again, not to be stuck with jurisdictions, not to be stuck with doctrinal categories. At the global level this is the Atlantic world problems of slavery and the fact that enslaved people may create insurance problems in Britain and, just like land policy questions in Wisconsin, may be about British investors in Midwestern lands.

Willard, actually I think there was a kind of assumption in his world that you could treat these jurisdictions as states with a clear citizenry and clear capacity to maintain boundaries.

Bill Clune: That makes a lot of sense. I tried to get at that in my comment to you in the email about agency. Willard would say, "Well the legislators had to respond to a lot of interest groups and they functioned as intermediaries," but he didn't give you a lot of the backstory of where these interest groups came from and the powerful economic engines that were at work.

Dirk Hartog: This is a very Wisconsin story. One of the things I learned years ago is that when the Wisconsin constitution was drafted . . . well it was drafted twice, in 1846 and in 1848, it was immediately translated into German. Why was it translated into German? Because this is right when there's a huge German migration. Germans, white, well they're all white, German men got off the boat in Milwaukee or Kenosha and voted on the Wisconsin constitution.

Bill Clune: They had citizenship.

Dirk Hartog: They had citizenship by virtue of arriving.

Bill Clune: Trump wouldn't like that.

Dirk Hartog: No, Trump would not have liked that. Basically they wanted the bodies. I've always wondered—I've mentioned this to students—what happened when they moved on to Nebraska or to Kansas or somewhere else? I assume they just kept their citizenship, but did anybody ever question that at a later point?

Bill Clune: Well, did they became citizens of the United States on arriving?

Dirk Hartog: A fact that insofar what is a citizen of the United States prior to the passage of Chinese exclusion when you begin to develop a naturalization system, nobody's going to question it if you are a white male.

Bill Clune: Yeah, that's right. You walk around where you want to.

Dirk Hartog: You moved around. Once you're in the country, once you passed quarantine, you were, I think, a citizen. Part of this is that . . . and I think I grew up, I think in my first book I wrote very much under the influence of both Hurst and Horwitz, who assumed this sort of a notion of these powerful things. In some ways, people could just move. If you didn't like the decision in one place, you went to another place.

Okay. How might this knowledge be useful in the professional lives of lawyers? I think being aware of the historicity of both the law and of interpretations of the law is useful knowledge. Beyond that, it might be helpful for them to see the fact which wouldn't have been as true in Willard's time of the numbers of debates over historicity and the law.

Bill Clune: Like legislative interpretation?

Dirk Hartog: Yeah, like slave interpretations or about the role of capitalism, debates over international human rights, the critical race theory debates over the significance of civil rights law. These are all, in some ways it's more civic lessons and humanistic lessons than direct practical instrumental: "This is going to shape how you make an argument before a judge."

Bill Clune: That is true also of legal process points like textual interpretation. How has a technique like originalism been used historically?

Dirk Hartog: I remember when Scalia came to Princeton to give his statutory interpretation lectures, and Scalia did make the argument, and I had to say that I didn't think, he wasn't stupid about it. Because there's so much interpretation out there and so many different ways of interpreting contextual evidence that looking to the text is the only safe ground and that you're better off because you're just opening yourself up to an indeterminate field of interpretation.

Bill Clune: Okay. I'm sure we're both on the same side as this, but the obvious response is his thing became a kind of formalism.

Dirk Hartog: Absolutely.

Bill Clune: By ignoring context he could choose whatever policy bias he wanted to in the words.

Dirk Hartog: Yeah. He's back-dooring during his own historical interpretation but without acknowledging it.

Bill Clune: Exactly.

Dirk Hartog: I understand that there is a sense in which it probably would not be a smart argument for a lawyer to make about a statute saying, "You know, there's 400 different interpretations."

Bill Clune: Right.

Dirk Hartog: They all have plausible historical pedigrees. I mean I always thought . . .

Bill Clune: Well, people are afraid of that kind of indeterminacy. How far are you going to stray from legal certainty and formalism?

Dirk Hartog: I've had this argument with people about the *Heller* case and the gun control cases, that I think the left might have lost no matter what, but one reason they lost is because I don't know if you follow this at all, there was this real scandal about this guy Bellesiles.

Bill Clune: No, I missed that.

Dirk Hartog: Michael Bellesiles wrote first a *Journal of American History* article and then a book which won all these prizes, which basically said eighteenth-century Americans didn't own many guns and most of the guns they owned didn't work.

Bill Clune: Whoops.

Dirk Hartog: The problem with his work is that he was a terrible scholar and he may have lied significantly, and the scandal of that came out just about the time that Heller was being argued. In some ways, the problem with historical interpretations is you better be good at it, or you're in trouble. He'd been trashed mostly by people with agendas, with right-wing NRA-funded agendas, but he was also wrong.

Bill Clune: Yeah, when you read about Lewis and Clark you see how important guns were to everybody.

Dirk Hartog: That's right. That doesn't solve the contemporary question about how do we get guns out of the hands of people who shouldn't have guns.

Bill Clune: Yeah, that's karma for historians, but the karma's also on all the rest of us.

Dirk Hartog: I think that the answer to your third question, how can law students benefit, is that they're going to have to talk about history no matter what they do. They might as well become more sophisticated at it. That it's everywhere in the material they're dealing with.

Bill Clune: I like that; you're always looking outward on history from some kind of window.

Dirk Hartog: Which is already historic to us. There is no non-historical legal claim and that can be shown, tort law, Palsgraf is a historical problem. It occurs with judges who are thinking about historical changes that are going on around them. There is no non-historical . . . In a way, it's exactly the same problem as law and economics. There is no non-economic moment or a private law or even for a public regulatory structure. Too much of the contemporary law school centers legal history as if it's legal history against law and economics, and I actually think that's a really stupid argument, because law students actually have to learn a certain amount of economics, or to think through an economic lens. The actors they're dealing with do want the least cost in their situations. There are more efficient and less efficient solutions.

No one is going to be harmed by having to read Coase.

Bill Clune: The same thing that you said about legal history is true about law and economics. If you're going to do it, you might as well get a little rigorous training in the thinking.

Dirk Hartog: That's right. You can't not think through this particular lens, and to do it unconsciously is the dumbest thing imaginable. This often becomes, and I think this is less useful though it's probably inevitable in the constitutional politics of the day, into an argument about originalism against anti-originalism. A little bit of originalism is inevitable, right?

Bill Clune: Right.

Dirk Hartog: You want to say to Trump, "You can't do away with birthright citizenship."

Bill Clune: Right.

Dirk Hartog: That's in the Fourteenth Amendment and it was enacted for a particular reason, which is because to undo *Dred Scott*, you had to create birthright citizenship. That's what the Fourteenth Amendment wanted. If that's originalism, okay, that's originalism. It shouldn't have to be a particularly interesting point.

Bill Clune: To the race conservatives' credit, they're urging repeal of the Fourteenth Amendment.

Dirk Hartog: They understand that they can't get away from that.

Bill Clune: Right.

Dirk Hartog: In other ways, does the Fourteenth Amendment require equality of voting right? I actually think you have to move in a different direction if you want to argue about that.

Bill Clune: Really. Not bringing in the Fifteenth Amendment.

Dirk Hartog: Yeah. You have a whole series of complicated questions or what equality of schooling means. My guess is if you were a litigant, or if you're the lawyer for a litigant in these situations, you have to actually argue the original, even if you think originalism is not a good historical strategy or is implausible historically.

Bill Clune: Absolutely. That's so much in my blood, so to speak. The touchstone is the words. You start there and work out and back and forth to a number of other things, but I never thought there would be a license to just say, well the words don't matter because society has changed so much, so let's just think about what would be good right now.

Dirk Hartog: My sense is there's a question how sophisticated does a legal advocate or a practitioner have to be about historical interpretations and about the streams of historical interpretations, which are of potential relevance.

Bill Clune: What would you say . . . Oh go ahead.

Dirk Hartog: No, you go ahead.

Bill Clune: One thing that I find certainly profound and rather thrilling in understanding legal history is that the battle between property rights and economic liberty and regulation started on day one and is still going on. I don't know if that's particularly consoling in a time when the pendulum's going the other way. That knowledge, it isn't as though you can walk into a courtroom and make immediate use of that, but it's a kind of anchor to understanding our entire legal system. That can't be bad for law students.

Dirk Hartog: No. I think some part of what's important about legal history, this is a different point, but I think it would come out of Willard's courses, I suppose my courses, most legal history courses, is some sense, this gets back to what you and I were writing about earlier, of longer periodization.

Bill Clune: Ah yes.

Dirk Hartog: Than just political history periodizations.

Bill Clune: What are political history periodizations?

Dirk Hartog: At least in the U.S., they're often tied to presidential regimes. Let's say the standard political history characterization of the late twentieth century is everything changes with Reagan.

Bill Clune: Reaganism, yeah right, or any of the presidents. Jackson.

Dirk Hartog: Yeah. That you pick your president, it's a presidential driven . . . With some categories, the New Deal becomes a different category. World War II, maybe the Progressives, but you have a certain kind of . . . It's American history survey knowledge instead of categories, and the assumption is that everything changes. Week one on progressivism then becomes week two on the New Deal, becomes week three on World War II, the Cold War, becomes Kennedy, Johnson.

Bill Clune: Like a checkerboard, you're hopping from one square to another.

Dirk Hartog: Yeah. Willard's work says, "Look, there's this kind of long consensus and a sense of conflict around exactly what you described, around a tension between property rights and regulation." I think Willard would have said, because he was such a Frankfurter student, that with the New Deal there's a fundamental change, but I'm not sure. He would also have been aware of the continuity.

Bill Clune: Yeah, it was similar to the Interstate Commerce Commission which was created earlier.

Dirk Hartog: Now today the periodizations would be wider if not longer than Willard because they would go to global issues about, again, the sort of interstate slave trade, the international slave trade. It might go to global trade. It might go to the mobility of people, it might go to the border and the movement of a people from Latin America or from China. Things that wouldn't have occurred to him.

Bill Clune: That's another point, it seems to me, about the usefulness of legal history, which again, I think almost everybody would intuitively understand. It would give you an insight into the problems that are about to happen, not just the ones that have already been dealt with. For example, international migration, and everybody knows about that now, but it's going to hit the legal system hard, and it already is.

Dirk Hartog: The politics of it, my colleague, Beth Lew-Williams has just published this new history of Chinese exclusion. Her book has two big features to it. The less surprising is how much this was a matter of international diplomacy. The more surprising is how much white violence shaped the movement towards Chinese exclusion, basically lynchings of lots of Chinese all across the West Coast. Chinese exclusion was a way to actually discipline this white population, which sounds a lot like Trump's alt-right people.

Bill Clune: Yeah, "Keep them out or we'll kill them." Like the new memorial in Montgomery that opened about violence against Black people.

Dirk Hartog: Yeah. There is also, and I remember talking to Willard about this years ago, there's also a kind of weird American lack of acknowledgement of a lot of this stuff. For generations, there has been no museum dedicated to slavery itself until the African American History Museum opened, and even that talks about much else besides slavery. Am I answering the questions?

Have law students expressed any skepticism? Here I actually have a story. When I taught at Indiana, where I taught before I came to Wisconsin, and Indiana in one of those moments of ill-thought-out curricular reform required all first-year students to take either legal history or legal sociology or maybe it was law and economics. I can't remember. There were three options. I, as a new law teacher, suddenly was confronted by 150 students in a legal history class, all first-year students, who despised it. I got the worst class evaluations. I think I did okay, I don't know, but I got the class evaluations. That was so terrible. I knew I was going to be fired instantly.

Eventually, I got the evaluations up to a bare mediocre quality, but then I came to Wisconsin and there were two things that were different in Wisconsin. One, it was not a required first-year course, and second, I was following after Willard, and students came with an expectation that they would like the course because he'd been such a great teacher.

Bill Clune: His reputation had a trailing . . .

Dirk Hartog: Had a trailing effect. The culture in Wisconsin, and to be blunt, Wisconsin was full of weirdo teachers.

Bill Clune: Exactly.

Dirk Hartog: I didn't look that weird.

Bill Clune: Somebody called them hunchbacks. I forget who that was. I think it was Lawrence Friedman with his usual wit.

Dirk Hartog: Yeah, Lawrence. I never had any trouble, skepticism. There's a standard understanding among legal historians who teach in law schools is that you can't assign them too much reading, which is a problem in a field where books are the currency. One of the pleasures of teaching here is that I can teach a course here and I can ask students to read a book a week, which law students won't do. Graduate students read two-and-a-half books a week, but that's the difference. The skepticism, I had a great time teaching in Wisconsin, but I always thought I got the trailing glory of Willard. I always remembered when we first moved there, or maybe a year after we moved, we bought a house. The lawyer who was handing the closing who was in his sixties said, "You're teaching legal history."

Then for an hour, he wanted to talk about Willard and what a significant force he'd been.

Bill Clune: That's a GP doing real estate work.

Dirk Hartog: Yeah. Basically he just wanted to talk about Willard.

Bill Clune: That's a great story.

Dirk Hartog: I think I experienced that several different times. He just had this reputation; I think he was understood as this legal historian, but he was also just a really smart lawyer.

Bill Clune: Yeah, you talk about pedigree too. Yeah. Frankfurter and Brandeis. Dirk Hartog: At twenty-nine being offered the Yale Law School deanship.

Dirk Hartog: I've never been sure about the question of the value, what students thought about the value of learning legal history. They weren't hostile to it. I think some got a lot out of it, some didn't. It's like most things pedagogically.

Bill Clune: It reminds me what you started out with: that legal history is more tolerated in elite law schools.

Dirk Hartog: I think it is an elite/non-elite. My great victory this year is two of my graduate students got tenure-track jobs at Columbia. For years, I assumed Columbia was just a corporate law basket.

Bill Clune: Oh Columbia Law School, not Columbia history.

Dirk Hartog: Yeah, Columbia Law School jobs. I'm thrilled. I do find it incredibly curious.

Bill Clune: Yeah. They have law degrees too?

Dirk Hartog: Yes, they both have law degrees. One of the two has all of the conventional credentials, *Yale Law Journal* and clerkships. The other doesn't. The other just came to graduate school, did finish her law degree, but then came right to graduate school and hasn't done any of the conventional certifiers of practice.

Bill Clune: This kind of is a little digression in the questions I started out asking, but one of the things about legal realism was the idea that there should be more social science training and social scientists on law faculties that became a big thing at Wisconsin while you were here and at other places as well, that there should be a "law and" component.

Dirk Hartog: Yes. Clearly that in the elite law markets I guess a PhD has become a credential, where when I went on the law teaching market, my favorite one was a letter I got from the dean of the University of Missouri Law School who tells me that he didn't want to interview me because he didn't see that I'd had any practice experience, and seeing that I'd been in graduate school, I would need an appropriately longer period of time.

Bill Clune: Right. You would have to be deprogrammed. Having gone into a cult.

Dirk Hartog: That's changed. I find it very odd. It's been great for my graduate students, but it's a surprising fact. In fact, I don't know if the realists like you, Bill, and Whitford and all the people at Wisconsin who came without PhDs, you would have trouble getting hired today.

Bill Clune: Well I have an MA and almost-PhD in Sociology from Northwestern. Did my prelims. Then came my law school job. My dissertation research got published but no dissertation.

So now it's not only a credential, but an essential one.

Dirk Hartog: Yeah, and I don't necessarily think that's a good thing. I was at a retirement event or a celebration of Bob Gordon at Stanford in February, and Bob was talking about how unimaginable it would be for his career—for him to have the career that he has in the present.

Bill Clune: Yeah, because he didn't have a PhD.

Dirk Hartog: Yeah.

Bill Clune: He was an autodidact in the field.

Dirk Hartog: It would be a loss for the field if there weren't a Bob Gordon.

Bill Clune: Yeah, really. The last thing I had is Hurst's influence on you and other legal historians. A question I wanted to ask, maybe it's part of this, but what did Willard do better than anybody else besides being first, and was he the first?

Dirk Hartog: No, it wasn't. There were others. There were really boring people. There was Julius Goebel at Columbia and there was Mark DeWolfe Howe at Harvard. There were people who were either of his generation or even older than he was. I think partly he was just smarter, to be blunt. He had a historical vision and one can react against it, one can argue with it. He was a genuinely brilliant historian, and one of the smartest legal minds I've ever come across. That's not exactly . . . As I think I probably say in that interview, I picked up *Law and the Conditions of Freedom* probably in a used bookstore, a little book, and I was just totally entranced by it, and this is in spite of the fact that he wasn't a very good writer.

One didn't get drawn into him by his writing.

Bill Clune: No, it has a density.

Dirk Hartog: He had these weird quirks, but the sense of his imagination.

Bill Clune: He combined meticulous detail with overarching vision and everything in between, and he could do a case as well as anybody. Then you talk about his ability to just get right in the middle of something and make it come alive, which is what you do with trial transcripts too.

Dirk Hartog: I don't have the gift he has. There's another way in which he weirdly, the fact that he was of his time with all those limitations, he was fully of his time. He read everything around. I'm told, I have this copy of his editions of Herbert Marcuse's *Eros and Civilization*. Somehow the idea of Willard reading that . . .

He embraced . . . there was a way in which he saw things in their largest view. Then he also had an eye for topics that others just didn't. In *The Growth of American Law*, the chapter on the Bar is just brilliant. I don't think anybody had thought about it at that point.

Bill Clune: Yeah, because even though he could be tedious, he could take topics that other people would have said, "Oh my god, you couldn't write anything interesting about that," and make it interesting.

Dirk Hartog: Yeah. One of the things, many of his students, Lawrence Freidman insofar as Lawrence was the student, is an exception, would do Hurstian things and they would become deadly dull. If you look at the pages of the *Wisconsin Law Review*, he got some student of his to do small claims courts and it's really boring. Some of it is just he had a capacity to see connections.

To situate things within a broad economic modernizing framework, that others just didn't have.

Bill Clune: I can see what you mean about a man of his time because one thing in the way background, being such a gentleman and just an epitome of a middle-class politeness gives us a genial anchoring to his work, but it's also that when he ever got into a story, he would pick it up, the details were related to some larger thing that was going on.

Dirk Hartog: That's right.

Bill Clune: At all times, either as an illustration or counter-example of it. It's as though all the details were carried along on a cloud. Cloud makes it sound too esoteric, but an organizing theme.

Dirk Hartog: Oh I know. He had such a deep structural imagination, which was shaped of his time. It wouldn't be the one, he didn't have much conflict. He did it by ignoring lots of things, but he has such a strong sense of how things work together. I wish I had his capacity.

I'm not apologetic, but deep down he was also a really arrogant guy. He knew who he was. I wrote about this a little bit in the introduction to the Bob Gordon's retirement . . .

Bill Clune: Really?

Dirk Hartog: By just basically constantly telling Bob what he should be writing about.

Bill Clune: Go ahead.

Dirk Hartog: Bob was not comfortable with that.

Bill Clune: It's true what you say about arrogance or confidence. He would give you the most cordial and polite feedback, banging out a reaction on his typewriter like he used to do with Brandeis and Frankfurter. It was wonderfully cordial. He treated you as an equal, but on the other hand, it's kind of like so sayeth Willard.

Dirk Hartog: I know, right.

Bill Clune: He wouldn't sign it that way, but . . .

Dirk Hartog: Yeah. There was some way in which the voice would come . . . He assumed the truth of what he was saying, and it was hard to argue with him exactly.

Bill Clune: Yeah.

Dirk Hartog: Actually one of the things your emails have made me think about is the virtues of his, call it consensus understanding of history, the sense that law has some kind of coherent underlying normative order I think is something that a lot of people have lost. I think that may have been rooted in his fifties sensibility, but it may be that not having it is a loss as well.

Bill Clune: It never went away, and it's having a big comeback right now at the national level.

Dirk Hartog: Yeah, it sure is.

Bill Clune: Although that would be a whole other long, long interview. Do you want to say anything about Hurst's influence on you and others? You've already said a lot. I don't know if this gets into successive of generations of legal historians or what. I mean I know there was this immediate diaspora of his associates. Lawrence Friedman and you and Bob Gordon.

Dirk Hartog: I think in a sense, if you were going to do the history of legal history, clearly Morton Horwitz's first Transformation book is crucial in the legitimation of legal history because it won the Bancroft Prize. It got a readership in the world of history that no work in American legal history has had before. Maybe this isn't quite an answer to your question. I still assign Hurst's *Law and the Conditions of Freedom* to my graduate students, and they all immediately make fun of his "we," which is so unfashionable today. Most of them come back and find it immensely compelling when they start thinking about writing their own work in a way that Horwitz today ends up seeming more old-fashioned, speaking less to them than Hurst does.

Bill Clune: It's more polemical, oddly enough, even though it's in the critical posture. It's in some ways more polemical than Hurst.

Dirk Hartog: Yeah. I think the idea that in some ways the cleverness of Horwitz's first book, not the legal realism book so much, but the first one, was that he ties legal history to the first-year law school curriculum and he shows how there was an economic history to each subject, property, torts, contracts. What Hurst does is he says it's all connected. That's in the end much more useful.

Bill Clune: Fascinating. It's not just him as a personal originator. It's an intellectual paradigm.

Dirk Hartog: It's something that a student has to confront and think through. I have this odd experience in the last five, ten years is that I've had a bunch of South Asian graduate students. For weird reasons, these are lawyers who decided to get PhDs; Indian lawyers who decided to get PhDs in legal history, doing South Asian topics. It's partly that I have a colleague, who works on legal history themes as well, so we've shared a bunch of students. They all find Hurst incredibly helpful as a way of thinking through the problem of writing Indian legal history.

Bill Clune: Pretty amazing. What a bridge.

Dirk Hartog: Willard would never have thought about it.

Bill Clune: We think oh Willard, Wisconsin, middle class, 1950s. Modern India?

Dirk Hartog: They are writing what we might call Hurstian Indian legal history.

Bill Clune: I had the reaction reading, well especially *Law and the Conditions of Freedom*. It was kind of thrilling to see what consensus meant was a consensus around growth and economic liberty and basically greed in some sense, constrained greed. I can make an immediate jump to Andrew Jackson and The Trail of Tears and property owners in Georgia and Tennessee kicking Indians out because they had gold on their land. It's all the same thing.

Dirk Hartog: Exactly.

Bill Clune: Say, oh yeah, this is the way it needs to be.

Dirk Hartog: My Indian students, for example, the problem, which in some ways, they're all writing about either just before or just after independence. What is a post-colonial society? How does a post-colonial society work? In some ways, that's what Hurst is writing about, what is a post-colonial society.

Bill Clune: Oh yeah, right. Okay, now you're all free, what are you going to do?

Dirk Hartog: You have to read it just the way . . . you have to also read about the Cherokee and you have to read about Georgia and you have to read about slavery, but in that context, you're not just reading about this group. Somebody controls the law and somebody doesn't control the law.

Bill Clune: Yeah. I don't think Willard ever gave the idea that the people who controlled the law were a special class of virtuous all-knowing men or something. He had this sense like, "Come on, you guys are scrambling around for money. That's what you do. Okay, I get it." It wasn't American exceptionalism in the sense of pilgrims saying that God gave us this land to grab. None of that.

Dirk Hartog: That's exactly right.

Bill Clune: This is marvelous. As you were talking, I thought man, a lot of people would love to read the transcript of this. I can feel them also getting jealous not being here, so to speak.

Dirk Hartog: This is fun.

Bill Clune: I've held you long enough, and it's been tremendously helpful. Thanks.

Interview of Herman Goldstein by Bill Clune

Abstract

This interview of Herman Goldstein (by Bill Clune), held May 10, 2018, discusses the impact of the American Bar Foundation study of the criminal justice system on the innovative criminal law courses developed at Wisconsin, namely Criminal Justice Administration, and Goldstein's courses on problem-oriented policing. Frank Remington was the director of research of that study and Herman Goldstein was a field researcher. Four radical changes from the previous model of teaching criminal procedure (which mainly covered Supreme Court cases) were: (1) the idea of an interconnected system, from first contact with the police all the way through to parole and corrections, (2) the pervasive role of low visibility discretion at every stage, (3) the differential impact of police interventions on different groups of people (e.g., homosexuals, poor, and minorities), and (4) the importance of distinct behavioral problems as to what occurs in the criminal justice system (e.g., street prostitution and public intoxication). An interesting instructional insight is how these features emerged in the classroom, for example, as Remington explored the appropriateness of aggressive police surveillance (e.g., wiretapping and stings), for various behaviors (e.g., street prostitution, shoplifting, organized crime, and terrorism). Important impacts of the Wisconsin work were changes in how criminal procedure is taught at many law schools, administrative regulations of police-citizen interactions (e.g., street prostitution and use of force), the development of alternatives to incarceration (e.g., intoxication and mental illness), and the prolific growth of the field of problem-oriented policing across research, policy, and practice, and of related fields such as environmental criminology.

On June 13 2018, Professor Herman Goldstein received the international Stockholm Prize in Criminology for his global impact on the improvement of policing. The prize—sometimes referred to as the "Nobel Prize" of criminology—was presented to Goldstein at the historic City Hall in Stockholm, Sweden.

Herman Goldstein: I was just talking with a researcher with a group from Harvard yesterday. She was sitting where you're sitting. They are searching the ABF field reports from the 1950s for material dealing with police harassment of gays. I empathize for her having to dig through all of those field notes because the files are not well indexed. That led to my reminiscing about the gay scene in the 1950s.

Bill Clune: Really?

Herman Goldstein: I was telling her that, in recalling some of those field notes, I almost became as bashful and turned as red as I did back then as a naïve kid in my twenties, never having seen this part of the world. Police officers were dragging me around at night showing me what then were the gay bars, and how shocked I was. I just didn't know how to react.

Bill Clune: It was invisible to straight people in the community.

Herman Goldstein: The responses were very dramatically different as to men, women, and where they came from in society. But one of the things I remembered most clearly since I spent my time in squad cars riding around, always in the back seat, was responding to complaints that the big stores in Detroit made about what they characterized as the misuse of their restrooms.

Bill Clune: Mm-hmm (affirmative).

Herman Goldstein: They would call the police and say, we've got a restroom on the sixth floor where there's a group of people that are misusing the place. The police would then go there, and through undercover operations, identify these individuals. When they were arrested, we often learned that they came from a cross-section of society. Their whole world collapsed in my presence.

Bill Clune: Yeah.

Herman Goldstein: They commonly asked, "What am I going to tell my family? What am I going to tell my kids?"

Bill Clune: And this took place in how many cities? Detroit and . . .

Herman Goldstein: We made observations in Michigan, Wisconsin, and Kansas. Three states. The study was conceived and advocated by Justice Jackson, and the plan for the study was to cover forty-eight states at the time. We got to three.

Bill Clune: Yeah. But you learned a lot in those three states.

Herman Goldstein: Oh, tremendous. Tremendous.

Bill Clune: So Wisconsin was one; Madison or Milwaukee?

Herman Goldstein: In Wisconsin we sampled Milwaukee first, and then some places up north. Smaller communities, Superior, some rural places, and then came down to Madison.

Bill Clune: Okay and at that time, had Frank already started at UW?

Herman Goldstein: Yes, yes. He was deeply immersed in revising the Wisconsin Criminal Code, and then moved over to helping write the Model Penal Code for ALI.

Bill Clune: What courses did you teach at Wisconsin after you were hired?

Herman Goldstein: My first teaching experience was to join Frank, Ed Kimball, and Don Newman in teaching the Criminal Justice Administration course, which at that time was sort of experimental for Frank. In addition to his basic criminal law classes, he had introduced this course for second and third-year students on Criminal Justice Administration, and that's what led to using the data from the ABF study. So we had a Criminal Justice Administration course, rather than deal in the orthodox fashion with substantive criminal law and with procedure. In the Criminal Justice Administration course, he started and intensified his commitment to teaching how the system operated.

Initially, the course would march students through criminal procedure starting with arrest and prosecution and the various other stages but focused on the middle of the system. It didn't pick up much of what police were doing. It didn't pick up much about the dynamics of policing. It didn't go very much into corrections. Then that got dramatically expanded.

Before 1964 when I got there, Frank and all the others teaching criminal law did what was traditional in law schools around the country. The teaching was based upon Supreme Court and appellate decisions. They had focused on those decisions raising constitutional issues. My guess is you could walk into most law schools today and it's still the case.

Bill Clune: Mm-hmm (affirmative).

Herman Goldstein: Such as what are the major constitutional issues that arise in the criminal process around arrest? How long can you hold a person? What can you pick them up for?

Bill Clune: Search and seizure.

Herman Goldstein: The search and seizure issues, yes. Yes, issues raised by years of accumulation of what was important. All of that was thrown for a loop by the ABF studies. By looking at the whole system, we came to realize that there was a hell of a lot happening up front in the context of policing that was of extreme importance and had got hardly any attention. More people were being processed and dealt with and interfered with by governmental authority before you ever got to the kind of constitutional issues that were being covered in law school. I realize now how dramatic the change was. Criminal law professors, who we assembled here at Wisconsin under the auspices of Ford Foundation and Russell Sage Foundation to review the Bar Foundation findings, just threw up their hands and said, "Oh wow. This is a world we never knew about."

Bill Clune: Really.

Herman Goldstein: Yes, the traditional teaching of criminal law assumed that all the cases went to trial, and the important issues related to the nature of the trial and outcomes, the role of the jury, etc. But the Bar Foundation study established that the vast majority of those cases were being plea bargained.

Bill Clune: Hmm.

Herman Goldstein: But that had not previously entered into the study of criminal law. It was in that period of time that several commentators started blowing whistles and said, "Wait a minute, what kind of a judicial procedure do we have for supervising plea bargaining?" That's when legislatures came in, and Frank was instrumental in writing some of the legislation, setting up procedures whereby if a prosecutor came in and said "This person wants to enter a plea. They're guilty of this charge," the judge had to go through certain procedures to establish that the plea was voluntary, that the accused understood the consequences, etc. This sub-rosa mechanism that was accounting for a high percentage of the cases was legitimatized and brought into the system, and procedures established for handling them.

Bill Clune: Okay, so you came to Wisconsin and joined the team that was working on the new Criminal Justice Administration course.

Herman Goldstein: That course and then I very quickly, I think in the second year, established a course on policing. I had the luxury of coming here under a Ford grant with no rigid obligations. It was essentially my agenda as to what I wanted to do. Every once in a while, Bill Foster would come down the hall and say, "We need somebody to teach evidence. Herman, you're going to teach evidence." I said, "I don't know anything about evidence." I wasn't a lawyer, so I just would laugh and run in the other direction.

Bill Clune: Nice try Bill. Yeah.

Herman Goldstein: I had the freedom to establish my own course and I did so bringing together materials that in those days were xeroxed and sold to the students. I gradually built that material up, formalized it more, and then started offering seminars which had a specific focus to them in addition to just the general course on policing. The course on policing ultimately acquired the title of Policing a Free Society or something like that.

Essentially, the criminal justice book influenced the book on policing. The flow of the book covers topics that had become the major themes of the criminal justice course. Initially we explored what the police do. What's their function? We explored the methods by which they tried to carry out their function, their use of the criminal justice system, their use of other systems, and then the big discovery of the Bar Foundation survey which was discretion. Before the ABF survey, no one even used the term discretion. It was widely assumed that the police just didn't have discretion. They enforced the law or did not enforce the law. The ABF documented all that discretion and explored it in great detail. Ultimately that led to a major movement to try to structure discretion and to adapt administrative rule making and some of the mechanisms of the process to the exercise of discretion, to see the police agency as an important administrative policy making organization, which didn't sit well with a lot of people.

We don't want police making policy, but we demonstrated over and over and over again based upon the Bar Foundation study that the officers were already doing it on the street, and they were doing it willy-nilly. Based on our work, and with national endorsement of both the ALI and the President's Commission on Crime, this led to widespread endorsement of the concept of rulemaking by police agencies to gain control of their discretion. It was in that period that police agencies all over the country started adopting policies governing their exercise of discretion. Prior to that if you looked at a police manual, it would address the question of how often you wash your car, you shine your shoes, how you wear your uniform, what happens if you show up late at roll call, but hardly a word about the exercise of public authority.

You could look at the manuals in those days and they had nothing about how the police interact with the citizenry. Gradually through the late 1960s and early '70s, police departments started enacting policies. One of the stories that has been lost in the recent concern about police shootings was that the number of shootings in New York City had skyrocketed. In 1972 we held a seminar here on campus for police chiefs from some of the largest cities, about fifteen of them. The subject of the seminar was gaining control of police discretion. Among the people that attended was the commissioner of police in New York City, Pat Murphy. He went home and adopted policies relating to the use of force.

Bill Clune: Lethal and other force.

Herman Goldstein: Yes. Larry Sherman, a sociologist, did an interesting study in which he documented the dramatic decrease in shootings in New York City after the policy was enacted. That would have been somewhere in the late 1970s.

The policies first and foremost were intended to narrow the authority that the police had by virtue of statutes. Up to that time, the police said "Well, we can use force up to the broad limits of the statute." The purpose of the policies was to restrict police authority. We now have a massive collection of policies on the use of deadly force that show how different communities chose to achieve that goal. In Wisconsin, interestingly, we came to realize that the needs of large cities and the needs of smaller communities were different with regard to not only use of force, but with regard to something like taking a person before a magistrate after an arrest: How much time should elapse? Well, the amount of time you needed in a large city was much more than what you needed in a rural area. So Frank and I were instrumental in Wisconsin in setting up a model that's still unique, which I complain still hasn't received the amount of attention it should have gotten. The enlightened legislature of the day provided in the statute that all municipalities will have a policy relating to the use of deadly force which will achieve certain minimum objectives. Then they should spell it out and file a copy with the attorney general. There's a collection of policies relating to the use of deadly force and with regard to several other sensitive issues in the state of Wisconsin.

Bill Clune: Mm-hmm (affirmative).

Herman Goldstein: Surveillance, body searches, high-speed chases, a lot of the discretionary decisions that got police in trouble. After the ABF study the results were so profound and so shook up people teaching criminal law, like Frank Allen at Chicago and Claude Sowle at Northwestern and Joe Goldstein at Yale and the people with the ALI, that the Ford and Sage Foundations gave funds for this purpose. Largely it was always Willard (Hurst) who was involved and said, "We've got to pursue this." Willard would get the foundations to set up these grants. For several summers we invited faculty members from various schools in the country to gather in Madison and learn about the process.

Bill Clune: Mm-hmm (affirmative).

Herman Goldstein: Faculty from the leading law schools were invited to come here and confer, using the Bar Foundation materials as their study guides. At that time, we were guarding the copies of the field data. You had to check out your copy because confidentiality issues were not fully worked through. We would have these daily meetings, and based upon their reading of those field reports the faculty members went off and reflected on the results of their having studied the materials in their teaching criminal law.

Bill Clune: That sounds like a mini-course in itself.

Herman Goldstein: Well, Frank and I started using the ABF materials extensively and introduced them into the teaching materials. Early on. So if you trace the teaching materials and their publication, you'll see increasingly their incorporation of ABF materials.

We're talking at various levels here but while all this was going on, I was beginning to develop courses specifically focused on the policing function.

Bill Clune: Right. One of which was Policing in a Free Society.

Herman Goldstein: Yes, and then I named other courses Selected Problems in Policing in the form of seminars.

Bill Clune: Oh yeah. Selected Problems, I remember that.

Herman Goldstein: They were timely in the sense that, for example, I think it was in 1972 that Wisconsin was one of the first states to move away from arresting intoxicated people to taking them into custody for their own protection. It was the first time police were given authority to put their hands on anybody in a form other than arrest.

Bill Clune: Hmm.

Herman Goldstein: So I think for two or three years, I ran a seminar on the way in which the changes were occurring in the law relating to intoxicated people. Likewise, there was a period of great activity when the legislature started moving to do something about domestic violence, to require arrests in domestic violence. We had a seminar on legislative changes relating to domestic violence. I don't know the depth in which you want to go into this, but I have the syllabi for all of these courses in my files.

Bill Clune: It sounds like those are the kind of topics that could work their ways into problem-oriented policing.

Herman Goldstein: Yes, yes. As you well know, Bill, reconstructing this stuff after all these years is sometimes very difficult. But it occurred to me once I learned that you and I were going to get together that there were two major leaps insofar as the teaching materials are concerned, the criminal law area, not just the policing.

Bill Clune: What were those?

Herman Goldstein: In the criminal law area, the first leap was to take cognizance of the criminal justice system, and that's why all these considerations were new at the time. The term criminal justice was new. It was an effort to be more generic, to cover the whole bit. Then you notice subtle changes when we went from cases to cases and materials. There even came a time when we switched the sequence of the terms to "materials and cases" so as to give emphasis to the former.

Bill Clune: Yeah.

Herman Goldstein: Which had great symbolism to it. The initial effort was to teach the system as a system and if you read the introductory materials to these volumes, you'll find great emphasis on that. You can't teach about the courts unless you know what's happening at the police end. You can't teach about corrections unless you know what's happening in the courts and vice versa. The very term "system," criminal justice system, was a creation of the Bar Foundation study. I don't know that it was ever used before that, but the whole thrust of the study was to see interrelationships. If I had an interesting case that I observed in policing, I would tip off the field observer who was present in the prosecutor's office or the field observer who was in the courts, and he or she would follow through on my case and see what happened to it.

Bill Clune: Yeah, when I think of system, I think of the full range of ways that citizens encounter criminal justice authorities starting with, I suppose, the police as the initial point of contact and going straight through the different steps of arraignment and plea bargaining and trial and sentencing. All of the people involved in all those sequential steps.

Herman Goldstein: Yes, and that was the big contribution of the Bar Foundation study and it was what Frank turned to in that second course that he established for the L2s and 3s. Subsequently, the subject matter for the second year and third year became the subject matter for the first year.

Bill Clune: So for 2Ls or 3Ls, it became a requirement in the first year. In my mind, check me on this, criminal justice administration is kind of a substitute for the procedure course but not for the course on crimes.

Herman Goldstein: That's right. Frank always maintained that all students had to have a course in substantive criminal law. They have to know what the elements are before you can prove a homicide. So that's why when we made the shift, there was the one semester on substantive criminal law, the next semester was criminal justice administration. In lieu of the old procedure.

Bill Clune: Got it.

Herman Goldstein: Frank always felt it was important to get me into the class to deal with the policing material at the front end. We got them to try to give a lot of thought to the fact that as the input agency, the police bring people into the system. Most of the cases that they brought in never went any further.

Bill Clune: Okay.

Herman Goldstein: I spent a few minutes just reviewing the book, and I'm leading up to when we switched to the problem orientation.

Bill Clune: Was that going to be the second great leap?

Herman Goldstein: Yes. That will be the second major shift—the problem focus. But in that first stage—limited to focusing on the system—can you imagine what we were saying in print? I couldn't believe we said this: the arrest of street-walking prostitutes has been a way of trying to keep that problem under control absent adequate evidentiary grounds for a lawful arrest. That was true of thousands of cases. By contrast, adequate grounds to arrest are usually present in the case of the down and out drunk and the offender in domestic violence. Even with regard to domestic violence, I remember police making arrests and bringing them into the system and the judge perhaps dismissing them. A better example was with the drunks. In the morning arraignment, court personnel would bring all the cases in. Then you'd see a shift in the courtroom. They'd move chairs around and push people back. They'd open up a door and all the intoxicated people would come out. They were nevertheless in court. The judge would look down and say "John, I saw you here yesterday. Bill, you were here yesterday." He'd say "You guys, stand back here and the rest of you guys go." The judge was saying "You're dismissed." Then he would take John and Bill and say, "Your job is to sweep up the courtroom."

Bill Clune: Hmm, okay.

Herman Goldstein: But they were going into court. The prostitutes were never brought into court. They just were picked up indiscriminately on the streets simply because they had been labeled a prostitute whenever they were seen. The prostitutes built the process into their schedules. They'd have their sex, they'd make their money, and then they'd go to a street corner and wait for the paddy wagon to pick them up because that was part of the routine.

Bill Clune: So the evidentiary basis was that they were just known to be street . . .

Herman Goldstein: Street walkers.

Bill Clune: Street walkers, they weren't observed . . .

Herman Goldstein: Having sex or anything like that.

Bill Clune: Taking money or anything else.

Herman Goldstein: No, no; no effort to acquire evidence of the transaction.

Bill Clune: It's kind of like a nuisance, like a vagrancy or something.

Herman Goldstein: Yes. "Mary, you're out late tonight, why are you so late?" Or "You're out early." The police had a social relationship with the prostitutes. They all knew them. In Detroit, they brought in around fifty every night.

Bill Clune: So they'd spend the night in jail.

Herman Goldstein: Yes.

Bill Clune: And then come before the judge and get released in the morning?

Herman Goldstein: No judge.

Bill Clune: Oh, no judge.

Herman Goldstein: They'd just walk out. Oh, the police may call headquarters to find out when they were last in for a health check. If they hadn't been checked recently, they might hold onto them and have them be checked for disease.

Bill Clune: Kind of police detention and supervision of a certain population as they saw it.

Herman Goldstein: Exactly; it was summary punishment, summary control, never got into the system. I pulled this out for specific description because this is what Frank would have said, "You have to study the system because if you don't, you don't even see these people. All those individuals who are entering a plea of guilty and are leaving, you don't see them." He would redraw a picture of the system and how it would operate and expose people at various points in the system where government was interacting with individuals on the assumption that they were . . .

Bill Clune: Criminals in some way.

Herman Goldstein: All these protections of government, however long they could be held, whether they could be questioned and searched. They just weren't even being looked at.

Bill Clune: Very good explanation.

Herman Goldstein: That was to force people to look at the system. Then Frank said he wanted to give more shape to what he was doing. That's when he moved toward the problem-oriented focus. I remember, I don't know if this is historically accurate, but I think I can almost claim that I remember the day when Frank shifted to the problem focus. He taught at 7:45 in the morning.

He always said he did it because there was a law school custom that you could get your parking space if you taught at 7:45 a.m., so he could always count on a parking space. I don't know if that was the case. In his skillful teaching methods and his use of the Socratic method, he would be teaching something like wiretapping in the context of the complexities of how the criminal justice system actually worked.

Bill Clune: Mm-hmm (affirmative).

Herman Goldstein: He posed a problem about some of these street prostitutes and maybe, in that context, raised a question of wiretapping them or using undercover officers to apprehend them and bring them to trial. The students would have some trouble with that.

Bill Clune: For drugs and prostitution and the like, yeah.

Herman Goldstein: But then he would shift gears so that the students would be enthusiastic about the use of wiretapping in the context of organized crime: "Of course, get a warrant for that" etc., etc. Then he'd switch gears and he'd say, "Well how about the use of an undercover operation or the use of decoys as between organized crime and street prostitution?"

Bill Clune: Stings and all that.

Herman Goldstein: And stings. Then he would shift to shoplifting—one of his favorites to engage the students—because he felt that some students had engaged in the behavior at some time in their lives, or knew someone who did. So he would shift to shoplifting: "How about undercover operations with regard to shoplifting?" "Oh no, no, no." He increasingly made the point that students and the public generally have entirely different attitudes about the use of government intervention, probing activities, investigative techniques, depending upon what it is that you're investigating.

Bill Clune: Okay, so you found different sets of interactions with the system depending on what the behavioral problem was.

Herman Goldstein: Exactly.

Bill Clune: You couldn't just consider the system in a sequence in the abstract.

Herman Goldstein: No. You had to put it in the context of a problem.

Bill Clune: Okay, right.

Herman Goldstein: That's what led ultimately to paying greater attention to the appropriateness of the choice of investigative methods in the context of specific behavioral problems. I remember having sat in on all those classes that he would, using the Socratic method, shift gears. The students would sort of gang up on him and reject the use of wiretapping in this particular setting and then he'd say, "Well, let me change the fact situation." He'd say, "The police department gets a call saying that somebody is threatening to blow up the Statue of Liberty." Then he'd pose the question of the propriety of using a wiretap to try to investigate that. "Oh, you can't allow that to happen." He had made his point.

Bill Clune: Early terrorism.

Herman Goldstein: Yes, so after a while he concluded, "There's no sense teaching this material unless you do it in some context."

Bill Clune: Okay.

Herman Goldstein: So that's why the book came to focus on specific problems: on robbery, on organized crime, on prostitution, on domestic violence. He began to teach in the context of problems. It was not a smooth ride by any means. I have trouble even recalling the change process. It is explained to some degree in the preface up front. Here's chapter two. It says "investigation." For all of chapter two on the top of the page, it says "investigation" on the left. On the right-hand side, it labels the page with the title of a problem. The problem approach goes to page 167.

Bill Clune: Okay.

Herman Goldstein: Robbery was the problem he used most often because it brings the possibility of bodily violence. Compared to organized crime which is group criminality.

Bill Clune: Mm-hmm (affirmative).

Herman Goldstein: Then he'd throw in something very common, like domestic violence, but now much more complicated given different social attitudes. When you surf the table of contents, you'll find references to car theft, which would generally be viewed as less serious.

Bill Clune: So each behavioral problem can be considered a crime but it's treated differently by the system at the different stages.

Herman Goldstein: Exactly. He put his finger on that and said essentially that the weight of the social norm, the social expectation as to how seriously we were going to treat this, was heavily dependent on the perception that the public had of the seriousness of the offense. Now, and this is where it gets even more complicated, is that Frank's view led me more and more toward my interest over the past twenty years. Why do we have to resolve all those subtle differences in the context of the criminal process? Aren't there alternatives to the criminal process? The first one that opened up was taking the intoxicated person into custody for his or her own protection. They said, "Screw the criminal law. Don't take them to jail . . . You're prohibited from taking them to jail." The preamble in the statute that Frank wrote on intoxicated people said, "This is not to be considered an arrest." For purposes of record, an intoxicated person could be picked up thirty times and honestly say, "I've never been arrested."

Bill Clune: We're not talking about driving under the influence.

Herman Goldstein: No.

Bill Clune: We're talking staggering around a sidewalk or something.

Herman Goldstein: Right, and it's very clearly defined.

Bill Clune: Public intoxication.

Herman Goldstein: But as you may remember from some exposures you may have had, I know in the fifties and sixties if I walked into a jail, 90 percent of the people in the jail were there for being intoxicated. They were in the drunk tank. This was minor behavior, but high in volume.

Bill Clune: Why did the cops even get involved? Was it because people complained? It was a public nuisance or something like that? Or they were a danger to themselves?

Herman Goldstein: It was a public nuisance and offensive or frightening to some. It's somewhat analogous to the issue we're concerned today with regard to the mentally ill.

Bill Clune: Mm-hmm (affirmative).

Herman Goldstein: The reality, Bill, is that there are not the resources out there on the part of government to deal with this as a public health issue so it falls to the police. In the past the only method the police had for dealing with it was enforcement. So Frank early on was a strong supporter of developing alternatives to arrest, and I picked up on that. A lot of my work has that focus. Phew, the distance we've come! I'm giving this talk at Stockholm in a few weeks about problem-oriented policing.

Bill Clune: You're gonna get a Nobel prize in Stockholm.

Herman Goldstein: It's not called a Nobel prize. I have to laugh at that because people don't know about that. "Oh, here comes the Nobel Prize winner." It's hardly that.

Bill Clune: Well, it's the top prize in your field.

Herman Goldstein: Hmm?

Bill Clune: It's the top prize.

Herman Goldstein: Yes, but what I'm talking about in Stockholm in a few weeks doesn't cover all this background of how we got there—the way problem-oriented policing evolved from Frank's early questioning of the way we taught criminal law.

Bill Clune: Mm-hmm (affirmative).

Herman Goldstein: Frank is urging: let's focus on the behavior, if you focus on the behavior, logic tells us we have to bring different alternatives to bear other than enforcement. Today, the best example of that stems from government having closed down the mental health institutions, presenting a different kind of problem today than it was thirty, forty, fifty years ago. The police must deal with mental health issues on the street. It's not an enforcement problem. It's not a criminal law problem. It's a behavioral problem they have to deal with, and they have to have a means for dealing with it. So now we do have a whole new set of separate statutes that speak to what police can do in taking the person into custody against their will. The major focus is to try to get help to people who are mentally ill. So the police end up being sort of nurses. I call them the street nurses.

Bill Clune: Triaging what should we do with this person?

Herman Goldstein: Yes, and we have to have the resources in the community, and we have to connect, for example with Dane County Mental Health in Madison, so that we can get them involved to ask, "What have we got here?" Is this a person who is okay on the street and we just have to get them to conform to some minimum requirements? Should the police consult with the family to decide what we can do? What kind of medical help are they getting? Is this a candidate for medication? Or is it somebody that has to be taken into custody? We have hundreds of people in the city now who have been placed under court order to take medications. If they can't be depended upon to take their medications, they may be required to go to a certain facility to get their medication each day. And if they don't show up, then they become subject to custody and treatment.

Bill Clune: So custody becomes in a way the substitute for arrest.

Herman Goldstein: Right. In the past, police arrested and then figured out what to do with the person. Now they try to figure out what to do and hopefully only take custody if nothing else works. That's just the one problem of mental health. Mike Scott and others have documented some 250 or so problems that the police are expected to handle.

Bill Clune: Now Mike is the head of the Center for Problem-Oriented Policing.

Herman Goldstein: Yes, at Arizona State. Our whole approach to policing is that you start off analyzing the problem: analyze it and figure out what to do. The answer might be, if it's a problem of people feeling insecure, it might be installing lighting in this area. That may solve the problem. We may not even come close to using the criminal law.

Bill Clune: I remember when I used to interact with you in the old days, I guess in the '70s because I came in '71, public urination was a problem, and one of the alternatives was putting . . .

Herman Goldstein: Putting urinals out on the street. We have hundreds of those alternatives now. Hundreds of them.

Bill Clune: How does that work . . . What's the route? It isn't an individual police officer who can get a Porta Potty located on a corner?

Herman Goldstein: No, but to the extent that we preach and teach problem-oriented policing, we are hoping that that officer, on analyzing the situation, concludes that the problem here is that there's not an easily accessible toilet. And the hope is that he has the connections to other city agencies to make this happen. I get so excited about this. I wish I . . .

Bill Clune: This is a fairly brilliant thing.

Herman Goldstein: Last night, I met with one of my best friends, Jim Dexheimer, a retired Madison police officer. He was very attracted to the whole concept. He's taken lots of courses at the university. He took my courses. He just lives and breathes problem-oriented policing. He tried his best to implement the concept in the Madison Police Department. He got some support but not always. We have some beautiful, beautiful local examples of problem-oriented policing at its height and Dex is associated with several of them. Last night, he had a celebration out at Olin Park with the people who worked with him in solving one problem, a big problem that occupied the police in Olin Park. Olin Park was on his beat. It had come to be seen by both the MPD and the public as a place where gay men went to meet each other and do what they want to do in the park, and this became so well known that the park was not used for any other purpose. Olin Park is a beautiful park.

For years and years and years Madison police just went into the park and used undercover operations, setting themselves up and arresting, among others, local lawyers, doctors, whoever went in the park for this purpose and to try to get the message across that you don't do this in the park. When Dex was assigned to the area that included the park, he was thoroughly immersed in the problem-oriented policing concept. He's a nature lover and a photographer. He analyzed the problem. Problem-oriented policing calls for in-depth analysis of what it is you're dealing with, and I mean really probing deeply. So he went into the park and did his deep probe and he realized the people living in the vicinity of the park would not go into the park. He decided one of his first objectives was to approach them and engage them. He arranged social affairs with the residents. As the police officer in the area who had a hobby of photographing wildflowers, he offered to share his collection of photos of all of the wildflowers from Olin Park. He said, "This is right next to you."

Bill Clune: Right.

Herman Goldstein: "But you're not enjoying it." He would then talk to them about the issues in the park and say, "There's a role for you to play in regaining the use of that park." He gained the interest of the City Park Department. He did surveillance to establish where the nests were, where these people met. He had the brush trimmed so there were no hiding places. Then he had the traffic pattern in the park altered, whereas before it accommodated cruisers who were going around looking for people looking to engage. He initiated other changes in the park. Then as the place started to look better, as the traffic pattern changed, as people were frustrated getting into the park and meeting their mates, he got neighbors to start reusing the park. He started planning concerts in the park to draw people into it.

As he restored use of the park, arrests declined. There's so much to tell about his case study, but one of the most interesting things was of special interest to social scientists, the people that I'm going to be talking to in Stockholm. They would ask him, "Well how do you measure what he did? We don't have any numbers. Where are the numbers?" Dex very creatively swept the park with a group of volunteer police officers picking up used condoms with sticks with needles or nails on the end of them before he started his project, and periodically thereafter. He counted the condoms as an indication of the degree to which he was reducing the number of sexual contacts in the park. That was not only a creative way of measuring success, it was a commendable initiative for a police officer, and the perfect capstone for a problem-oriented policing project.

Bill Clune: There was a book when I was in graduate school in sociology, called *Unobtrusive Measures*, by Webb, Campell, and others, on counting occurrences through indirect measures.

Herman Goldstein: I remember that same work. They measured such things as the interest that people had in certain football and baseball games, between the quarters and innings, when people would go to the bathroom and not go to the bathroom, by the volume of sewage.

Bill Clune: Yes.

Herman Goldstein: One of the best examples of problem-oriented policing we have in Madison is the elimination of the riots that occurred on Halloween when the police and others in city government just repurposed the phenomenon. It is now a musical event.

Bill Clune: Mm-hmm (affirmative).

Herman Goldstein: Frank started talking about how we've got to have more alternatives for dealing with behavioral problems that arise in the community. You only get at the alternatives if you look at the problem. So what's the problem? The problem was young people rioting on Halloween. That's an event that occurs once a year. That's how you define the event.

Olin Park is an event that extends over a period of time, but not into the winter.

Bill Clune: Yeah.

Herman Goldstein: In problem-oriented policing, problems get defined in a variety of ways, usually based upon place, offenders, times of day, seasons of the year. We've got police officers now out there who think in these terms and have been taught problem-oriented policing along these lines.

Bill Clune: Whereas back in the day, police only did one thing. They might walk into a riot with shields and billy clubs and tear gas.

Herman Goldstein: And still do in most situations. In my Stockholm talk, I had to acknowledge that problem-oriented policy is still relatively rare. I did not want to portray an unrealistic situation. The vast majority of police in this country still operate in an enforcement mode.

Bill Clune: Okay.

Herman Goldstein: Where's the violation here? If you show me the violation, I'll deal with it. Otherwise, why did you call the police?

Bill Clune: Mm-hmm (affirmative).

Herman Goldstein: In trying to advance problem-oriented policing, we start with the assumption that policing is not just law enforcement. Policing is dealing with 250 or so different behavioral problems that arise in a community.

Bill Clune: Mm-hmm (affirmative). Your course, you always had one course—Policing in a Free Society. Was the other main course Problem-Oriented Policing, and they both had a book?

Herman Goldstein: No, I didn't actually label the course as problem-oriented policing. I usually offered two seminars in a semester. In one, we all focused at the outset on a specific problem—like sexual assault, or convenience store robberies—and set out as a group to explore the problem in depth, drawing on how it occurred in a number of police agencies. In the other seminar, students were initially introduced to the problem-oriented process and then each student was offered the opportunity to select a specific problem to research as it arose in a given community.

Arrangements were made for them to engage with a local police department. Each student would share their work as they proceeded on their individual projects, getting input and ideas from the other students. Toward the end of the semester, they presented their individual projects to all students taking the seminar—drawing contrasts between their findings with all of the students. The push was to be as rigorous in their analysis as feasible, and to be creative, going well beyond traditional legal analysis. They each wrote a report which was ultimately presented to representatives of the agency with which they had chosen to work.

Bill Clune: Convenience stores, that's another one I remember you used to talk about.

Herman Goldstein: Yes, convenience store robberies were a common focus. Motels that got a reputation for accommodating troublesome activities was another. As to both of these problems, solutions often took the form of proposing regulatory codes; making environmental changes (e.g., lighting); staffing; changes in management; etc. But such efforts often extended to taking civil actions—including shutting down the businesses as nuisances.

Bill Clune: The drug houses.

Herman Goldstein: Actually ripping the buildings down. Here is an illustration that I'm using it in my talk. A group working in a problem-oriented mode in Cincinnati this last year went into a four-block area where there was gun violence, and these are some of the things they did. They improved the lighting. They demolished several buildings, always of course based upon evidence that they've collected. They discovered that drugs were flourishing because along the street cars would stop and deals would be made through the windows of the cars. So they had the whole area posted as no parking. That got enforced, and the drug problem was eliminated. They found an empty lot and they created a playground. They organized the neighborhood. It takes various different mechanisms for doing that.

Bill Clune: Mm-hmm (affirmative).

Herman Goldstein: So you have police agencies that become very proficient, like Cincinnati.

Bill Clune: What kind of staff within a police department . . . is it like public administration staff? Or do some of the police officers take to the approach and become the managers of it?

Herman Goldstein: Some officers become very enamored with it. They just say, "This is the greatest thing I've done since I've been on the force. It's so satisfying. I'm getting something done." In Cincinnati, their police department was out of control. They were put under a federal consent decree with the condition that they had to adopt problem-oriented policing.

Bill Clune: Mm-hmm (affirmative).

Herman Goldstein: The Cincinnati PD had several presentations at this last conference that's held annually, and the officers in charge made their presentation. They're also traveling to Stockholm. They reported that their city manager told them and told their city agencies that in Cincinnati every city agency is a part of the police department.

Bill Clune: Yeah.

Herman Goldstein: Because they all have responsibilities. They have to fix the lighting. They have to change the traffic patterns. They have to clear up the parks. They've got to become involved and they do.

Bill Clune: So some kind of organizational change within cities can be part of it, ideally should be part of it.

Herman Goldstein: Yes. It's exciting stuff. A massive literature has become available, a lot of it by criminologists, especially environmental criminologists. There's much tension within criminology between those who want to change the behavior of people and send them to prison and have them come out and be good people and the environmental criminologists who say, "We're going to prevent crime by reducing opportunities for crime."

Environmental criminologists have hundreds of projects that they have done where they apply some of their methodology, highly rigorous methodology, in measuring the number of thefts that occurred. When they altered the environment they then measured the number of thefts. They've developed a whole vocabulary. They also have a vocabulary that describes diffusion of benefits. For example, you not only benefit from the reduction in thefts in an area, but because that parking lot becomes safer, the area in the vicinity of the parking lot also becomes safer. They always include that as a measure. I've worked with some of these people and it's a happy marriage between the interests of police and police drawing on the work of the environmental criminologists. For me a success story is when an officer who understands the problem-oriented concept checks out the literature on environmental criminology and says, "What they have learned has application to the problem that is in front of me."

Bill Clune: Mm-hmm (affirmative).

Herman Goldstein: Hopefully they will make greater use of this kind of analysis. Enforcement falls by the wayside.

We're societies, hopefully we're organized, we try to live together. Sometimes we don't quite make it and our "social agreements" are disrupted. We try to establish a social norm, and I'm increasingly impressed by the power of the social norm. I think so much of what policing should be about is reinforcing the social norm. We have enormous potential in achieving good by strengthening the social norm. Look at what we've done with smoking.

Bill Clune: Mm-hmm (affirmative). I can just see it with sexual assault and the #MeToo movement as well. I mean, I remember the reform in criminal law that defined degrees of sexual conduct. That hadn't been there before, and now if you think about sexual assaults on campus, you can so clearly see it as a norm that's broader than just the criminal law.

Herman Goldstein: Yes. So that big, big, big picture to which I was referring is you just see that police are left to deal with residual problems that come to their attention because it's happening. Left to their own devices, more of it might happen unless somebody steps in and says, "You don't do that." I criticize the police severely for being too vulnerable, to taking on more and more and more things.

Currently for example: the opioid epidemic. It's become a police problem. Police leadership is now pointing fingers at the pharmaceutical industry. The medical profession is in a much better position to control the opioid epidemic than are the police.

Bill Clune: Yes. In our neighborhood, a young guy overdosed, and the police came when somebody called 911.

Herman Goldstein: You call them when something goes wrong. That's the definition of their role and they will be pressed to assume more and more and more things unless they stop and say, "Wait a minute. There are other ways in which to deal with this." Yet, in our society, the police are thought of as having their mission defined for them by the law, and we see them as a ministerial agency and we don't want them to be advocates and to be policy makers. But essentially they should be pushed more to speak out to do that because they have the knowledge with which to do it.

Bill Clune: What was the alternative to the environmental approach in criminology?

Herman Goldstein: Well, there are various schools of criminology. Some of them will focus on who commits crime and what factors in their background and makeup and upbringing may have contributed to their crime. So causes of crime. Others will focus on the rehabilitation of criminals. Are they rehabilitatable? There's various different schools. The school that I have been relating to most directly is the environmental, as I described earlier.

Bill Clune: Okay. In your problem-oriented courses you took problems and had students work on them.

Herman Goldstein: Yes, I always put students to work on specific problems. For example, if in the period of time when the legislature had acted, and we said, "Okay, they changed the statute with regard to intoxication, I want each one of you to take a county in the state, go out there and nose around and find out how the county is altering their practices in order to implement the intent of the statute."

Bill Clune: Mm-hmm (affirmative).

Herman Goldstein: Because in some places they ignored it. Milwaukee for a long period of time just continued to arrest intoxicated persons found on the streets. They didn't have the facilities to detox them. This slow adjustment blows me away. I'm retired and I've been less and less involved for twenty years. This obligation I have for next month has brought me back into these unsolved problems. I feel that I have twenty different projects that I could identify for young academics to take hold of. I'll give you an example that I attribute to my good friend Dex who is very thoughtful about these things. You're familiar generally as a local citizen with the Mifflin Street Party.

Bill Clune: I've never been to it, but I've driven by it.

Herman Goldstein: Yes, and the police have done a good job in bringing it under control. It's not the reckless event that it used to be. But it's still scary, especially all these buildings that these kids live in. They come out on the porches. Police worry that the porches might collapse, that the participants might get drunk and fall off.

Bill Clune: Yes. Herman Goldstein: Yes, but Dex raised an interesting question. He says, "Why as a society are we content in saying, well this year we got through the Mifflin Street problem and there were only X number of arrests." If you were to go down there, you would see a massive group of young kids, I understand the freshmen and the sophomores get into it in a big way, who are intoxicated beyond their capacity to handle the liquor. They're falling down. The local detox facility closes. The Mifflin Street party begins. They have had their fill by three or four o'clock in the afternoon as I understand it."

Herman Goldstein: Yet this continues to go on. It's so outrageous when you see it. These young coeds, that's an improper term these days, these young college women and men experimenting with liquor and getting soused. We don't rush in there and put up temporary detox facilities. We don't bring a bunch of doctors in there and immediately meet the needs of these people.

Bill Clune: The kids are around saying, "My friend or somebody over there is in really bad shape, needs attention." I mean there's some great demand for it right there.

Herman Goldstein: Yes, and why haven't we developed a social movement that says it's wrong to get soused to the point where you are endangering your life, just as it's wrong to smoke cigarettes?

Bill Clune: Yeah. Okay. Well, I think we've covered a lot of ground. I feel fortunate to have spoken with you weeks before you're getting this award. I mean that's just a phenomenal achievement.

Herman Goldstein: Yes, I have become very rusty on the sequence of all of these developments. But a lot of it has come back to me through your questions. One of my regrets is I don't have the same collegial relationships. Just to be stimulated in my discussion with you today is refreshing for me. I have a feeling that if there were one or two or three people out there with whom to chew over these questions, I'm ready to start running and thinking anew about where it would take me because one of the things that excites me, Bill, is that in the scheme of these things, in how to deal effectively with patterns of behavior, we have not given adequate credit or attention to the large number of advocacy groups relating, for example, to domestic violence, sexual assault, child abuse, most recently the #MeToo movement. We are redefining how society responds to these behaviors and producing results far beyond what we were able to do in the use of the criminal law.

Bill Clune: I thought of the #MeToo movement when you were mentioning social norms and how norms become social actions, for example, people getting dismissed from their jobs is not police action, but it's a very significant penalty.

Herman Goldstein: Yes. I was reading a little bit about current problems in Sweden and their concerns about migrants. The fundamental question is how do you acclimate? How do you integrate a large number of people into your society? Some aspect of the change is going to involve the police. So it gets defined as a crime problem, but it's really an integration problem.

Bill Clune: Assimilation problem.

Herman Goldstein: Assimilation problem and establishing the social norm. I was reminded of an incident in which I became involved. I was patrolling in Amsterdam with a police officer, a lieutenant, in the Red-Light District. There were two men who did not speak Dutch, but Dutch supervising police officers are required to speak four languages. One of the men came running up to the lieutenant and said, "Lieutenant, Lieutenant." He explained to him that the other guy had taken a screwdriver and was going to attack him with it. In the States if that had occurred, that would be a pretty serious thing. The officer just saunters up to them and says, "I want to talk to you, come here." First he says, "Screwdriver, where is the screwdriver?" The guy brings out the screwdriver. The officer takes the screwdriver away and puts it in his back pocket. It's a seizure of some kind, but we're not going to make any fuss over that in this setting. He then talks to the two guys. They have an exchange that I understood because, for the most part, it was in English. Then just before he sends them on their way, he says, "I just want you to know, we don't do that here. We don't do that here." I thought, "Man, he was teaching a social norm." It was his contribution. We don't do that here. In the States, those men may have been arrested, put into the system, probably sentenced, substantially.

Bill Clune: Great example. Okay, this was really wonderful and thank you so much.

Herman Goldstein: Yes, okay. Very good, Bill.

Interview of Stewart Macaulay and Bill Whitford by Bill Clune

Abstract

The *Contracts Law in Action* materials and course book grew out of other contracts books that emphasized law in action/legal realism, such as Macneil, Kessler & Sharp, and Fuller. A law in action approach to contracts can be understood as an empirically oriented alternative to casebooks that feature contract formation (offer, acceptance, etc.) and doctrinal analysis.

The Macaulay/Whitford book begins with remedies which severely constrain the empirical odds of successful litigation. Lawsuits based on lost profit ("you promised to give me money"), or expectation damages, almost never succeed because of a variety of defenses, such as the obligation to mitigate damages, reasonably foreseeable damages, and others. The rule that successful parties do not recover the costs of litigation means that many recoveries are not financially worthwhile. Restitution as a remedy is based on a distinct conception of damages (restoration of losses). Other law in action themes are relational contracts, inconsistency of doctrines (doctrine and counter-doctrine), the contextual background of cases, and the dominance of more powerful parties. Relational contracts between parties whose transactions are embedded in ongoing relationships, such as employment, marriage, and commercial supply agreements, are based on trust rather than legalities, and disputes are usually resolved through negotiation rather than litigation. Inconsistency of contract doctrines (doctrine and counter-doctrine) increases the uncertainty of recovery. Research on the contextual background of cases reveals unanticipated consequences, strong arguments neglected on appeal, and multiple rounds of judicial and legislative maneuvers that result in mixed or unclear success by the winner of a single case. The dominance of one party to contracts, characteristic of consumer transactions and employment, means that consent of the less powerful party is a formality, and the more powerful party has virtually all practical rights and remedies (including binding arbitration).

The Wisconsin Progressive tradition can be seen in attention to cases and legislation that attempt to redress imbalances of power (e.g., restrictions on do-not-compete clauses, automotive lemon laws) which are somtimes successful but often unsuccessful because of the legislative and judicial influence of powerful elites in legislatures and courts.

Origins of the Wisconsin contracts book

Bill Clune: Who developed and taught Contracts: Law in Action? Kind of quick background.

Bill Whitford: It grew out of the use of Ian Macneil's book—

Stewart Macaulay: Well, it grew out of the Fuller book, Kessler and Sharp . . . . And then the Macneil book.

Bill Whitford: Yes, and the Wisconsin supplement—

Stewart Macaulay: And the Wisconsin supplement—

Bill Whitford: That was the key thing.

Stewart Macaulay: That's right.

Bill Whitford: And then we used the Macneil book, because he was considered the core originator of the relational contract school with Stewart, and it was the first teaching material from the relational contract's perspective . . . 1970, about?

Stewart Macaulay: Yeah.

Bill Whitford: And the *Wisconsin Law Review* article has these details. The Wisconsin supplement got so big that about '78 or so, after the Danzig book came out, which had contract case background stories, some from our materials, and we assigned the Danzig book, we just decided it was silly to ask the students to buy the Macneil case book, because their assignment sheet was crazy. We just took cases from the Macneil book and put them into the Wisconsin supplement. And it's a testament, amongst other things, to the wonderful resource that we had at the time, at the Wisconsin Law School, that made the development of teaching materials feasible, and that was the duplication center here, run by Ruth Saab and David Ward.

Bill Whitford: They were very efficient, very cooperative. And it made things possible . . .

Stewart Macaulay: I think that's right.

Bill Clune: So what, were the Fuller and Macneil books closer to the law in action goals than other alternatives?

Stewart Macaulay: I think what you'd have to say is that the Fuller and the Kessler and Sharp books were very legal-realistic in the sense of theories, ideas, approaches of how the judges decided cases, and this sort of thing. We were the ones putting the law in action stuff in the supplement.

Bill Whitford: What we now call the book, actually, *Contracts: Law in Action.*

Stewart Macaulay: Yeah, the relational contract and these sorts of things. And trying to put things in context. That is, giving background of the case. What happened after the case was decided? And very often, when you could that find out, it was fascinating that people did not just pay their judgment.

Bill Whitford: Yes, a case is an event in a longer story. I would say this about Fuller, and then Kessler and Sharp materials. There was the old Langdellian Model, which still exists, we now call the bar review courses, but if you go back to a Langdellian model, often associated with Williston, though perhaps a little unfairly. It was what our late colleague Jean Braucher called the sacred, in that wonderful article about the sacred and the profane. It was to try to create what Willard talks about in his memory of his contracts course at Harvard. He said, it was a geometry course, taking a few propositions and working out analytically what the implications of them were, and then looking for cases that illustrate those implications, and they can order the rest of the cases.

Stewart Macaulay: The things that didn't fit this were wrong—

Bill Whitford: And not taught. And they were forgotten, and so it purported to be empirical in the sense that the ideology behind it was we're going to look at the cases and figure out the law, but it wasn't really that. It was figuring ideologically a set of principles that one would want to apply in a free market economy to a contract. And then, figuring that when there's a gap, there needs to be interpretation. And so, Fuller begins to break from that in a very legal, realistic way, going back to the thirties really, in a lot of different ways. But his empiricism is kind of intuitive, it is armchair empiricism, but it's illustrated very clearly by beginning the course with remedies. And that just says right up front, the parties are bringing the lawsuit because they want a particular result. This is the most important part of the doctrine that Fuller figured out: what remedies were being granted to these people, and why they wanted them, and whether they're adequate to their aims, so it begins to break away from the doctrinal approach.

Stewart Macaulay: The second case in our book makes the important point that if you win the lawsuit, normally, you don't get your lawyer's fees, which is a simple little point to make as you're going through there, but it opens the door to saying, "Wait a minute." Fuller talks about the expectation interest, putting you where you would have been if the contract had been performed. Well, minus the cost of getting it. And you're making a very important point right there.

Bill Whitford: That's the law on the ground kind of thing.

Stewart Macaulay: Yeah.

Bill Whitford: Kessler and Sharp differed from the Langdellian tradition in a different way and reflected legal realism in a different way. Particularly, emphasizing the inconsistency in decisions, so that this image that there was a kind of seamless web, and really emphasizing that are dual lines of precedent, so there's a lot of choices that the judge has; which line of precedent are they going to cite.

Stewart Macaulay: They had this wonderful heading in one of their chapters. It's called, "Rule and Counter Rule. Over Corrections, and Over Generalizations."

Bill Whitford: But it's still focused very much on what goes on in court. Unanticipated results after appellate decisions.

Bill Clune: So that's terrific. Give me an example of something unexpected that happened after the appellate case was decided? That you mentioned before, where it didn't work out, or it did.

Stewart Macaulay: You very so often, if you get ahold of lawyers afterwards, you discover that the case was settled and that the kind of settlement was surprising, and one of the things we do in Contracts II, more than in Contracts I, is we have the pressure for settlement, especially in the big cases. There we do the story of a couple of the settling judges. These are judges that are the great arm twisters. They are rather famous for this kind of thing, and so we bring them front and center at that stage and talk about . . . And also, it's partly how qualitative things like material failure of performance, or the question of excuses for impossibility or impracticability, and that sort of thing. And when they are that highly qualitative, there's always a good argument the other way, and that leads you into a position that you get your arm twisted to settle the darn thing.

Bill Clune: So in this arm twisting, aside from I guess just leveraging the pressure of the settlement, do they bring in some arguments that did not prevail on appeal, and so that give them some weight?

Bill Whitford: Who's the "they" in there?

Bill Clune: The ones who are settling. The lawyers and the judge and the settlement procedure, or just the lawyers.

Bill Whitford: Oh, sure.

Stewart Macaulay: Sure, and what's the name of the judge? I'm blanking on thejudge who was the great settling judge we—

Bill Whitford: Judge Robert Merhige, Jr.

Stewart Macaulay: The CEOs of the two corporations that were involved, and they would come out to his house and have mint juleps, and he would send them into his screened porch, and was basically telling them to settle the darn case!

Bill Whitford: He was considered . . . He was criticized for being unjudicial in a lot of these efforts.

Stewart Macaulay: Yeah, but he really was the extreme case of this kind of thing, but not the only case. You get all kind ofpressures.

Bill Whitford: Increasingly, right?

Stewart Macaulay: Oh, yeah!

Bill Whitford: Because now, the big thing, the vanishing trial, is a big theme in law and society now. The cases just don't get tried. You go down and talk to downtown lawyers and they just say cases just don't get tried.

Stewart Macaulay: Summaryjudgment.

Bill Whitford: That's where all the action is. You stay away from jury. There could be a trial, but you stay awayfrom the jury.

Bill Clune: Yeah, not to mention arbitration.

Bill Whitford: Well then, arbitration is a second way to avoid jury trials too. In arbitration, you can have a trial.

Legal realism and contracts law

Stewart Macaulay: But it does seem to be that one of the things you should recognize, through talking about legal realism, you're talking contracts. This was one of the great places for legal realism: conflict of law is the other big place where the legal realists were hot and heavy. But here, in contracts, you're talking Karl Llewellyn, who's a major player. And you're talking Lon Fuller. Now there's a pair of superstars of legal realism and jurisprudence. And in contracts we've got them both, and, on the other side, I suppose I'd add Bob Scott, who basically says that the realists got it all wrong. What we need are certain, efficient rules, so he's counter-revolution.

We start with remedies. Then we go to long-term continuing relationships, then the good old-fashioned consideration doctrine, and reliance, these kinds of things. Employment is the next thing, which is one of the modern kinds of things.

Bill Whitford: Franchise relations.

Stewart Macaulay: Yeah. And then, we have a long note at this point. About things like master supply agreements and these things. And master supply agreements, of course ideally, these are not legally enforceable. Or not legally enforced beyond a tiny degree, but you set a structure for everything. And we tell the story that I still think is fascinating, the Boeing 787, about carbon fiber, fancy new engines, and the pieces of the plane were to be made by various sub-contractors, and the pieces were all to be sent to Seattle, and they put them together there, and of course, they didn't fit. My son Phil, the engineer, says it was the world's greatest Lego project! But what happens is the Lego pieces aren't the right size. But the story is just fascinating. Nobody thought about suing for damages. That isn't what happened. Boeing sent its engineers out and took over the sub-contractors. Shaped them up, straightened them out, and got the planes. It was kind of a self-help, specific performance.

Part of it was nobody had experience working with carbon fiber, and it turns out that it isn't just super aluminum. But I was just fascinated by that story, because it is a kind of remedy, and it's nothing that the law could help with very much.

Contract "remedies" that don't reach courts

Bill Whitford: We do, in terms of what you're asking about problems that aren't solved—

Bill Clune: That don't reach courts.

Bill Whitford: Courts. You know, it's hard, because that kind of case is not easily accessible public material.

We very early got to interviewing the lawyers about the case, so we could find about a case that did get to court, why did it get to court? Why didn't it settle? What happened afterwards? But if you take a case that never got to court, then you have . . . well, Stewart is an avid reader of the *Wall Street Journal*, so he picks up a lot of the big stuff, because the *Journal* will cover it, so we get these anecdotes that way. But increasingly, in the commercial area, there's now scholarly articles about some of these practices. This is what my son Josh does, and there's increasing literature from law and elsewhere about practices such as the supply chain that Stewart's talking about, so it gets easier, but it isn't easy to incorporate in a first-semester course. It's not obvious as to how we could get talking into all the different things the first-semester course, but this is not just about the relational aspects of our materials, but that's at least part of the story. We're trying to teach a relational contracts course without totally disclaiming the responsibilities that a first-semester course needs to do.

Reasons for teaching traditional doctrine, doctrinal conflicts, restatements, UCC

Stewart Macaulay: These people may have to take the bar exam if they don't practice in Wisconsin, so— Good old-fashioned religion is still there for bar exams—

Bill Whitford: I guess lawyers still need to be able to distinguish holding and dictum, a case, that's part of being a lawyer, right? You either hire a lawyer, or a law firm hires a law school graduate—

Stewart Macaulay: And also, it's part of what you might call the legal culture. You have to sound like a lawyer. If you've never heard of *Hadley v. Baxendale*, a partner might look at you and wonder if you went to law school.

Bill Clune: A kind of a culture, yeah.

Bill Whitford: Yeah, we're very big in the materials on this legal realism thing we were talking about earlier. The kind of Fuller thing, and that came to be called deconstruction. That is to say, the theory of precedent falls apart, there's rival lines of precedent and different ways to interpret things. We're very big on that, or I always was, and not strictly the relational stuff—

Bill Clune: I was just reading about the uniform commissioners on state laws, about how they outlined the common law and put it into the form of rules.

Bill Whitford: Statutory form.

Bill Clune: Statutory form, and so, this is kind of a side point, but it almost begs the question of how do they deal with conflicting precedent?

Bill Whitford: The whole restatement project was all wrapped up in that problem too, you know? It's a restatement project, the core idea behind the restatement project, and they had restatements in all kinds of areas, was that there was a coherent body of doctrine. It was Langdellian in its conception. And they morphed through it in a variety of ways. We talked about the restatement second, that was the neo-formal way. It just blew through a lot of the inconsistencies by coming up with what Stewart calls a qualitative standard. Some kind of phrasing in the rule in a way that can accommodate both lines of precedent. But doesn't give you a concrete rule that will give clear indications about how a case should be decided, where everybody would agree, that these are the implications of a restatement principle, in this fact situation. They had a disagreement about that.

Bill Clune: They reached a level of generalization above the conflicts, and they concealed them.

Bill Whitford: That's right. Restatement section one, everybody should be nice! Something, that's an exaggeration, a parody—

Stewart Macaulay: But Llewellyn would have given you a long lecture on good faith.

Bill Whitford: Yeah, he certainly would.

Stewart Macaulay: Which is—

Bill Whitford: Probably part of being nice.

Stewart Macaulay: Which is part of being nice to someone.

Bill Clune: That thing does come through in his writings.

Stewart Macaulay: But the other thing it recognized too, a move we made, many law schools taught a contracts course, which was sort of an introduction. There's this grand thing of contract floating out of the air.

And then, in the sales course, you got article two of the uniform commercial code, which always struck me as, you sort of had to undo what you were taught in the first semester. But we made the choice to launch an article two in the first course. And I think you could defend it, because article two had splashed over into other areas, and so often they apply it even when it's questionable.

Bill Whitford: The restatement second is similar because article two had a big impact on the restatement second, which comes out in the 1980s, and article two came out of the 1950s. So the restatement which applies generally to contracts was heavily influenced by article two.

Bill Clune: Interesting. To what extent is article two in the legal realist/law in action tradition?

Stewart Macaulay: I think it is very much; it's Karl Llewellyn blocked here and there by Wall Street lawyers.

Bill Whitford: Part of the legal realist part is he had to get the damn thing enacted, because it is ultimately statute, but he was trying. He was somebody who believed that law could really shape human events, even in the contract area. Where the impact of law and how it shapes human events is mediated because the parties have this agreement. So parties have a great ability to displace what the law says through the details of their agreement, so it's not like criminal law, you know? Where you can just say, "Thou shall not smoke a reefer." Or something like that. It's mediated.

Bill Clune: He strongly believed that law could have an impact.

Bill Whitford: But he also strongly didn't believe in Langdell, and he believed in the deconstruction of the Langdellian vision. He was an early law in action guy as well, he was very definitely. So he tried to mold all that together and create a different kind of statute.

Stewart Macaulay: And recognize one of the great things where Bob Scott gets very angry at Llewellyn, Llewellyn had this notion, that judges have a situation sense.

And they may not give you a nice law school argument that you may be able, as a law professor, just to carve up their opinion.

Bill Whitford: They have a judicial culture that tries to get to the right answer. And smart people will have a substantial consensus of opinion about the right answer. He wasn't big on the polarization of the judiciary, which was a very Ivy League attitude in those days, right?

Stewart Macaulay: Absolutely! He's generalizing from Learned Hand and Ben Cardozo.

Bill Whitford: From the culture he was in, because he grew up in Columbia Law School, he was part of the East Coast elite. The same kind of period that Brad Snyder writes about, he doesn't write about Llewellyn, but he writes about the intellectual elite, starting from Woodrow Wilson, right through to Franklin and Eleanor Roosevelt. He was really part of that.

Stewart Macaulay: Oh sure, sure. "Empirical" statutes illustrating law in action?

Bill Clune: I'd love to have some of those guys back on the Supreme Court. In any case, so is there such a thing as a more or less empirical statute? I think of article two, but I also think of a thing I was corresponding to Bill about, the insurance code that Spencer Kimball did, which reflected so many specific situations, like what happens with suicide? Do you get life insurance awarded if you commit suicide?

Bill Whitford: Oh, that's very true, I think you could study that, because Spencer Kimball probably hasn't been given due credit for what an innovative guy he was in the legal realist tradition.

Stewart Macaulay: I think that's right!

Bill Clune: He was very much a student of Willard's.

Stewart Macaulay: That's right!

Bill Clune: Willard was the one who called the law school's attention to Spencer.

Bill Whitford: And Ed Young pushed him out as dean after Bill Sewell's time as chancellor.

Stewart Macaulay: Yes, yes. And Sewell of course, presided over some of the first protests against the war in Vietnam, and the regents didn't like that he didn't shoot all the students who protested, and so he got pushed out, and Ed Young got in. And Sewell had made promises to Spencer. And really, promises that would have bolstered the law school.

Bill Whitford: So much for contracts.

Stewart Macaulay: And Ed Young basically just told him, "I'm not honoring any of that."

Bill Clune: So do you think there's such a thing as a more empirically based statute? Or another way to put it, was there a trend towards statutes, which were closer to law in action?

Stewart Macaulay: Insofar as Llewellyn in article two talks about custom, and practices and things like that. That's where I see an empirically based statute. And again, we have Lisa Bernstein tell us, we've got custom, but we have a counter-custom. We always do "X" except when we don't. That's how customs tend to be.

Bill Whitford: They're hard to discern.

Stewart Macaulay: Yeah. And just what is it under these circumstances. And she would say, "who's custom are we talking about?" It may be a certain elite in the organization has this, but this is the way ordinary guys do it. But nonetheless, that is a place where you start looking for empirically, how is it done? I still remember the plans for our house, and I'm told they are quite typical this way. The architect didn't draw the windows for the whole house. He had typical windows, and the builder was to take that as kind of the starting point, and then you were to be consistent with that, make the window that would fit in over here. You couldn't just take it and stamp out a one size fits all.

Bill Whitford: You've got to consider the political process, because how is a statute going to be drafted? It's going to be drafted by elites, which was certainly the case of article two of the commercial code; there were some interest groups that got involved, although late, and they had impact. But the early part of article two of the uniform commercial code was strictly an elite-driven process.

Bill Clune: So business oriented?

Bill Whitford: And not interest-group oriented.

Bill Clune: Oh, elite, but not an interest group, okay, yeah.

Bill Whitford: Yeah, elite academics, but also there were some elite lawyers, but they were top of the bar and interested about what would make good law, and then later in the process, interest groups, particularly department stores. Macy's and so forth got involved through their lawyers, but they get involved in a certain interest-group position, a buyer protection kind of approach. A lot of statutes in the contracts area, a lot of statutes are not general like article two, they are particular. And they are very interest-group driven, and they are very law in action driven. That is to say, they really know what goes on on the ground. And we even tell a story of that kind of thing, with a very different kind of a statute. The insurance code would be some kind of in-between, because I think you'd find that Spencer Kimball was attuned to interest groups. He kind of had to be in the insurance area, because legislatures were kind of captive to insurance companies, and he had them involved in the process, but it was nonetheless a comprehensive code.

But a story we tell, which is a different kind of statute, but a kind that probably is more common in the contract area than article two, is the ski hill story. You had a Wisconsin Supreme Court decision, fairly radical, progressive. It dealt with ski hills, where they have you sign a kind of release of liability when you buy the ticket. Like limited liability. And the Wisconsin Supreme Court interpreted those clauses, as what the common law calls exculpatory clauses. Clauses that limit the contractors' liability for negligence. In a way that was almost impossible for the ski hill to win. Or they would have had to redraft their contract clauses. And then we have a story about how the ski hill enterprises, which have influence in the legislature, had to decide whether to go to the legislature and get an act that would reverse that Supreme Court decision.

In fact, what they did was, they complied with the decision. So this is a good example of what you meant, because I was thinking that this story is going to lead to a statute, but it didn't. What it led to was, now something you have to sign, which is a separate document that has in red, it's big and bold, and that complied with the Wisconsin Supreme Court decision, that just says "I agree not to hold the Ski Hill liable even if they are negligent." It uses the word negligence.

Bill Clune: I know I might break my leg, but I agree anyway.

Stewart Macaulay: Yeah, and part of the argument is half the fun of skiing is the risk of breaking your leg! I mean, isn't that what it's all about?

Bill Whitford: But it has to use the word negligence in capital letters and all, but we thought initially they would seek protective legislation. We followed this case when it was on its way up in court, we even had the lawyers in to do a kind of mock argument here before Supreme Court decided the case, right here in Lubar.

Bill Clune: Willard mentions repeatedly that the great majority of legislation is special-interest legislation.

Bill Whitford: That's right. We've got to think of some good examples for them in the contracts and materials there, but there are many, right? Special statutes that are like that, that are even responsive to the decisions, just overturning them. But that's a kind of law in action, different kind of statute, but through the political process. It's not the academic process.

Stewart Macaulay: And there is the point that I would make, that we did, in time, get more and more politics into those contract courses. It was not simply this grand thing handed down by a bunch of British judges long ago. Where this really comes up is kind of the era of Ralph Nader. And you get all of these reforms that are coming along and this kind of thing. And then what happens? And arbitration is one of the things that happens, but there is a whole series of things that we go from that, and now, you look at a world that's quite different on this, and the same thing with employment. The employee at will, and all those kinds of things.

Bill Whitford: Well, the Fullerton lumber story is an excellent story. We could go through that if you want, but that's an example in our materials. Well, it's now in Danzig, but Danzig got it from us.

Bill Clune: Interesting; so I can't resist asking you talk about Fullerton Lumber.

Bill Whitford: We can tell the whole story, it's an old case now. When we started it wasn't an old case. It was 1954, if I remember right. '56? Basically it comes out of Clintonville. This is up northwest of Appleton, and there's a World War II vet who had been employed by a lumber company that had many outlets based in the Twin Cities called Fullerton Lumber that had an outlet in Clintonville, but before he comes back, they're going to put him in a managerial position in Clintonville, and they have him sign a non-compete clause.

He goes to Clintonville, he's very successful, he builds the Fullerton Lumber company up, the outlet there. Come I think, 1954, eight years later, he decides that he can go in business by himself and he's built up the relations with customers, and all this kind of stuff, so he opens up Torborg Lumber and Supply in competition with Fullerton. Takes most of Fullerton's employees, we learned this. You don't learn this in the case, but we learned this in the record in the Supreme Court case. And opens up Torborg Lumber and Supply, so Fullerton sues to enjoin Torborg Lumber and Supply as a violation of the non-compete clause.

They take it all the way up to the Wisconsin Supreme Court, and they win. And in order to win, the Wisconsin Supreme Court has to change common law precedent. The reason Torborg did this, again in a lot of detail about what we call severability, but the clause that he signed, the non-compete clause that he signed was a ten-year clause. There's always been a rule of reason in contract law that non-compete clauses have to be reasonable; if they are unreasonable and excessive, they're unenforceable. This is a principle that goes back even to England, and you could call it a pre-statutory antitrust law, because it had a pro-competitive kind of effect, not so much a protection of the little guy, but more a pro-competitive, or at least that was part of the rationale.

Torborg's lawyer had advised him that under Wisconsin precedent, ten years was excessive, and given that the ten years was excessive, the whole clause would fall. The court wouldn't just modify it down to a reasonable period under existing precedent.

And Wisconsin Supreme Court reverses that precedent, basically, and adopts another common law rule from another state that gives the court the ability to just strike the excessive parts and enforce the rest, so the employer basically won, and they said three years would be reasonable. Ten years was too long. So they enjoined Torborg for three years.

Bill Clune: Three years from, I don't want to get into detail, but how much time had passed already of the three years' time?

Bill Whitford: No, three years from the time of the injunction, so that's a very important point, because already over a year had passed by the time it gets up to the Wisconsin Supreme Court.

So that's what you know from the Wisconsin Supreme Court precedent. It changed the old rule, so casebooks like it, because it shows the old rule, it shows the new rule, so you can kind of teach a lot in one Supreme Court opinion. It has an asinine dissent in the Fullerton Lumber case about the courts shouldn't be making contracts for parties. So you can teach a lot.

Well then, we follow up what happened afterward. Stewart did this research, by contacting the lawyers and stuff, and what we learn is, while the only person enjoined was Torborg, and Torborg Lumber and Company won the competitive battle. I think Fullerton hadn't closed up yet, but their sales had tanked. I think there were three lumberyards in Clintonville, but Torborg was number one. Torborg then filed bankruptcy, he took himself out of the management of the company and substituted his wife, Betsy.

Right?

Stewart Macaulay: He took a job somewhere else, so he wasn't even in Clintonville working, he was off in Appleton as I recall.

Bill Whitford: Green Bay I think, but in any event, commutable, but he transferred his shares. Fullerton was really out to make an example of him; we learned that because not only did they get the injunction, but after they got the injunction they pursued an action for damages, because there had been this year plus when Torberg was not enjoined, and they had lost a lot of sales. They lost that in the court below, because the local judges, they liked Torborg. He was local. And Fullerton took that to Supreme Court, so in the two Supreme Court opinions, they won the judgment for I don't know, $ 36,000 or some kind of damages against Torborg, but Al Torborg got rid of his shares, sold everything, put everything in Betsy's name, and here you get into a lot of uncertainty about how he did this, he was discharged in bankruptcy, but he didn't have any assets; Betsy owned everything. Now that raised a lot of questions for a person like me who teaches creditor and debtor rights, and Fullerton had good lawyers, we know that. They figured out a way to do it, and we didn't research that part.

And then after the injunction period ended, guess what? Al Torborg was the president of Torborg Lumber and Supply again.

Stewart Macaulay: Fullerton at this point left with its tail between the legs.

Bill Whitford: They closed their branch, and we used to have pictures of Torborg from students of Clintonville; they would go by and take pictures standing by Torborg Lumber and Supply, which won the war and lost all the battles, two Supreme Court decisions, but then Stewart followed it up further, because this case got into the legislature, and it showed how legislation works. So the local assembly person from Clintonville, who knew Torborg, he was an important businessman in town, introduces an individual bill that changes the Supreme Court decision on the issue of severability that said even though it was a ten-year covenant, the court could cut it down to a reasonable covenant. And Stewart gets the mark ups, and it's marked up a little by the legislative reference bureau, but ultimately it passes. It's one of these different kinds of legislation we have today, but it's one of these things legislators pushed for constituents and got on the books. It sounded like it was small-businessman oriented, and it basically says if the covenant is excessive in any respect, boom! It's out. I call it the no-divisibility rule.

This is a wonderful thing to teach, because you've got all doctrine in there, but all this law in action stuff. So that statute gets passed, and that really does have some impact on the way covenants are drafted, non-compete clauses are drafted around Wisconsin, because you have to draw them narrowly, because if they go over the line, you end up with nothing. And we teach that, that this little rule about divisibility is probably the most important principle involved, because what you want to do is to get covenants drafted reasonably in the first place.

Stewart Macaulay: And you can make the point that the old way was draft them very broadly, because in a sense, yeah you could knock it down, but you might not do it and it's going to cost you a lot of money, so in effect, even one that could be knocked down would have a deterrent effect—

Bill Whitford: One point was that Fullerton had kind of won the war also, because although Torborg won the war in Clintonville, they sent a message to their managers. They were subject to being held up so to speak, by all their managers and all the successful ones in all these small towns around Wisconsin.

But they taught a message, you can do this if you want, the next Torborg in whatever town, but we're going to go after you with both barrels running. Torborg had to go to the Supreme Court twice and declare bankruptcy. And he won, but a lot of people aren't going to want to do that.

Bill Clune: So like a three-year thing would be okay from there on?

Bill Whitford: Yeah, and you probably make it two years, because what's the most important from the employer's point of view is to have a covenant in those first months when the person is stealing all your business. But the story doesn't even end there, it's a wonderful story from a law in action point of view, because then the Wisconsin Supreme Court changes, and it gets more pro-business, more conservative, and the employers begins to bring cases up from covenants that weren't reasonably drafted. And Gableman writes an important opinion within the last ten years that misinterprets this no-divisibility statute in a really contorted way. It's more complicated than this, but more or less, it put back the original Supreme Court decision in Fullerton Lumber, which I call free divisibility.

Stewart Macaulay: I would never say it in class out loud, but maybe after class, I might ask a question about Justice Gableman.

Bill Whitford: Well what we should have in the materials is just a little note on how much the Wisconsin manufacturers in commerce contributed to his election campaign. That's what we should put in there.

Stewart Macaulay: I kind of think so.

Bill Clune: Doesn't that kind of invite litigation? Since every time there's a possibility of excessive . . .

Bill Whitford: It doesn't, employees just don't challenge the covenant, because they're not going to win the litigation, or at least it's going to be expensive litigation. The nice thing about the no-divisibility statute was you could win on summary judgment. Once we establish that it's excessive, we win. Nothing much to appeal on.

Now there's a whole set of issues, qualitative standards ondivisibility, the whole set of issues that the powerful party can litigate.

Stewart Macaulay: But notice the story we've just been telling; this is the kind of thing you get into a contracts course.

Bill Whitford: Yeah, that's a whole legal process story, totally.

Stewart Macaulay: And that was sure not in my contracts course in the early 1950s, I tell you!

Bill Whitford: But it's a good example to come back to the question you asked on law-in-action-driven statutes. That little story about how this non-divisibility statute got put into the Wisconsin statutes is a story about an awful lot of statutes dealing with contracts, where they come from, and they aren't some academic, elite-driven thing.

It's also a good understanding of the impact of court decisions on the ground, you know? That's what drove this statute, this no divisibility statute, this little assemblyman was a friend of Al Torborg, and he was totally aware of the kinds of things you wouldn't find in that first Supreme Court's decision with Fullerton Lumber. You wouldn't find any of that in there, but the assemblyman knew that.

Bill Clune: What about the lemon law in Wisconsin?

Stewart Macaulay: I had a little responsibility on that, because a student of mine from sociology of law was working for the legislature, and he phoned me and asked, "What did I think of the lemon law?" Because he had sent me a copy of the draft at that point. And I said, "The only thing that strikes me is how do you finance using it?" And so, he responded by going to the Democrat who was working with these things, and put in a rather ample if you win you get attorney fees, which has been cut back since.

Bill Whitford: I used to teach about the lemon laws, it just deals with autos that can't be easily repaired. You already had, as a lawyer, the arguments you needed built into the UCC, and the problem was that they were subject to some interpretation, because they are always filled with a bit of qualitative standards, but there were a number of so-called lemon laws passed around the country. Ostensibly, to give the consumers rights. But really they cut back into some of the arguments possible under the UCC, they were really dealer protection. Auto manufacturer protection, but they vary. Now some lemon laws in fact, expanded on the consumer protections available in the UCC. And they often performed a very important law in action role of calling the buyer's and the public's attention to something that was perhaps already there buried in article two, but lawyers didn't know about it and they weren't advertising, and they weren't generating a case load.

Now a lemon law comes in Wisconsin, and suddenly you get lawyer advertising, and then you've got lawyers just advertising, "I'm the lemon-law king, if you've got a problem with your car, bring it to me." And that is important, but Stewart's quite right, one of the key things you want to look at in the lemon law is whether the consumer is really protected, and they vary. A lot of them contain arbitration, or informal dispute settlement kinds of provisions that you can't bring in court action under the lemon law, unless you've exhausted your administrative remedies, is the concept, but basically, if it's gone through the auto and dealer manufacturer's dispute mechanism, which is often structured to be a series of hurdles, so that you just get tired out. You go one level to another, to another, to another. A little like health insurance companies now do when you dispute some coverage decision.

And others have arbitration provisions that are designed to facilitate consumer remedies, and the industry hates them. An example, I don't know what the law is now, but in New York, where they set it up, it was very easy, quick to get an arbitration, and the arbitrators were appointed, I don't know, by the court somehow. But they were often young attorneys just out of law school. They were hanging their shingle; they weren't employed by the manufacturers. One way to make money was to arbitrate these lemon cases, and they came at a lot of decisions that were very pro-consumer, and the auto manufacturers hated the New York lemon law, where other lemon laws were manufacturer protection. People in those states would have been better off with something from the UCC.

Progressivism in contracts law?

Bill Clune: I've often thought of law in action as having a progressive slant. Of course, special-interest legislation is law in action both when consumers don't win and when we see workable remedies.

Stewart Macaulay: Plea bargaining is law in action, and plea bargaining isn't exactly the way I would like my legal system judged. Conning people into doing various things. It's a game where the first guy to get in and help the prosecutor out gets a much lower sentence.

Bill Whitford: Well yeah. Like everything in the world, Stewart, plea bargaining has its good side and its bad side. Taking the sentencing power away from the judge.

Stewart Macaulay: That's probably the good side.

Bill Whitford: Well, this can be, right? It can be a good thing.

Stewart Macaulay: Yeah, yeah. It depends on what's your objective, but in any event, the point is that law in action could help elites, it can be very power-driven and so forth. It's really a question of how do we deliver, or fail to deliver law?

Bill Whitford: Yeah, I don't think of it as a progressive issue. I think of it as what are you trying to do in law school? I mean, at least in terms of what you're talking about in the curriculum. We haven't talked that much about it, but I mean, what are you trying to do in law school? You can make an argument there. People make it. What you're trying to do in law school is to get people through the bar exam, learn the vocabulary. They come away with a vision of law that's Langdellian. That's okay, that's what law school is supposed to do. Teach how you talk that way. You can distinguish holding and dicta. You can pass the bar exam, and there are other things a lawyer has to know, of course, but that's not law school's responsibility.

Bill Clune: I guess the extent is a progressive theme in your course. It's the unearthing of things that don't look much like the public good. I mean, it's showing who wins and who loses and why.

Bill Whitford: Oh, there's a lot of critique. That's true, because we're progressive. And in some ways, law in action is very progressive. Depends on the circumstance. The classic example are contracts of adhesion, which Kessler had a lot to do with, Kessler and Sharp are one of the predecessors, but in the old Langdellian thing, well it's a contract. They signed it. There might be some issues about whether there was offer and acceptance. That's the agreement process that you, especially with the internet, do by clicking "accept," right? Other than that, that's it!

And that got trashed in the thirties, Llewellyn, but also Kessler, and that's a law in action way of talking about these documents. And it clearly had a progressive impact, because it takes it out of the traditional concept of contract. Political parties agreed, of course.

Bill Clune: So, I'm looking down the list of my questions. What about the question of what topics does the book cover, and how these topics match and differ from other books in the field?

Bill Whitford: I think a good way to articulate it, because it gets onto these things that I sort of feel like we haven't talked about enough. The kinds of compromises you have to make in putting together a first-year course, because of your multiple objectives. But if you look at the difference in book one and book two, as we used to call them, our Contracts One and Contracts Two courses, because what we've done is to push many of the doctrinal problems that would dominate a conventional contracts course into Contracts Two, and you could make arguments for including them in the mandatory contracts course, Contracts One. We touch on offer and acceptance and consideration in Contracts One, but we go in more depth in Contracts Two and we certainly don't go into it in the kind of depth most contracts courses do.

Then, you have the whole issue of interpretation, right?

Stewart Macaulay: Oh, I think that's right.

Bill Whitford: We touch on it just a little, but the in-depth coverage is all in Contracts Two. There's a huge remedies issue called conditions, which is a combination of interpretation and remedies. We don't get into it by name in Contracts One. We get into it because we have the substantial performance rule, right? In chapter two. We get into it conceptually, but not by name and all its parameters until Contracts Two. And then, you have the area that Stewart loves. The unexpected we call it. Impossibility and frustration of purpose, but you know, hurricane whatever comes through and to what extent can parties alter the obligations because the contract doesn't provide for what should happen if a category five hurricane comes through.

We put all this in the second course.

Bill Clune: A little paradoxical, but more doctrinal things go into the second course?

Bill Whitford: Well, we have doctrinal stuff, but I mean, we do it because we've got what? Four credits in the first semester. So we start with remedies, where if you're going to have to teach doctrine, and teach the Langdellian ideology, or whatever, I believe, and I believe Stewart believes, remedies are where you want to start. Because you get right to the expectation principle, and its exceptions, which are the key doctrinal issues. And not what you do when the letter of acceptance crosses in the mail with a letter of abdication, which people like to start with as relatively simple problem, but it's not so important.

So we started off with the tough doctrine. Then we have a big chapter, which is where the relational stuff is. To show the kinds of compromises you have to make, we started off, it's nice, because you can fold in a little offer, acceptance, and consideration into it.

Stewart Macaulay: If you do this, I will give you money.

Bill Whitford: It happens all the time in the extended family, and often mostly it gets worked out without litigation. But you get the occasional case where somebody doesn't like the result they're going to get under a will, and they bring an action as a contract. And you've got a lot of doctrinal cases there. So we're teaching how to use a concept that's often used in relational contracts, any contract embedded in social relations. That's a concept from Mark Granovetter, a famous sociologist, whose kind of the equivalent of Macaulay and Macneil in the sociology field, the grandfather of the school. These cases teach a lot of doctrine, but they are together because of the fact situations. They are all in extended family contexts.

That's why they're in our chapter two. We're teaching all these cases which are embedded in social relations and you have to think about them in that way, the way contracting relates to everything else.

And then as Stewart mentioned, in the same chapter, we go on to employment, franchises, and we have this long note on commercial relations. Now, in book two, the second course, we go much more into commercial relations, which is the heart of the academic literature in relational contracts. And a lot of the thinking about relational contracts takes place in commercial contracts these days. We don't do it except with this long note in our first book. Why? Because these are first-semester students.

The advantage of trying to start with the theoretical point about contracts being embedded in social relations starting off in the family and employment, is that students come to class with some sense of the social context in which those contracts are embedded.

But I'm emphasizing that we've made compromises, because from a theoretical point of view, we like to be talking about commercial contracts. That's what we debate with our colleagues in other law schools. It's in that area. But in a first-semester course, you're trying to do so many things, you can't totally ignore teaching doctrine, which is what we start off with, sort of, because you have to know, that's part of your job, is to teach the holding and dicta, whatever, we try to do it in a more complicated way than just that. But you do need to be able to read an appellate opinion and analyze it. Figure out how it's useful in a legal argument and things like that.

And then we go on, we save our final chapter, it's focused verymuch on consumer transactions, another area of social embeddedness. I mean, another social context people are familiar with, and has a strong regulatory thesis. And that's truly progressive, the most progressive of the book. Is that fair?

Stewart Macaulay: Well it's also got warranties in it, it's got—

Bill Whitford: Oh no, there's a lot of stuff that would be considered to be conventional contract stuff, but we always teach it in the consumer context. The Fullerton Lumber Company case comes up in that context. That's an employment context, but mostly, it's consumer context, and the theme is anti-freedom of contract. That is to say, contract, you need to regulate freedom of contract a bit. Why? Well you have to look at the embeddedness of social context.

Bill Clune: So lemon laws could go in there.

Bill Whitford: Yeah, lemon laws go in there. We talk about a lot of doctrine. I just mentioned the restraint of trade stuff and the non-competes, and there are other rules. The warranty rules start with the common law. They all have their consumer protection aspect to them. Warranty is more complex than just that.

So, we wanted to get that consumer protection perspective. We're teaching a bunch of doctrine about the regulatory rules. A lot of bar review stuff, when you come to warranties and things like that. A lot of Uniform Commercial Code article 2 in that chapter, right?

Stewart Macaulay: Absolutely. And contracts of adhesion.

Bill Clune: What about contracts of adhesion?

Stewart Macaulay: You're talking about the statutes of a private government. Then I think you're much closer to what's going on, and not necessarily a benevolent government.

Bill Whitford: Because of Llewellyn. Llewellyn was appreciative of the fact that contracts of adhesion had to be regulated and it's all in article two. So there's some nice statutory construction stuff. So that's our first-semester course. And we've left out relational contracts in big business, which from our point of view would be the big thing we've left out of the first-semester course. Except for a few notes, like you mentioned about the

Boeing Dreamliners and stuff. But they're kind of like teasers. That focus is on the second book.

Bill Clune: So with EPIC you are deemed to accept the arbitration clause by continuing to work there. This is really saying you don't have any freedom of contract with the employer.

Bill Whitford: We've got these equivalent every day with your credit card. They'll send you, "These are the new terms and conditions now." They're probably just email it to you, but they used to send it in the mail, and there's a provision in there, by continuing the use of your card, you've consented to these new terms and conditions, and the new terms and conditions will include a consumer arbitration clause that you have to arbitrate any disputes, and you can't turn to a class action.

Bill Clune: Arbitration with our sympathizers.

Bill Whitford: And of course, it will also affect your interest rates, because if you're amending that, it will be more boldly disclosed, but the way you agree to new interest rates is by continuing to use your card. Now, when you get the mailing you probably, like most of us, just don't read it through. You just throw it in the wastebasket.

Stewart Macaulay: If you continue to read.

Bill Whitford: Or you could get it on email, and it's just one of those emails you don't open.

Bill Clune: Sometimes they'll say, "Do you want an email of it?" It's kind of like would you want an email of a long, boring document?

Stewart Macaulay: Which you cannot change.

Bill Clune: You cannot change, right.

Bill Whitford: Or you can drop your card.

Stewart Macaulay: That's always open to you if you want to do that.

Bill Whitford: I did that once. It was the year I was kind of off, because I was getting chemo, so I had time, and I read one of these things that came through from a credit card company, and it included a consumer arbitration agreement. So I told them I protest the consumer arbitration agreement. Because I had time, so I read it. And they said fine, we're terminating your card, or I think they didn't terminate the card at the time—

When it expires, your current card expires, we're not renewing it. I think that's what they did.

Bill Clune: So that's probably right, we've got the power, we set the terms.

Bill Whitford: I have my freedom of choice. Fortunately, credit card's a competitive business. If I terminate one card, you end up having to deal with your auto-pays. It's no problem getting another card, right? If your credit rating is up there.

Bill Clune: Yeah. I have agreed to many contracts without knowing it.

Bill Whitford: Somebody sends you a form saying, in the worst examples, "You agree that your first born would be a hostage," or something. "If you tie your shoes in the morning, you've agreed to this contract." You know, if you get a memo from your boss and you're an employee, the odds that you are going to read it are probably higher than if you get something as a filler with your monthly bill from the credit card company.

Bill Clune: So their freedom contract was ability to quit.

Bill Whitford: But that was Jim White's example. There's got to be some limits on this.

The other example that Stewart uses is if you breathe, you agree. But you can't specify something like if you tie your shoes in the morning, you've agreed to this, whatever. Mostly the case-law limitations that have been developed have not proven effective, because today they just have you click on an "I agree" box. Click on this, when you order things you have to click the box that says you accept the terms and conditions. Then click it. That element has very simply eliminated any influence of these decisions that say there's some limit on the ability to specify ordinary human actions as acceptance of terms.

One of the best progressive examples of using form contracts in that context is where you get neutral third parties basically to draft a form contract. An outstanding example of such contracts is the American Institution of Architects where the Trade Association of Architects has drafted a form contract to be used by owners and building contractors, with the architect kind of standing in the middle. And they are still used, right?

Stewart Macaulay: As far as I know.

Bill Whitford: That's not a bad solution, because you want to have a form contract to fill in all the things that you want to just rely on the common law or article two, you know, whatever article. That's not a bad solution, because it doesn't mean you need it to be part of the bargaining; you wouldn't want it to be part of the bargaining between individual contractors, there's too much money going into something that's only marginally important in the terms of the contract.

The Wisconsin contracts book and others

Bill Clune: What does a standard book look like compared to yours?

Bill Whitford: Well, we've left out coverage of a lot of doctrinal areas that make our course seem, to some people, heretical. Particularly, limited coverage of offer and acceptance and consideration. Limited coverage of the whole interpretation area.

Stewart Macaulay: Let's just say, what would a more typical book be? Well, you begin with offer and acceptance, you form a contract. Well, you have to have offer, acceptance, and consideration. And one of the things that always bothered me so much with that is you're taking some of the odd little quirks that don't come up very much, and that's where you begin. And of course, when you're beginning, you're going slow. You're putting big emphasis on it.

Then we have to interpret the contract. And how do we do that? Then we perform the contract, or we don't perform the contract, is the idea. And these finally, because you didn't perform the contract, then it's damages. One of the great problems of all this is in many ways, the hardest thing for many of the students to deal with is damages, because it's numbers.

They went to law school because they weren't good at numbers, you know. So this tough thing, you put it at the end of the course, which means you don't teach much of it.

Bill Whitford: You ran out of time.

Stewart Macaulay: You run out of time for the hardest stuff.

Bill Whitford: And I would even say myself, and Fuller certainly thought that if you want to get at the key theoretical concepts in contract law, it's not freedom of contract, which you can teach in offer and acceptance—that you mean by freedom of contract. It's why you enforce contracts at all. That's the key policy question from a law and economics point of view. And that you get at through teaching remedies. It's what you're trying to achieve by enforcing contract.

Bill Clune: That's expectation damages and stuff?

Stewart Macaulay: Well, yeah. Fuller says that you can have expectation. You could have reliance, and you could have restitution. These are the three big kinds of things.

Bill Whitford: But why expectations? I think the key, from that point of view, from the point of view of debating dogma, doctrine, the key question is, why should somebody earn a profit simply because he was promised it? Why should we protect that? That's the number one question in contract law.

Bill Clune: Why do you say that starting with remedies, and in particular the expectation measure of damages, allows you to get, better than other approaches, to the key policy/theoretical question underlying the law of contracts?

Bill Whitford: The key question is why the law of contracts enforces a "fully executory contract," one that has been agreed to by both parties but has not been performed on either side. Some people regard the breach of a fully executory contract as a moral wrong. That may be, but morality clearly is not the reason the law of contract has chosen to provide a remedy for breach of the fully executory contract. That can be seen by law's adoption of the expectation measure as the basic remedy for breach. Why should we want to put the non-breaching party is as good a situation as performance, when that party has incurred no expense towards its own performance?

Consider, for example, a contract between an actress and a movie studio in which the actress agrees to perform a particular role in a planned movie for a set amount, and then the studio breaches before filming has begun. If the actress wins her entire salary as expectation damages, then she will have received a large amount for doing nothing. We award this remedy nonetheless because we think it is efficient to encourage the actress to rely on the studio's promise. She may have an investment opportunity that she can accept without first waiting for payment, or she need not expend resources searching in advance of performance for contingent employment opportunities for the same time period in the event the studio breaches. We can encourage these kind of reliances by providing her the promised compensation, either through the studio's performance or through damages for breach.

Qualifications on the expectation principle further show that encouragement of reliance on unperformed promises, which is deemed economically efficient, is the true rationale for the law's enforcement of fully executory promises and selection of the expectation principle as the primary measure of damages. One principal qualification is the mitigation principle. If, for example, our actress has another acting opportunity of comparable quality (and for the same time period) presented post-breach, her claim against the studio will be reduced by what she could have earned elsewhere, whether or not she accepts the alternative acting job. This is because she could have protected any possible reliances on the studio's promise by accepting the alternative job, so a rule mitigating her damages in this circumstance does not discourage her possible reliance on the studio's promise. The mitigation principle ignores immorality of the breach, if any. The law of contract clearly thinks there is nothing wrong with breaking a promise if it causes no damage as measured by the expectation principle.

Starting a contracts course with remedies makes it much easier to focus a student's attention on the contrast between an efficiency and a moral rationale for the law's rules. Nothing in the law's rules of offer and acceptance illustrate the distinction so well.

Stewart Macaulay: And, recognize again, as delivered, it's almost a freak situation that you'll get the profit.

Bill Whitford: Well that's true, we teach it that way, because we start off in the law in action aspect, starting with remedies.

Stewart Macaulay: Absolutely, I want to raise the question, but I also want to come around very quickly and say, in a sense we've got the two great meta principles. One of them is, dammit, a deal is a deal and if you can't carry it out, by God, you've sinned! You know, this is terrible! Another is—

Bill Whitford: A man's word is his vow.

Stewart Macaulay: Exactly! The other is, the world changes, you've got a little give and take.

Bill Whitford: We start teaching the exceptions to the expectation rule right in the very first case, which introduces the mitigation doctrine. It's doctrinally the big exception. And in the second case, we introduce the big law in action point. Yeah, you're going to get your expectation damages, but no attorney fees. So we're talking about the exceptions right from the beginning. But at least we're starting off with that theoretical issue.

Bill Clune: What is the mitigation issue?

Bill Whitford: Yeah, you're going to get your expectation damages, but if you could've avoided the loss by reasonable actions you don't get them.

The mitigation rule is a huge exception, doctrinally, and then we ultimately come to Hadley and Baxendale, which is another famous exception to the expectations principle.

Stewart Macaulay: And then there are damages with reasonable certainty.

Bill Whitford: We get into that and then—

Stewart Macaulay: It turns into being a huge kind of thing. What do you mean by reasonable certainty? And that gets you into new businesses. What's a new business? If it's an established company, are they a new business when it's a new product?

Bill Whitford: A traditional doctrinal book like Murray follows the chronological approach and is just oriented towards bar review. He doesn't even do a good job of introducing you to the complexities of how you interpret a case, because he edits the cases down so that you're not really having to deal with the difficulties of case interpretation, but let's leave that aside.

In our course, the way we start is with remedies. We ask an awful lot of the students in that first chapter. This is a criticism that Stewart and I have faced often with the materials.

Stewart Macaulay: You bet.

Bill Whitford: And we're doing it in the first weeks. And the doctrine is hard, if we just focused on the doctrine, which involves some simplified law and economics where you very studiously stay away from any of the terminology, but you have to understand that the idea, the expectation damage is to get people, not just an incentive to perform, but to encourage people to rely on contracts, because they're either going to get performance, or they get the equivalent of it. You start introducing some of this kind of thinking, and we're introducing all the law in action, all the exceptions, all the practical stuff, and we haven't even talked about the most difficult doctrinal thing.

And then you get into restitution, and restitution is one of these early realist things where you have two rules, you have expectation and reliance as a kind of a corollary. And then, you have restitution, this kind of comes from a totally different sense of justice. It doesn't have to do with expectation thinking; it is totally different. And there are cases where the restitution line of cases conflict with the expectation line of cases. And how do you resolve that conflict? And you know, it's fairly deep thinking, and it's really difficult.

Stewart Macaulay: In Great Britain they had the courts of law and the courts of equity. It's part of the legacy of that.

Bill Whitford: The restitution materials, at least the way I taught the course, is a place where I really hammered on the idea that students bring with them, and was part of the Langdellian tradition, that law is all a seamless web. You find it in some of the law and economic stuff now, you know? It all makes sense, it's seamless. It's like Willard talks about geometry course and the corollaries all make sense. There are a few cases where the judges got it wrong, but it all makes sense, and then we hit the restitution line of cases, and they just are in conflict with the expectation line of cases, and it doesn't all make sense. And you might have to make compromises, and the law can be an ass. It can have some results that are just crazy, and we have some of those results, like *Oliver v. Campbell*. In the hypothetical version of the case, where the lawyer recovers the full $ 5,000, it's just kind of silly, it seems like, but the doctrine fairly points in that direction.

Stewart Macaulay: Yeah, and one of the things about the traditional approach, there aren't a lot of cases. You get one or two cases and you've got it. This sort of thing, and it sounds like you're giving answers. That's one of the things where our students will get very upset by our materials. At least in my experience, because, what is it I'm supposed to learn? I mean, there's this thing, but then you tell me that isn't always true!

Bill Whitford: And then the student knows that you will examine him/her, how am I going to write the exam, they ask?

Stewart Macaulay: That's right.

"Law in action/policy questions" on contracts exams

Bill Whitford: And after the exam, we're going to judge you on what we regard as the quality of your arguments, and the quality of the arguments is not the way an English professor would do it. A way that a judge, or an educated lawyer would think is that it's a persuasive argument, because we're always putting them in that position of arguing for a client. We aren't so law in action, well we are occasionally, but not usually on the exams.

Does law have any ability to impact the behavior of private contractors—that would be a law in action question. We've had questions like that, and they're hard to grade.

Stewart Macaulay: Very hard to grade.

Bill Whitford: But an easier grade is what would an educated lawyer regard as a persuasive legal argument in some fact situation. You can work law in action into the argument, but you have to figure out how to work it in.

I always have had a question on my exams that was oriented towards the policy and law in action side. I usually tried to build a few little benchmark things into those question which you really should mention in the answer. I can use those to have a little objectivity in how I graded those. And I gave a four-hour exam, and it was forty-five minutes or an hour. So it was not the major part of the exam. But I did it.

Because I knew students looked at the exams in the next year in order to know what they should study.

Bill Clune: Forget about all that law in action.

Bill Whitford: I didn't want to signal that. I wanted to signal just the opposite, and that's why I was kind of insistent on always including one question like that. Not that it helped me on my chore of ranking students from top to bottom. It didn't help me very much.

Bill Clune: So I fear I am running out of your patience and time with you, so next questions: where does the knowledge about law in action in the book and in the course come from? Empirical research anecdotes? And was there discomfort among students with a law in action approach? Those are two different questions.

Bill Whitford: The first one is easy. All of the above, right? I mean an awful lot ofit is anecdotes, but if we can find empirical research, systematic empirical research, usually qualitative, not quantitative, fine. Great. Sometimes it gets harder to incorporate into the casebook format. We tend to try to stay away from methodological issues in a Contracts I course.

Bill Clune: Well, the relational contracts area started with some well-known research by Stewart Macaulay and others.

Bill Whitford: It started anecdotally. It was more qualitative research.

Stewart Macaulay: Yeah, anecdote's okay, but in the sense that I had certainly gone out and done empirical research.

Bill Whitford: Well you had, although what we included in the materials was very often just your interview snippet, right?

Stewart Macaulay: Yeah, yeah.

Bill Whitford: Then there was this story about the Boeing 787, there was a story. Usually not such a complicated story.

Bill Clune: Another thing you mentioned is digging into case—

Bill Whitford: Individually.

Bill Clune: And background.

Bill Whitford: Yeah, and we did that anecdote about Fullerton Lumber, and we use it for so many wonderful things. Remember when Danzig took it out of the book?

Stewart Macaulay: Yes.

Bill Whitford: We just put it back in, remember? We got permission, I guess. It did so many things.

Use of the Contracts Law in Action book and approach at Wisconsin and other law schools

Bill Clune: I can't remember, does the article talk about the places that adopted it other than Wisconsin?

Bill Whitford: No, no, I'd have to get you that data.

Bill Clune: Roughly, like how many law schools, what kind of law schools? Anything you can think of as a—

Bill Whitford: Well, we were the only place where it became used in all the sections.

We talked a little about that in this article, and that I think was important to its acceptance at Wisconsin, amongst other things. We were kind of immune from the argument for years about why are you teaching contracts this way? This doesn't help me for the bar review course. To use our materials in another law school, you're teaching a very different contracts course, and as a teacher, you're always being held up that way, and that can be a problem.

Stewart Macaulay: But there were at least four or five people that used them quite regularly for a long time.

Bill Whitford: Ten to twelve.

Stewart Macaulay: Well yeah, but I'm thinking of four or five who really—

Bill Whitford: Well, I think you should expand it at ten just because you're remembering four or five, but I think there were more. But anyway, we could go through a few of the names. I mean, certainly Jean Braucher was, she taught at Cincinnati, and then Arizona, and became a co-editor in the book and always used the materials and became one of the team. And then Sandy Meiklejohn at Quinnipiac, who else are you thinking of? The guys at Denver, it began with "T."

Stewart Macaulay: Tom Russell, legal historian. It'll come to me. What's my name again?

Bill Whitford: There's two or three—

Bill Clune: And Lipson.

Bill Whitford: Lipson, well he started using it here when he came here, and now he still uses it. Went back at Temple—

Bill Clune: And Hendley, you've got Kathryn Hendley. Well, she's here.

Bill Whitford: She's here. And Mitra Sharafi uses it here, but there were a couple other people at Temple, and a guy at Rutgers, Camden, it was a very good guy. Jay Feinman. There was a guy at Rutgers, Alan Hyde, employment guy, regularly used it. There was a guy at Hastings, now at Fordham, Ethan Leib.

I don't think he teaches contracts anymore. There are a couple of guys at Miami, Rob Rosen, and there were some others at Miami. Bob Gordon used it when he taught contracts, but that's quite some time ago that he even taught contracts. Carl Bjerre at Oregon uses it when he teaches contracts. We're forgetting some people.

Bill Clune: Some of these people were very closely connected with Wisconsin. You may consider Wisconsin diaspora or network or something. Other people just adopt it.

Bill Whitford: That's right, yeah. Others just adopted it on their own, and to the extent that we had connections with them, we met them through that.

Stewart Macaulay: And we did a couple of times stage a conference here, that was the nice thing about having the contracts fund with the royalties for the book to be able to do this, and we brought people to ask what do you want in the next edition? That was the kind of basic question we were asking them. And of course, to me it was fascinating, it was more law in action. They were always pushing to give us more detail about where these cases come from, what they're like and so on. But of course, that was so like predictable . . . We selected the people who would take that position.

Bill Whitford: There's a guy in New England who's always used it. Peter Enrich. One thing about the casebook that I think of is historically important, but different from most casebooks: From the very beginning, the first edition, we've assigned all royalties, we've never gotten them personally, to something that's now called the Contract Enrichment Fund, and it's run by the UW foundation, accounting-wise. For the enrichment of contracts, more or less, and that fund has been used by our research assistants, copyeditors for the book, and to run a variety of conferences. Including Stewart's festschrift in that book that was produced.

And it still exists out there. It funds the Kidwell lectures, but now it doesn't do much else. Seriously. It's helped us maintain this fellowship, that's what Stewart's comment reminded me of. I don't think you'll find very many casebooks like that. At least in my case, one of the motivations in setting this up was that for years, 50 percent of the purchasers of the materials were right here at Wisconsin. 50 percent is approximate. And we were requiring it of students, and I just felt guilty about keeping the royalties.

Stewart Macaulay: Right with you on that.

Bill Whitford: Guilty about personally profiting from requiring my students to buy. I didn't have any control over the market price. I couldn't go through the publishers and say, "You have to discount the price for Wisconsin students."

Bill Clune: Yeah, that's very good. Not that it's necessarily uncommon out there among a lot of professors to assign their own books, right?

Stewart Macaulay: And of course, this thing now, $ 190.

Bill Whitford: Well, the prices are ridiculous. We first started, this story is told in here, is how we move from duplicated materials to commercially published, and we had to choose a casebook publisher, and we had an offer from Foundation Press, considered to be the principal, the largest casebook publisher, but this little publisher out of Virginia called Michie, offered us much better copyediting.

So we went with them, and we needed the copyediting, but this is another limitation of the expectation principle, they promised all this copyediting, and they didn't deliver.

Stewart Macaulay: We were in a good position to sue them!

Bill Whitford: There wasn't a good remedy in contract law, and so what we learned is we had to do the copyediting right here in house, after that first go-around.

Bill Clune: Based on your own law in action.

Bill Whitford: Kidwell was the main actor in that department while he was alive.

Bill Clune: So, what about now, is there any discomfort among the students? For example, social science, not law, and how did you handle it?

Bill Whitford: I think there definitely was discomfort, but I think we were helped through Wisconsin, because everybody taught it.

Stewart Macaulay: You had that, and you had also, I think, that so much of it was the law in action part, was you could feed right in. We're teaching you to be lawyers. This is what lawyers do.

Bill Whitford: Those were the kinds of arguments we made. And we were helped by the fact that law in action is so pervasive, not just in the contracts, but in so much else of the curriculum here at Wisconsin, so it doesn't seem, you didn't get as much of, "this is not what I came to law school for." As you might elsewhere.

I had this experience at Boston University. I visited there one semester in the 80s. It was a spring semester; I didn't teach contracts. I was brought in to teach, my main course was the garden-variety soup-to-nuts, UCC course. Article two through article nine. It was a bar review course, taken by second or third year students at BU. But I did articles three, four, five, I think, but I didn't cover seven. You always didn't teach eight, this is more than you need to know. Eight is really taught in a securities' law course.

And I tried to introduce a little of our law in action kind of approach, especially with article two. It was a very hard sell at BU. Partly, it was that I had over one hundred students, about, but why were they taking it? Because they were preparing for a bar exam, and the UCC is all over the bar exam. So it was partly, in any law school, it would have been a bad audience, but I felt it was partly because they're not prepared by getting this kind of stuff in their other classes at Boston University. It wasn't just the particular students who were taking it, but it was also the institution to some extent.

Bill Clune: So we could talk about an organizational culture of law in action.

Bill Whitford: Yeah, I think we had a critical mass here, you know? It affected the acceptability.

Contract drafting vs. standardized contracts

Bill Clune: It makes me realize one thing we haven't talked about. Oddly, it seems like you're talking all about litigation, you haven't talked about contract drafting.

Stewart Macaulay: Yeah, that's quite true.

Bill Whitford: We don't talk about it as much as maybe we should. That's been a movement in the contracts field around the country to focus entirely on drafting, and everything gets boiled down into how does it affect the ultimate drafting decision. Not how a judge would decide the case, but how would the contract drafter respond to all this information.

I'm not against that way of thinking but to think of that as the whole picture is to lose an awful lot.

And I would say the way they're teaching this, how you design a contract, design literature, it's called, they're all imagining big Wall Street firms with no real financial restrictions, how much resources they put into drafting a contract, how you would do it in some kind of ideal world. That's the milieu they're thinking about. And an awful lot of contracts aren't drafted in that kind of context.

Bill Clune: You just go with contracts of adhesion, which are drafted.

Bill Whitford: Yeah, and you think about poor Al Torborg, who comes back from World War II, and he gets thrown a document in front of him that says, "sign this, and we're going to make you a manager." Sounds like a good job, right? And he signs a ten-year covenant. He had no idea that he even signed it, let alone what it means, until after he gets to Clintonville and discovers he's a pretty goddam good small-town lumber mill manager, and he's not making enough money, and Fullerton, they're making a lot of money off of my skills.

Stewart Macaulay: And when he talks to his lawyer, his lawyer says, "This is no good!" That is part of this story also, how Torborg checked with a lawyer on this, and the lawyer said, "It's no good."

Bill Whitford: Yeah, in fact, the lawyer might have been the friend of the assemblyman who started the legislation, not so much Al. But the lawyer was embarrassed about the fact that he gave the bad legal advice.

Stewart Macaulay: Which was good legal advice in the sense that he probably fought for it!

Bill Whitford: Only bad from a point of view of hindsight!

Bill Clune: One of the odd things about the stories you've told, I think of law and economics, is that a lot of contracts and contract holdings are anti-competitive, they're not efficient, they're anti-efficient. The lumber story being one of them.

Bill Whitford: Of course. You can't escape your Marxism, I mean, the ultimate tendency in capitalism is to monopoly, right? Or something like that. Any particular contract actor is not interested in more competition; they're interested in less competition.

Stewart Macaulay: Absolutely!

Bill Whitford: Well, Josh Whitford worked in the supply chain stuff. Turns out some interesting examples, because he finds some of these, the original equipment manufacturers. The supply chain literature comes from when the vertical integration method of organizing industrial production broke down, so even Boeing has got all these suppliers. It used to be that General Motors made their own clutches, made their own brakes, made their own transmissions, all these things. Those days are long gone.

But according to Josh, the original equipment manufacturers, when they are picking, it's all contract, but it's all carefully controlled contract, but when they're picking suppliers, they are interested in having suppliers that are not totally dependent on them. So they want their suppliers to limit the percentage of their output that any one original equipment manufacturer buys. Why? Well because, if they decide to cut their orders because of some dip in the sales, or whatever, they don't want to kill the supplier.

They want the supplier still to be out there so that they be available in the future.

It's forcing the suppliers to share their technology. A supplier might be a very good supplier. It has a real unique technology, which, if you could capture all of it, it would give you a competitive advantage, an increase in demand for your product, but it also inhibits your flexibility.

Maintaining the competition is the result. So, Josh writes about that tension.

Bill Clune: Okay you guys, what a wonderful tour of the magical kingdom of law in action and contracts. I'm kind of dazzled at this point. I will have a transcript made and make it available to you, with no obligation to read it all over again, and we will go on from there.

Stewart Macaulay: Wonderful group of people to hang out with, and—

Bill Whitford: Bill, here's footnote nineteen of the article, you asked where it's been adopted and that we list it.

Bill Clune: You know, you talked about the sacred; when I think back to my first-year contracts course, there was something exhilarating thinking about free and equal parties entering into agreements to benefit them both. It was kind of up there in the clouds, I guess.

Bill Whitford: It was; it's very much arguing you know, arguing about applying principles, but that's clearly true. Law and economics has gotten onto it because this is where the geometry is playing, now it's algebra, I mean, or calculus. I mean you can't really have a publishable article unless the middle two-thirds of it is a bunch of equations. And all that works if you make certain assumptions about human motivations.

Stewart Macaulay: Assuming perfect competition, assuming zero transaction costs, I mean get things like that.

Bill Whitford: Rationality, people are profit maximizing, they don't care about anything else, they have unlimited time to figure things out.

My old law school classmate, Alan Schwartz, is probably the parody of formalist law and economics. The classic example, probably.

Stewart Macaulay: Yeah, I think so.

Bill Whitford: We were in the same law school class. He always advocated that you should teach algebra in first semester law school, and he's at Yale; probably algebra and calculus, because you can't really study law without knowing how to do this stuff.

Bill Clune: You can't really study law without calculus. Har, har.

Bill Whitford: We used to have these arguments about accounting in the first semester. All lawyers should know accounting. Well—

Bill Clune: We had a little accounting course. It was a revelation to me as a literature major.

Bill Whitford: In the practice of business law, there's some utility to that. But to have to know algebra and calculus is ridiculous!

Stewart Macaulay: So many of us went to law school because we didn't want to do math.

Bill Whitford: The only thing you really need to know it for is to read this literature, which appears in the best reviews.

Stewart Macaulay: That's right, that's right.

Bill Whitford: And I have to confess that I don't even bother with most of those articles. And I could take a remedial course, I was a math major in college, so at one time I used to know how to do that stuff. I don't know how to do it anymore.

Bill Clune: But that's the neo-Langdellian part. All you need to do is read formal logic or math, and you understand all you need to know about contract doctrine.

Bill Whitford: That's true. I mean, in the purest form, we're probably parodying Langdell. I would say in the debates of the school I grew up in, usually Williston substituted for Langdell.

Stewart Macaulay: But the thing I find fascinating, is that Williston was a great progressive.

Bill Whitford: He was, and in contracts, he was, but I mean, we used to parody him, Williston versus Corbin, and Williston as the formalist, but he was in his day kind of a legal realist. There is this kind of legal revisionist literature about Williston, and so now I use Langdell as my bad guy.

Bill Clune: Well, Langdell was a botanist by training. As was Williston.

Stewart Macaulay: There are institutions called law schools. They're part of universities. We're always at a little peril, but they're not closing the doors tomorrow afternoon. These were people trying to create a place to study law in university, and what's new? They were facing a viewpoint where there's no place in the university for schools of fencing, dancing, or law.

Bill Clune: That's Langdell, right? Because the history of the Harvard Law School he was wrapped up with the effort to transform legal education from an apprenticeship to a science.

Stewart Macaulay: Yeah, yeah. And you had to have some principles. You had to have something that was obviously a university, and again, it was an era in which sort of applied philosophy was essentially what you had.

Bill Whitford: I mean in one step you've got . . . The teaching of principles was so economical; you could have the large classes—

Stewart Macaulay: Oh, and that was very important.

Bill Whitford: That gave the law school kind of its own cash cow, a protection in the university setting—

Because if you tried to make it like the medical school, with lots and lots of clinical built in, you know, they would have been pushed out and said, why don't you just stay with apprenticeship?

Bill Clune: Right. That's a good note to end on. Thanks so much. This was brilliant.

Interview of Cecilia Klingele and Keith Findley by Bill Clune

Abstract

This interview with Professors Cecelia Klingele and Keith Findley is about the course they teach, Introduction to Criminal Procedure, which is the modern version of the course on Criminal Justice Administration developed by Frank Remington and Herman Goldstein. The course emphasizes exposure to the whole system of criminal justice in chronological sequence, the ubiquitous prevalence of discretionary decision-making, disparate impacts on population sub- groups, and criminal justice reform.

Whereas traditional courses in criminal procedure are organized doctrinally, Fourth Amendment, Fifth Amendment, and Sixth Amendment, this course is organized sequentially and introduces Supreme Court cases as they relate to each phase. The chronological phases reviewed in the course begin with how crimes are recognized in the system, the decision to investigate and investigative methods—call and response, proactive policing like stop and frisk, undercover investigations and surveillance, and problem-oriented policing. Then follows the decision to charge, roles of the lawyer and prosecutor, pre-trial discovery practice, including disclosure decisions by the prosecutor, plea-bargaining, the plea, plea negotiations, what plea to offer, a bit on trials (very few occur relative to pleas), sentencing decisions by the prosecutor, and, time permitting, sentencing decisions by the court. The course covers the important Supreme Court cases as they relate to the chronological stages, but fewer cases are included than in traditional courses because these cases are considered as remote from the real practice of criminal law and are rarely encountered in discussions withpractitioners.

The course emphasizes the central role of discretionary decision-making. Discretionary decision-making feels uncertain for students, and discretion is a difficult concept involving reasoned judgment between competing legal principles, rather than arbitrary, unmoored or biased judgments. In the final examination for the course, students must engage with the legal sources that guide discretion, such as the supplemental statute pack, ethical principles, and ABA standards. The teachers strive to convince students that formulation of policies and standards, such as use-of-force policies, and differences between policies, can make a real difference.

Students have direct experience of how discretion operates through non-classroom activities such as police ride-alongs and simulated plea bargaining, assisted by the observations and commentary of prosecutors, judges, and defense lawyers. In addition, four evening discussion panels are mandatory—on policing (with police chiefs), prosecutors, defense attorneys, and judges. Students get to ask questions. Panelists discuss their roles and the exercise of discretion. All of these activities are generally well received by students.

Disparate impacts on sub-groups and criminal justice reform are emphasized throughout the course. Professor Klingele made anonymized slides of quotes from observations of students in their police ride-alongs for discussion in class. Students can see their classmates talking about such issues as profiling or where economic disparity played a role in someone being entangled in crime in some way. Inequalities also appear in the details of police investigation, appointment of counsel, and standards for indigency. In computing who qualifies for appointed counsel, students see that it is only the truly destitute who qualify and that there is a large middle group of non-affluent people who will be unable to afford an attorney. Further on disparate impact, the materials include sections on stop and frisk, the use of force by police, and mass incarceration and its causes.

The course requires and conveys extensive empirical knowledge about the realities of the practice of criminal justice. Both professors are consumers of social science research which they naturally bring into their teaching. They also have extensive contact with and observation of the system and its various actors, for example, informal interactions with police and prosecutors, and service with various agencies and groups, such as the Police and Fire Commission, the Board of Public Defenders, and the Children and Family Youth Justice Bureau. The non-classroom activities experienced by students in the course require regular interactions by the professors with police, lawyers, prosecutors, and judges. Thus, the empirical knowledge base of the course comes from both formal and informal research, much of the latter embedded in continuing experience in the field.

Bill Clune: Recording. Transcription usually works well. I'll send it to you when it's done. I guess we can begin. So, first question, what does the book cover, and your teaching, how does it match other books, how has it changed over the years? And is it used elsewhere?

Cecelia Klingele: Sure, I can answer that. First of all, it is currently not used elsewhere. Every once in a while, people ask me if I want to turn it into something for national consumption, so far my answer is, "No, I don't have time to do that." Plus, we have tried to retain a little bit of a Wisconsin emphasis, and I'd have to give a lot of thought to how to convert that to a national book without losing what we have that I like.

Bill Clune: Go ahead, sure.

Cecelia Klingele: I should have brought the book. Do you have a copy of the book?

Bill Clune: Oh, no. I could have–

Cecelia Klingele: I can send you one, if you don't have–

Bill Clune: Yeah, I have it. Yeah.

Cecelia Klingele: You can see the table of contents, the basic answer is that we cover important exercises of discretion in the law, discretionary decision points, beginning with the Commission of Crime, all the way through . . . There is a chapter on correctional supervision, but we rarely get to it, just because there's so much ground to cover in this class. Then we go through from Commission of Crime to the decision to investigate, investigative methods, decision to charge; I'm skipping over all the policing stuff, there are a lot of mini questions in there. Then role of the lawyer, decision to charge, discovery practice during the criminal process, including disclosure decisions by the prosecutor, the plea, plea negotiations, and what plea to offer.

Keith Findley: Then we have the role of counsel of both the prosecutor and the defense lawyer.

Cecelia Klingele: Right before decision to charge, I think, is where we did that to introduce the role of the lawyer and it has some ethics pieces to it. Then after plea negotiation, then we have a little bit on trial–they shouldn't do a ton on trial because there aren't a lot of trials–sentencing decisions, and then correctional decisions. Again, that's a chapter that we often don't get to really cover because we run out of time.

Bill Clune: How different is this from other approaches to criminal procedure?

Cecelia Klingele: Many of the schools have two crim. pro. classes, there's the investigation and then adjudication. One is going to go from reporting of crime and investigation issues to the Fourth, Fifth, Sixth Amendment stuff. Then the other one is the bail to jail class: it's going to cover trial practice. Actually, it usually goes past jail and does a little bit of appellate process and sometimes even habeas process, too.

Keith Findley: Most of my experience, at least, is most of the traditional criminal procedure courses are organized doctrinally, Fourth Amendment, now we're going to study Fifth Amendment, whereas our course is not. Our course is organized sequentially as you work your way through the criminal justice system. It doesn't artificially compartmentalize things under doctrine, but rather, addresses them as they come up in context of investigating or litigating a criminal case.

Cecelia Klingele: First we go to crime and crime reporting, we talk about the universe of crime, how much bigger it is than is ever reported or detected or processed. The first question we really look at is how does crime come to the attention of the criminal justice system. We break it down into four parts, let's see if I can remember them. First is call-response: somebody calls and tells the cops to come, and we talk about what are the pros and cons of that approach, resource constraints, how much . . . We look at 911 calls and what percentage of them are false 911 calls and how police can be driven that way. The second is police go out and find it on their own, so that's where you introduce *Terry* and stop and frisk, and you get some of that Fourth Amendment case law in there, but thinking about it in the context of "how do we find out about crime?"

Third is undercover investigations, and so we do a unit about how police go out and try to find it, but they do it stealthily, and what's the law on that, and of course, there's not much law on that. We talk about the importance of these decisions, including the decision to employ civilian informants, the dangers of that, and how little regulation there is of that practice. Then finally, we talk about problem-oriented policing and community-based approaches, but also look specifically at some of Herman's work on identifying crimes as problems and responding more proactively, rather than the reactive call-response method. That's how we're trying to get some of those doctrinal points in there, we don't want them to leave the class unfamiliar with the really big constitutional cases, but I always tell them, if there's anything specific you want to know more doctrine about, we have advanced classes for that.

We have policing classes, we have four, five, six, we have sentencing and corrections, but the idea here is to give you an overarching view of how the system operates and the interrelatedness of the decisions made at different points along this chronological timeline.

Bill Clune: Okay.

Keith Findley: So one of the consequences is that we spend a lot more time looking at policing, I think, as a study, than does most criminal procedure . . . Most criminal procedure courses, to my understanding, only view policing to the extent that it affects Fourth Amendment or Fifth

Amendment. Whereas we look at it more systematically and that's sort of the law in action angle. As Cecelia was describing, it occurred to me, one way you can understand the difference in the way we teach it is that if you're going to organize the course doctrinally, you're going to start the Fourth Amendment typically with a discussion of *Katz v. United States*, which answers the fundamental question, "What is a search?" We don't start with *Katz* because we start with when does the law encounter Fourth Amendment issues, and that is with investigative stops. Well, that's *Terry v. Ohio*. So, you understand Fourth Amendment doctrine evolving in the context of how it actually applies in the street, rather than purely from a theoretical perspective.

Bill Clune: Okay.

Keith Findley: I don't know if that makes sense to you.

Bill Clune: It does, absolutely. You mentioned the problem thing, in Herman's interview, one thing he says is that an awful lot of what police do doesn't result in arrest, they do other things with people, like he uses the old example of putting drunks in jail, which then got changed to taking them to detox, and so on.

Cecelia Klingele: Unless detox is full, in which case we take the drunks to jail.

Bill Clune: You get into that?

Keith Findley: Yep.

Bill Clune: Yeah.

Cecelia Klingele: Yeah, the decision to arrest is another of the discretionary decision points that we emphasize, and we talk about arrest and its multiple purposes.

Bill Clune: Okay.

Keith Findley: If you're looking at it only doctrinally, you're going to miss so much of the criminal justice system that doesn't invoke the formal criminal justice apparatus of the courtroom. Our approach, in order to understand how criminal justice is actually administered, you need to go beyond just those cases that actually get reviewed by courts.

Cecelia Klingele: We talk about that a lot in the context of the exclusionary rule, too. We talk about how the exclusionary rule is premised on the principle that law enforcement, their goal, is to have successful criminal prosecution, and therefore they'll be deterred by the prospect of exclusion. Of course, there are many cases in which that's the case, but there are also lots of cases where no one cares if it gets prosecuted or not. They want to get the gun off the kid who shouldn't be running around the streets with a gun, and whether he ends up prosecuted is peripheral. In those cases, the exclusionary rule does nothing.

Bill Clune: Herman talks a lot also about the experience with prostitution in Detroit, right?

Keith Findley: We still talk about that, at least I do. Where the exclusionary rule is completely irrelevant to controlling what is unlawful police misconduct because they had no intention of ever charging these prostitutes, and so it's never subject to judicial scrutiny. So, it really engages the students in thinking more broadly about the limits of law—

Bill Clune: The police don't do that. Just take them in jail for a night and let them loose.

Cecelia Klingele: The whole nature of policing prostitution has changed because so much of it now is online and the meetings take place all in private residences. That said, there certainly are cities where there still is a very public presence for prostitutes, and not much has changed.

Bill Clune: People do complain about it as a nuisance sort of thing. I was interested in what you said about starting with a discretionary decision about what to do about crime.

Keith Findley: What to pursue.

Cecelia Klingele: That goes with the idea of police making choices about where to look for crime, and sometimes they just go where the calls lead and sometimes they actively try to find stuff, and other times, they solve problems, but we want them to see right away from the beginning that it's not like the criminal justice system passively encounters all of it. There are decisions being made about how to use limited resources and how to allocate legal authority, from the very get-go.

Once they get that, it becomes much easier to engage [students] in conversations later about things like disparate impact on minorities and racial disparities within the criminal justice system, because they already have a framework for seeing that where the police go is a choice in many cases.

Bill Clune: Okay, that was great. Now, how has the content of these materials changed over time? It sounds like an awful lot of what was there originally is still there.

Cecelia Klingele: We've tried to keep, I think, the core goals, and focus, and frameworks, but the order of the materials and the way it's set up has changed a lot. When I redid the materials, gosh, how many years ago is that now? A lot.

Keith Findley: You had redone them when I started teaching this in 2012.

Cecelia Klingele: Okay, so I think I had redone them in, gosh, maybe 2011.

Keith Findley: Probably.

Cecelia Klingele: Yeah, I bet I did. When I first redid them in 2011, and then we updated it again I think in 2015—

Keith Findley: We've done periodic tweaks, but no major overhauls since then.

Cecelia Klingele: No. The materials had been subject to lots of periodic tweaks before, for probably twenty years, and so, they were just a little . . . They were cluttered, there was a lot . . . There were a lot of news articles that were twenty years old, and things of that nature where we just felt like, gosh, there were better, fresher examples that would resonate with students that we wanted to draw on. There also were just little places where there was material that may once have seemed timely or relevant, but no one could remember why we were teaching it. My goal was to clean it up to make it feel fresh and current for the students. There was a time when the New York stop-and-frisk litigation was going on, there was just so much to draw on, it seemed like a good time, so we did that.

When I did it, I did go back and look at the original hardcover book and many other earlier versions. I talked with Walter and contemplated reorganizing it, going back to the problem-based model to try to follow the case examples like they had done. It was just really hard to think how we were going to be able to cover the foundational materials the students needed to be able to go into prosecutors' offices or defense offices feeling competent—or at least ready to learn—without organizing it a little more chronologically. Obviously, there's just more law in many ways. We tried to keep the model of teaching them many kinds of law, not just constitutional law, so that flagship constitutional cases are scattered throughout, but we also have regulations, and we have ethics rules, and we have ADA standards.

Keith Findley: Statutes.

Cecelia Klingele: Statutes. What we want them to do, is be able to leave that class with a sense of where you look for guidance, both for control and authority, but also for guidance on how to exercise discretion well. We talk about internal policies and have several examples of policies. I actually want to add, for discussion at least, the new Philadelphia charging policies, which I have a copy of. So, we want them to see models of what good guidance looks like, and I know a lot of that comes out of the spirit of the original materials, which was really looking to administrative law and policy within departments to guide discretion.

Bill Clune: Right. Is there still a Problem-Oriented Policing course of the kind that Herman offered?

Cecelia Klingele: No. But I do teach a course on the Role of Police in a Free Society in alternate years. When Michael Scott took over, he taught two courses, one was Role of Police in a Free Society—Herman's flagship course—and then he did a seminar that partnered students with police agencies. In that, they had to come up with a problem to solve with the police, which seemed like a great class. When he left, obviously we lost those classes. Then we actually lost Role of Police, I think, for almost four years. It may have been four years. This was when national interest in policing was going through the roof and all of a sudden, we'd been teaching it when no one was teaching it and we weren't teaching it any more. It just seemed wrong, so I offered to take that on. I certainly don't do it nearly as well as Herman would, but we at least have his class, a class bearing the same name, and he and I have talked about it before. So, I now alternate that with Sentencing and Corrections, and teach each one every other year.

Bill Clune: You've talked about some of the impacts at the ground level, ordinary citizens. You've talked about the system, the problem approach, you talked about regulation and management of police discretion. Then you mentioned disparities of resources, too.

Cecelia Klingele: I would add that we go back and forth on what the course requirements are going to be. In my dream world, this class would be four credits.

Bill Clune: I can't believe it's not.

Cecelia Klingele: Well, yeah, right. This is a perpetual problem, that really, it is a four-credit class and the students, that's their biggest complaint is that this is a fricking four-credit class, and I'm like, "Yes, I know, I'm trying." I've cut back a lot because really, five would be fabulous. We've tried to cut back. We used to have some outside reading that they used to do—do you still do that at all?

Keith Findley: I don't. I suggest the books and I actually offer them extra credit on the exam if they work those books into any of the answers in a meaningful way.

Cecelia Klingele: You're so smart. I should do that.

Bill Clune: Clever incentive.

Cecelia Klingele: That's nice. Yeah, because there are so many great trade books out there right now, that offer different lenses to help them understand with greater depth the operation of the system, that we used to require them or give them a choice between a couple, but it's just too much work. Because in addition to the course materials, they have to do observations of the criminal justice system, and then I have them pick, I make it clear my strong preference is that they do a ride-along with a police agency and then write me a paper about the exercise of discretion by the police officer. But since you have to sign a "I waive away my life" waiver to go on those, I feel like I can't require them to do that for the class. So, I also let them write about the exercise of discretion by a sentencing judge if they go to an argued felony-sentencing hearing.

Keith Findley: I also make them do an out-of-class exercise like that and I give them the choice of going to an argued felony sentencing or a police ride-along. Then they have to write a very short reflection paper on it.

Cecelia Klingele: Yeah.

Keith Findley: We also then, in addition, we have four sessions that we hold jointly—

Cecelia Klingele: Didn't we do it for three years now?

Keith Findley: At least, yeah.

Bill Clune: You two?

Cecelia Klingele: Uh-huh (affirmative). In the evenings.

Keith Findley: They're four evening sessions that are mandatory. The first one is a policing panel, where we bring in police chiefs and Sheriff Mahoney, as well, he usually comes, to talk about their role and answer questions. Then we have a prosecution panel, a defense attorney panel, and a judges panel. Again, for those, I make them write a short reflection paper after each one of those.

Cecelia Klingele: Yeah. I don't. I should, but I don't.

Keith Findley: It's not much, but—

Cecelia Klingele: They talk broadly about their role, but then we also ask them specifically to reflect on the exercise of discretion in their jobs, and then students get to ask them questions. When we started those, I thought the students weren't going to like them, that they were going to think it was busywork, but they adore them. They think that they're just like the best thing ever.

Keith Findley: They like the ride-alongs a lot, too.

Cecelia Klingele: That's true.

Keith Findley: They love the ride-alongs and they love these panels.

Cecelia Klingele: I know. It hurts our feelings a little bit, but that's their favorite, is getting out and seeing this stuff, and not surprisingly. We also, some years, we haven't done it mostly because I'm lazy, I'm sorry, I should do it again—

Keith Findley: No, no, because it's hard logistically to pull it off—

Bill Clune: Yeah.

Keith Findley: We're talking about something else now, there's another thing that we've done that's logistically even more challenging, but Cecelia—

Cecelia Klingele: It's really cool. I should do it this year, if I can set it up. We bring them in on a Saturday, and they have to come . . . They only have to be here, the students, for half an hour, so it's not too bad, they don't resist.

Keith Findley: But we have to be here all day.

Cecelia Klingele: We have to be here all day.

Keith Findley: Because we stagger them for thirty minutes—

Cecelia Klingele: We do a mandatory . . . It's a plea negotiation. We give them a packet and we assign them; they're either a defense attorney or a prosecutor. We have several different versions of the prosecution facts and several different versions of the defense facts.

Keith Findley: Both the prosecutor and the defense get different bits of information about the same case, like you would in the real world.

Cecelia Klingele: Yes, and it's secret from each other, but then they get to decide what to disclose in a negotiation. We say, "You're going to come in, you're going to negotiate for ten minutes on the resolution of this case," and what we do, what takes a lot of work, is that we bring in volunteer attorneys, prosecutors, and criminal defenders—

Keith Findley: So we may have like six or eight of these—

Cecelia Klingele: Simultaneously.

Keith Findley: . . . simultaneously, and the students—

Cecelia Klingele: All day long.

Keith Findley: . . . come in and do it, so it's going on all day long, and we have to bring in volunteer attorneys to sit in and supervise and give feedback on each of these—

Bill Clune: So you have like six, eight attorneys?

Cecelia Klingele: During the day, but the attorneys don't stay all day.

Keith Findley: No, they will come for a few sessions.

Cecelia Klingele: I think twenty-four attorneys it takes to run this, usually. So, it's all a big effort. Although they're super generous . . . they always come in and do it. Sometimes we get the U.S. Attorney, and the D.A., and a lot of people will come, because they think it's really fun and we feed them lunch.

Bill Clune: That's very cool.

Cecelia Klingele: The students negotiate for ten minutes, then the lawyer's supposed to give them feedback for ten minutes, then we have ten minutes fudge time to make sure we stay on track. It's always fun because the students feel really awkward. They're like, "Well, how do I negotiate? What am I supposed to do?" You're like, "Yes, go find the law. Oh, right, there isn't any. Oh." They're interested. It's just that they have to stumble around and feel what that feels like, to not have law that tells them what to do—

Bill Clune: I'm all alone, determining somebody else's fate.

Keith Findley: We can preach at them all we want in class about how important the exercise of discretion is and about how unguided it is, and all that. They don't get it; the light doesn't go on until they have to exercise that discretion without any guidance from the law. This isn't really a training in negotiation; that's the vehicle. It's an opportunity to get them to experience decision making, discretionary decision making.

Cecelia Klingele: It seems so much more effective than having them do an argued-motion hearing, which would be a more traditional experiential activity, to argue the Fourth Amendment case law. That's not really what lawyers are going to do all day.

Keith Findley: That's right.

Cecelia Klingele: They're going to do this; they're going to talk. It's also really fun because the students who think of themselves as progressive typically, end up so punitive. So it's really awesome when the prosecutors are like, "This is an easy probation case, people," because it is a total probation case, and they're all ready to send people to prison for two years.

Keith Findley: It's also interesting then when we get back into class and debrief the exercise—

Cecelia Klingele: That's my favorite.

Keith Findley: . . . to see the wide range of dispositions that they come up with, all of which are perfectly acceptable under the law.

Cecelia Klingele: Right. Then we share the different facts and we start to talk about, "Well, how did the fact that the defendant was detained pre-trial, did that make a difference, versus the scenario where she's not?" Or the one where you have a really angry victim versus the victim who's like, "Whatever." So then they get into one in which she's deportable and one in which she's not deportable.

Bill Clune: So you can take common facts with different approaches.

Cecelia Klingele: Ask them how it matters—

Bill Clune: How many different factual patterns do you have?

Cecelia Klingele: We only have four fact patterns. Yeah, because it's two defense, two prosecution, and they can match up in various ways. It's in the debriefing that they think about, "Oh yeah, what did affect me or not, and would a change have resulted in a different disposition, or would it not have?" They love the contact with the practicing bar, too. It makes them feel cool to have a real attorney there, but for us, what matters is, yes, the fact that it feels awkward and uncharted—

Keith Findley: Unmoored.

Cecelia Klingele: Yeah. That's good for them. We try to be really conscious of the burden we're putting on the police, and I have been even more conscious of it in the last few years because the number of ride-alongs has gone up. So, we ask them, or at least I do in my class, to try not to go with the City of Madison police, knowing that some of them will, no matter what we say. What I say is, when you go home on spring break or wherever you go on spring break, try to set up a ride-along there.

Keith Findley: That's what I say, too.

Cecelia Klingele: Or go home for a weekend and go in your local community. They do. Then I also throw out the names of all of the near suburbs. Fitchburg does a lot for us, Middleton and Verona do a lot for us; they're pretty generous.

Keith Findley: The police seem pretty happy to do it.

Cecelia Klingele: They're very friendly. Last year, they worked really hard—we had a student in a powered wheelchair, and Madison worked with her to find a way to get her out with one of their community officers all day, which was great.

Keith Findley: They, I think, really see it as important in terms of community relations to build trust and receptiveness in the community. Most the departments I'm familiar with, at least, are pretty receptive to doing it.

Cecelia Klingele: They're good. I'm trying this year to . . . I made progress this summer and now I've sort of slowed down a little, but I'm trying to get out with all of the departments that routinely take our students, so that I can just thank them and just see what's going on. That, so far, has been really good. It may take me a while to get to all of them, but—

Keith Findley: Yeah. Good for you.

Bill Clune: What different lawyer roles do you deal with, with the students?

Cecelia Klingele: In the questions, so even in the examination, we often put them in some non-traditional roles like counsel to the police departments.

Keith Findley: That's true.

Cecelia Klingele: Which they don't always even think of. I always make a point, and especially because I don't know if . . . This is super anecdotal, but I've seen an increased interest in policing from my students in the last few years, which is funny, because nationally, applications are down. But I have a number of students who are interested in careers in law enforcement, and so I point out that we have lawyers who become police officers.

Keith Findley: When we bring in police on our panel, we often bring in Chief Mike Koval from Madison Police Department, he's a lawyer. So, they get the message that going into law enforcement is one thing you can do as a lawyer.

Bill Clune: Is David Couper around anymore?

Cecelia Klingele: He's around, but not doing—

Bill Clune: Okay.

Cecelia Klingele: . . . this stuff very much.

Bill Clune: Yeah, you mentioned being on advisory boards and things. When I was thinking about legal history and legal process, and the roles of lawyers, a lot of good points, I think it was with Walter Dickey actually, when I did that interview, he said they don't just end up representing a client in a criminal proceeding, they become legislators, they become on boards of various kinds, they become policymakers, and all this. So, lawyers become very powerful people in society. It's, I think, to me, very relevant to see in the system as a whole and a lot of the issues surrounding it and not just a gun for hire.

Cecelia Klingele: It's hugely important and I make that point to them all the time, that because it's a diploma privilege class, everyone takes it and not everyone does criminal law. And I said, "This is about you being an informed citizen. You're going to advise your city council. You're going to vote. You're going to be a leader in your community, and you need to understand how this works and all of the complexities—on top of the fact that all your friends are going to call you when their kids get pulled over for drunk driving. Everyone wants you to know something, but the fact is that you are actually going to need to know this for leadership." And that's why I get a little heated when every six months or so I'm asked if there isn't some way that I can teach this class as a one credit add-on to some crim. pro., add-on one credit to crim. law, so that it would meet the diploma privilege.

Bill Clune: Oh, that—

Cecelia Klingele: I just am like, "Absolutely not." It's a full stop. No. People need a class and I'm not . . . Even someone the other day was like, "Why not two credits?" No, no.

Keith Findley: That question, very interesting.

Cecelia Klingele: I'm getting it all the time. I teach both classes and—

Keith Findley: Oh, yeah.

Cecelia Klingele: I have offered to trade a credit of crim. law for a credit of crim. pro., I would go for that trade, I would do a three-credit crim. law and a four-credit crim. pro., if I could get it, but—

Bill Clune: Yeah, I'm surprised it isn't that way.

Keith Findley: Yeah, that makes perfect—

Cecelia Klingele: Yeah, it's about the credit allocation in the first and second semester. The students are weighted too heavy in the spring right now, have too many credits, and they need the extra credit in the fall.

Keith Findley: That's what drives it.

Cecelia Klingele: Right, it has nothing to do with the subjects.

Keith Findley: It's the numbers, not the subjects.

Cecelia Klingele: I also feel like if I let go, I'm not going to get more, I'm only going to get less because, yes, there's a big push to try to make a combined class that meets both requirements because Marquette has one.

Bill Clune: Is that because somebody else wants some room in the first year or something?

Cecelia Klingele: No, it's that Marquette has one. It makes students happier, and the students who don't like criminal law don't have to take the class. My whole point is, I don't care if they like criminal law, they need to know this to be educated citizens.

Bill Clune: Oh, I see. I see the connection there. Okay. Yeah.

Cecelia Klingele: We've done that with trust and estates, so it's required for diploma privilege, but it's now a two-credit option, so students can just take a two-credit mini version—

Keith Findley: I must say that my experience has been that a lot of students who come into this with no interest in criminal procedure wind up finding it really engaging. Because it is so real in everybody's lives, and it's not just dry reading of doctrine. I think the students actually do find it very valuable and it's so topical.

Cecelia Klingele: Right.

Keith Findley: It's so easy and so good to tie it into what's going on in the news all the time.

Bill Clune: Yeah. Even when you read the definition of a crime, it's like, "Oh." Yeah. So you think that it's good to have the substantive law crimes first and then procedure after?

Cecelia Klingele: I think so. Students often get confused because they expect the classes to be more similar, and of course they're totally not. Criminal law, I teach it, but honestly, it's not that much fun. We make it work, but it's very technocratic. It's about developing a skill set to read a statute, to understand how to apply it, just building-block basics of law school, really, is what we're doing in that class, and crime just happens to be the subject matter that we talk about. Because we don't teach that class particularly doctrinally either, we teach it as sort of a skill-building statutory reading class.

Bill Clune: Which it is, yeah.

Cecelia Klingele: Crime's almost peripheral to criminal law. So, this class, a lot of people expect it to be similar and some students find it very difficult to make the transition because they like the structure of criminal law, it's very formulaic, you can predict it, the answers are more clear. Whereas criminal procedure, I don't know if you get this, but I constantly get it, "This isn't a law class, this is a sociology class."

Keith Findley: I never get that.

Cecelia Klingele: What am I doing wrong? But every time, that's all that they say. I hear a lot of it.

Keith Findley: You probably just do that side of it better than I do.

Cecelia Klingele: I'm not a real lawyer, I'm a fake. I practice sociology without a license all the time, right?

Bill Clune: Well, it's insecure, that's like you were talking about a plea bargain, you put out determining somebody's fate with discretion, that's an insecure feeling. When you have a formulaic thing, "Here's the statute, what are the issues under it, here's a fact situation," you feel more in control. Macaulay and Whitford were saying the students love, offer an acceptance, because it has nothing to do with anything, but it's clear, right?

Cecelia Klingele: Yes.

Bill Clune: Okay. Disparities of resources, race, and social status, I think you've already mentioned that in the context of where the police go, I think is what you said.

Cecelia Klingele: It's everywhere.

Keith Findley: It's everywhere.

Cecelia Klingele: I feel like it just comes in at every opportunity. The cases provide examples, but student observations when we debrief them provide opportunities to talk about this. I've started pulling out quotes from the ride-along summaries every year, quotes about things the students have seen that fall into categories of things we're talking about, and I'll pull up student slides, and I'm hoping to build a big body of these. I'll depersonalize them, so I'll say, "Rural Agency, Wisconsin," or "Metropolitan Agency, Minnesota," something like that. So it's not identifiable who said it or what, and I get rid of the names in it, but they can see their friends talking about seeing, "Just last year, some of your classmates saw this happen . . ." That fits into . . . It's often things like profiling and other sorts of . . . Or someone, in some instance where it's clear economic disparity, played a role in someone being entangled in crime in some way. I think that makes it more real for them, but I feel like we talk about it . . . You can't not talk about race and class, and economics—

Keith Findley: It comes from police investigation, to appointment of counsel, and the standards that are used to determine indigency.

Cecelia Klingele: Yeah, which we do teach. I was going to say that in the role of lawyer, that we spend talking about indigency standards and actually making them compute what those are, so they realize that indigent isn't poor, indigent is like destitute, and then think about what that means for all the people like them, who don't actually feel like they could just go out and afford counsel, but are expected to pay. Then we talk about *pro se* issues in that context.

Bill Clune: Yeah. I have this image of criminal, in some sense, two systems, those who have no resources and no status, and are processed through like objects, and then those who have effective representation who have more effective control over it, even at the earliest points.

Keith Findley: Then there's actually those in the middle, who are not poor enough for appointed counsel, but actually don't have the resources to get any kind of representation. I think that's partly what Cecelia's talking about, is the students realize that there's these gaps that are really consequential.

Cecelia Klingele: Sometimes they see those, too, in their observations, when they're . . . I used to require, I think, a lot more observations than I do now, just again—

Keith Findley: Yeah. Me, too.

Cecelia Klingele: . . . because of the credit requirement. It's not fair to them, even though it's so much more helpful to what they're learning. Also, though, I cheat and I put it in my first-year class, so my 1Ls in the more technical class still have to go to a court observation.

Keith Findley: Good for you.

Cecelia Klingele: It's helpful, it makes that class also a little less dry and brings it to life a little more when they see the people affected. When they do go and observe, often what they're seeing are both the racial and economic disparities, and the differences in quality of counsel. Which even they can recognize.

Bill Clune: I'm thinking of what are the materials that reveal the impact of resources for students. Do they come out of the printed materials in the book or do they come from experiences?

Keith Findley: It's in the book, some of it. For example, the standards for appointment of counsel are in the materials.

Cecelia Klingele: Right. I would say that we have . . . So many of the cases in the book involve obvious issues of race and racial disparity, that if you're talking about the case correctly, you're going to observe for the students, "Oh, where are the police located? What does this side of town look like? What were the races of the officer and the defendant in this case?"

Keith Findley: When you're talking about stop and frisk—

Cecelia Klingele: Well, we have some of the stop-and-frisk materials are readings on that disparity. We also have a course website with supplemental materials, where we have links to radio programs, and some videos, and things like the full court order in the new stop-and-frisk case, so they can also look at some of those materials and that's where we put a lot of emphasis.

Keith Findley: One thing that we've added to the materials in recent years, that I don't think were there much before, is whole sections now on police use of force.

Cecelia Klingele: That's right, we did add that, just a couple years ago.

Keith Findley: Of course, that's both topical and important.

Bill Clune: Less than lethal force or including lethal force?

Keith Findley: Including lethal force. It's timely, it's topical, but it is also inherently about race, right?

Bill Clune: Mm-hmm (affirmative).

Keith Findley: It's just steeped in that, so that comes through very prominently there.

Bill Clune: Yeah. Wow, like you say, there's so many issues in the newspaper every day.

Keith Findley: Yeah.

Bill Clune: It makes me think, I had this experience with relatives who were arrested in Washington, D.C. The landlord called them in basically because they backed out of a contract which hadn't been signed yet, so she punitively called the police and said that they had stolen jewelry. So, I went into immediately overdrive and said, "You have to get a lawyer," and we contacted someone we knew, who had been a district attorney, and got her in there talking and knew some of the police. Once you're in that system it starts to grind away at you. There was this very strange assumption that somebody who complains about a crime is telling the truth. They should have been actually arrested for false arrest, because they lied about it. Anyway, that idea, it's a necessary system, but a dangerous one if you're caught in that, right?

Cecelia Klingele: I know. The idea and the presumption of innocence, when I teach it in the first year, it's hard any more to even say that's a thing. Because once you get in the system, it's the opposite.

Keith Findley: They must have been arrested for some reason.

Cecelia Klingele: That's right, clearly, they did something wrong, or no one would have called the police.

Keith Findley: Right.

Bill Clune: Really, that presumption of innocence vanishes in a second, yeah.

Keith Findley: There's actually quite a bit of empirical work on that.

Bill Clune: Really? What is that empirical work like?

Keith Findley: Well, it's assessing the way jurors' attitudes about guilt or innocence when they're confronted with a case. There's a strong sense that they think the person must be guilty of something. Even if they're in somewhat equipoise, it's rarely an actual presumption of innocence. There may be an equipoise at the start and as soon as they hear any incriminating evidence, the presumption is gone.

Bill Clune: Right. Why are you sitting there in that chair—

Keith Findley: Exactly.

Cecelia Klingele: Yeah. "I'm not sitting in that chair; I've never had to sit in that chair."

Keith Findley: It's absolutely logical—

Cecelia Klingele: So, clearly—

Keith Findley: . . . the presumption of innocence is counterintuitive, it's counter-logical, so of course they're going to assume the person must have done something. Why would they be arrested and why would the state be marshaling all of its forces against them if they didn't do something?

Cecelia Klingele: Right.

Bill Clune: Okay. Let's see, where are we time-wise? Especially for Cecelia.

Cecelia Klingele: We're good, it's only 1:15.

Bill Clune: Okay. Yeah, we're moving along. So, we've already gotten somewhat into question three, law in action and traditional teaching. Cecelia, you mentioned that it's sometimes seen as criminology—

Cecelia Klingele: Tons of our students love this approach. It feels real to them, it feels grounded. They find it fascinating. But then I get complaints.

Keith Findley: Maybe you're just more approachable, so they level with you and tell you.

Cecelia Klingele: Mine sometimes will say, "This feels like a glorified sociology class, this sounds like what we talked about when I was in undergrad in criminology." It also is true, though, that I find students regularly underestimate the intellectual rigor of the class. I try to warn them about this along the way and give them discussion problems to work on and write through, and to try to help them see that it's often the ones who think this is the easy class . . . I did share with you a few years ago, I think, one of my favorite student emails. A student did incredibly poorly, like got a D in my class. He emailed me and said, "Professor, I do not understand how this is even possible because this is the easiest class I ever had in law school." Therein lies the problem.

I think sometimes . . . Discretion's a difficult concept and so, we try to drive it home that discretion doesn't mean just doing what you feel like. As I always tell them, it's not the decision between eating oatmeal and Froot Loops for breakfast. Making that choice isn't an exercise of discretion, that's just a decision that you made. The exercise of discretion requires reasoned judgment between competing legal principles that are equally available to you, that you can justify logically. Even though we try to help them, give them that intellectual framework for approaching these questions, some of them just feel like, "Oh, it's just an arbitrary choice; I'll just do what I feel like doing," and what is there to say about that? So then they get to the exam and rather than engaging with the supplement statute pack and using ethical principles and ABA standards, and applying constitutional reasoning, and acknowledging the complexity of the issues we present them, they just have some incredibly superficial response to the material.

So, of course those students are dissatisfied during the semester because they're not doing that deeper work. Quite frankly, that reflects the nature of practice. That's what we see when we go into the courthouse. There are a lot of people who actually wield a lot of legal authority without being very reflective about what they're doing. What we want to do is move them forward and get them past that point, but I don't know that we're always doing it. If we were, the courthouses would look a lot different than they look. That, I think, is the frustration of this class. It matters so much that getting it right is really critical and getting it right is really hard.

Keith Findley: I haven't had the students complain to me like that, but I'm not sure that, that means they aren't feeling. It may truly honestly be just that they are expressing what they're thinking to Cecelia, not to me. It could be because there are certainly some students in the class who really embrace this approach.

Cecelia Klingele: For sure.

Keith Findley: . . . because there are some very active, engaged students who are really into talking about it all and thinking deeply about it all. Then, of course, like in any class, some students who don't speak up about that. One of the indicators I get also, that for many students that they may not be fully embracing it is the parts that the students really, almost universally, want to talk about is the case law. They're still there, they're still in law school, so clearly, they feel much more comfortable engaging with that stuff. I don't know if you've experienced that—

Cecelia Klingele: Oh, yeah. Even more than statutes and regulations. They don't read the statutes and regulations, they skim them, they're not sure what to do with them. It really takes a lot of work to help them see how the formulation of a use-of-force policy, and differences between different policies, could lead to different outcomes or presumptions on the part of law enforcement. You have to work really hard to help them see why this matters because it does require a lot of really careful analysis and it's more intellectual work than naming what the case holding is.

Bill Clune: So, it's supposed to be thought-through discretion with the proper considerations.

Cecelia Klingele: Right.

Keith Findley: Which I think what Cecelia's saying is that is the definition of discretion: it is a reasoned process of judgment, not just decision-making, based on all the relevant and appropriate criteria.

Cecelia Klingele: Right. That's hard. It's a hard concept.

Bill Clune: Well, there is such a thing as unbridled discretion, as with a dictator . . .

Cecelia Klingele: Well, but in law, it would be abuse of discretion if you don't follow that reasoning process, right?

Bill Clune: It's supposed to be the rule of law.

Keith Findley: What she's talking about is the appropriate exercise of discretion and that is not unbridled, it's not totally unhinged and unmoored.

Bill Clune: Interesting that you mention skipping over statutes. I've been reading . . . I'm having to try to understand four different fields of the law, and one of them is legal process and there's this debate about giving students not just cases, but statutory material, administrative regulations, various kinds of original things from the administrative process, for them where these writers say most lawyers encounter more of that than they do judicial review of administrative discretion. It makes sense that it's somewhat difficult to say, what do you make of this statute before it came up framed in a case, and you can look at what the judge said and think about that way. There's more pre-digested material for thinking when you have a judicial decision, but that's not what you often encounter in practice, so it takes some effort to do that.

Bill Clune: I guess we talked about, how do you convey exposure to broader issues?

Keith Findley: Everything that I'd say about that, though, is that I think our perspective is that the broader exposure to broader issues is—

Cecelia Klingele: That's what makes you a good lawyer.

Keith Findley: . . . essentially to the professional training of lawyers.

Cecelia Klingele: Especially in our system.

Keith Findley: Now, the trade-off you may be alluding to there is, does our approach mean there's less coverage of some of the Fourth Amendment case law for example? Yes.

Cecelia Klingele: Sure.

Keith Findley: We don't cover as much case law. Our approach, though, is that the rest of this stuff is equally as important and should not be neglected, and we're going to give you enough Fourth Amendment law, and enough Fifth Amendment, Sixth Amendment, that you understand the basic principles, and you're poised to learn the rest of it in a subsequent class or when you get out into the real world.

When you go into all of . . . You're not going to remember them anyway, right?

Cecelia Klingele: To be fair, most of them will be overruled by the time you graduate, so really, the theory of law changes so fast. What I tell them is, I want you to understand this at a level where you see the Fourth, and Fifth, and Sixth Amendment case law as a conversation between judges who are weighing competing interests. The interest in efficient law enforcement action, the interest in protecting civil liberties, and how both of those things are balanced matter, but you can see in the cases that these interests sort of rise and fall, depending on where our focus is in any given context.

If you understand this area of law as a balancing of those interests, then the fact that cases get overturned is going to be less shocking to you or make you question the judiciary. You'll see this more as just values and norms changing over time, and you'll be able to jump into that conversation at any moment in time and find case law that helps you at the time. That's relevant. I want them to understand how this law is formed and what it's surrounding and what are the interests at stake. I don't need them to know today what the rule is on searching a glove box necessarily.

Bill Clune: It also occurs to me as you've talked that there's so much law other than judicial review, as in the legal process area. There's police regulations, there's statutes, there's guidelines, and all of that's much more a law in totality than Supreme Court cases in particular, highlighted aspects of the whole process, right?

Cecelia Klingele: Right.

Bill Clune: The proportion is just vast, it's probably 95 percent not supreme courses, but law that applies to—

Keith Findley: I was a public defender for six-and-a-half years, and six months of that, I was in the trial division. I can tell you those trial lawyers don't read case law.

Cecelia Klingele: Right.

Keith Findley: Occasionally, sure, they read something, they become aware of the big picture, but it's not what governs the way the law is practiced on a day-to-day basis.

Cecelia Klingele: They tell me that every year. I hear that. Annually, I do a one-hour Supreme Court criminal law update session at the State Public Defender Conference. Every year, it's my great distress. The lawyers tell me, "This is the only time a year I pay any attention to the Supreme Court telling me what I need to know. That's it." That's their only continuing ed. in this area. Because they're too busy and it doesn't come up very often.

Keith Findley: And it usually doesn't determine the outcome of their case.

Cecelia Klingele: Right.

Bill Clune: Do you bring social science into the course, for example, criminology and impact studies on what is really happening out there?

Keith Findley: I'm sure we have some of the criminology scholarship.

Cecelia Klingele: I would say even, when it's in the legal scholarship, it draws on it.

Keith Findley: Sure.

Cecelia Klingele: One article on plea bargaining looks at psychological profiles of people who are most likely to plead guilty and talks about what are the structures and constructs that can lead to pleas that have absolutely nothing to do with guilt and innocence, and have much more to do with case load, pressures, and risk aversion, and age, and gender. That's the one that's jumping to mind, but I know we have little things like that kind of scattered throughout the material.

Keith Findley: Yeah.

Bill Clune: You mentioned that hardly any of the cases go to trial.

Cecelia Klingele: In terms of the universe . . . DOJ has a picture, a little graphic, of the criminal justice process that's very elaborate, and pretty, and multi-colored, and it starts with this sort of big line that comes in, it's supposed to show you that if you channeled crime into the system, you're only catching a little bit. I'm like, yeah, except that it's like this much crime, all this stuff that's going on every day, and then there's this little sliver that we actually notice, and then of that, it just shrinks as you go along.

Bill Clune: Crime is much bigger than—

Cecelia Klingele: It's pervasive.

Bill Clune: Really.

Keith Findley: The data of the convictions that are obtained, it's somewhere around 97 percent is by plea. The federal court is, what, 95?

Cecelia Klingele: I think.

Keith Findley: But that's only the ones that result in a conviction, so in the materials, we have a section on . . . We have more on the plea process than we do on the trial process.

Cecelia Klingele: Yeah, because that's where the work is. We also talk, and we didn't mention this before, we talk about diversion—

Bill Clune: That's interesting.

Cecelia Klingele: . . . we talk about formal diversion, we talk a little bit about treatment courts, because those have become a big deal. We did mention bond, the bond decisions are another one that we talk about. In that context, we introduce some limited, but real, conversation about risk tools, which are becoming increasingly common throughout the criminal justice system.

Bill Clune: What's that?

Cecelia Klingele: So, actuarial risk-assessment tools are being used in some places even by street-level cops, for street diversion. They're being used most prevalently at the bond decision and at sentencing, and then in correctional supervision. They're designed to classify individuals who come into contact with the system as low, medium, or high risk of re-offense.

Bill Clune: That is automatically bringing in social science . . .

Cecelia Klingele: My fear is that I do . . . Do you . . . I show the materials where I have scenarios and I make them in class do bond, on the spot, bond decisions, and I give half the class the Connecticut Risk Assessment one-page tool and I tell the rest of the class to just use the traditional rules. Then I have one of them play defendant, one play prosecutor, one play defense attorney. In real life, of course, these arguments are made with almost no information, so we do it that way, too.

They just have to make stuff up on the fly and just do it. Then I'll ask my class judges, "So, what's our decision going to be for bond?" The best is when you talk to people who used the risk tool and of course, all of them come up with different numbers using this apparently very simple tool—

Keith Findley: This objective—

Cecelia Klingele: Right. It's supposed to give you this objective advice and they all are all over the place, which makes my point nicely and I don't have to spend a lot of time with it.

Keith Findley: I'll have to pick your brain on how to do that, I've not done that—

Cecelia Klingele: It's kind of a fun one, too. I like it.

Bill Clune: That's fascinating. Keith, did you say something that there is a lot even before plea bargaining?

Keith Findley: Well, I think most criminal activity never gets caught, and among that that's caught, most is not charged, of that that's charged, much is not prosecuted fully. What I was talking about was just the three-to-five percent that go . . . Of the convictions, it's 95 to 97 percent that are obtained by plea, the others are by trial, presumably, but that's only talking about those that actually result in a conviction, which is just a very small piece.

Bill Clune: So there's a piece of it that's an arrest, but no charge—

Keith Findley: Absolutely.

Bill Clune: What is that? That they investigate and then let people go?

Cecelia Klingele: Or the police want it to go somewhere and the prosecutor's like, "Nah."

Keith Findley: Or the police just want it for the harassment value, or—

Cecelia Klingele: Or they never refer it at all.

Keith Findley: Right. There's all kinds of reasons. Prosecutors do actually refuse to charge on a lot of stuff that's brought in.

Bill Clune: I'm wondering how expert knowledge and research works its way into criminal law and procedure. You take any environmental sustainability problem, there's a huge amount of available technocratic expertise that you can apply to almost any problem, water quality, anything. How has criminology, over these many long years, worked its way into the teaching of criminal law?

Cecelia Klingele: I think there's two layers to this. One is just the fact that we tend to be heavy consumers of psychology and criminology literatures, and so it's what we know, so it's what we talk about when we talk to our students about this, and we assign some of it. The other, though, is actually much more legal and not sociological directly, and that's the work we do. We spend a lot of time on the ground, whether it's hanging out with—

Keith Findley: You mean in our own scholarship and participation?

Cecelia Klingele: Yeah.

Keith Findley: Yeah.

Cecelia Klingele: We hang out with cops, we hang out with policymakers, we hang out . . . I am trying to think of the last few weeks. I've been in Mendota, talking to the people who run the mental institution. I've talked with both kids and adults. We're in the prisons, we're in the jails. You're on the police and fire commission. We get to spend time with people doing this stuff, and they ask us questions and tell us about what they're doing. So, a lot of it is organic, that although obviously we're not practitioners in the same way . . . Well, Keith, you still litigate.

Keith Findley: Not much anymore.

Cecelia Klingele: Right.

Keith Findley: I used to litigate a lot, so I had a lot of contact with the world that way.

Cecelia Klingele: We're hanging out with these people.

Keith Findley: We are and we're reviewing . . . We're both doing a lot of field research that's drawing on data from what's happening out there in the real world, including the way police are doing their work.

Bill Clune: So you do a lot of empirical research, both informal and formal.

Keith Findley: Yeah. I think that's true for both of us.

Cecelia Klingele: Yeah.

Bill Clune: And you consume the literature, the secondary literature.

Keith Findley: I think we both pay a lot of attention to the psychological and the criminological literature.

Cecelia Klingele: That's important to us and we think about the intersection—we think of systems a lot and work with that. We both have pretty heavy service obligations that connect us to what's really happening, or we try to find synergies, I think, between the volunteer work and service stuff we're doing.

Keith Findley: Yeah.

Cecelia Klingele: I'm on the board as a federal defender and as part of that, meet every two weeks to do case staffings with some of the defense attorneys here in town, and so I get to hear about their litigation and what their litigation strategies are like, and what are the issues coming up. That kind of work.

Bill Clune: Police and fire, things like that, you see system issues, I assume, that jump right out at you, as opposed to particular case issues and the business that comes before them.

Keith Findley: Yeah. Right. It's rarely individual cases, unless it's a case of police or fire officer discipline, that we see.

Cecelia Klingele: But you get to see recurring themes. I get that, I do some work now with Division of Children and Families Youth Justice Bureau, where it started out as doing some training of the judges, but then we just continued as a work group to talk about what are the issues in the system across the state, disparities between counties' responses to similar problems. Then you can take all that back to the classroom.

Bill Clune: You said that this particular course is not taught, to your knowledge, in another law school.

Keith Findley: I think that's directly attributable to Frank and Herman, don't you?

Cecelia Klingele: That it's not?

Keith Findley: No, no, that it's different here.

Cecelia Klingele: Oh, that we do it.

Keith Findley: That it's different here . . . Because they created it.

Cecelia Klingele: Insofar as other schools go, I would say, senior-level faculty still know, remember, feel warmly about both of them. Lots of people around the country feel very strongly about their influence. Younger scholars have less familiarity with them directly, although Herman is known still by the younger policing scholars. They know who he is, even though they don't know him personally.

Keith Findley: I will say this from my work with the Madison Police Department, he is still revered there.

Cecelia Klingele: Oh, yeah.

Bill Clune: Yeah.

Keith Findley: Within the police department.

Bill Clune: Yeah, he walked on water.

Keith Findley: I didn't mean to cut you off.

Cecelia Klingele: Oh, no, no, no. I was going to say, I think the younger people know less, but they're hungry for it. Whenever I'm talking to other criminal procedure people about what to do, a lot of . . . When I was at the Crim. Fest this summer, the annual meeting of the criminal law professors, a number of them told me that based on conversations in prior years, they have started having their students do ride-alongs and court observations. Their students love it, too. Of course they do, right?

Keith Findley: Of course, yes.

Cecelia Klingele: So now they are true believers. That's not about what Keith and I are doing, that's about what Frank and Herman were doing.

Bill Clune: Well, Herman, in his interview, gives this anecdote that when the ABF study came out, it was a bombshell in criminal law nationally, and Joe Goldstein came from Yale and other people came from Harvard, and I think—

Keith Findley: Yeah, I had Joe Goldstein.

Bill Clune: Yeah?

Keith Findley: In advanced criminal procedure.

Bill Clune: Oh, did you?

Keith Findley: Yeah. Yeah.

Bill Clune: Okay. So, I got the idea that they went back and somehow changed their courses or the way they taught students. I don't necessarily mean in the first-year criminal procedure course, but in some way. In fact, it was after that, that Frank got the offer at Harvard, which he turned down two days later, what a guy.

Keith Findley: Yeah.

Bill Clune: Of course, the ABF study was the study of the police and what they did, and the amount of police discretion, that was the bombshell, how much discretion there was exercised. I got the idea that it profoundly affected the whole field and yet, I also know that people still teach Fourth, Fifth, and Sixth Amendment courses.

Cecelia Klingele: They do. I think it is also true that you can't get through law school anymore without hearing about discretion, and that wouldn't have been true in earlier times.

Keith Findley: Yeah. Discretion's not a secret anymore. It's not hidden. I think that, that absolutely had a profound effect across the country, that discretion is out in the open, but it wasn't before. Right?

Cecelia Klingele: Absolutely. I think that, that, even for people who teach more traditionally, it's a non-controversial point. It's essential to the functioning of the system and everyone knows that and acknowledges it. I do still think that there are divisions in the ways that criminal and law procedure are taught more broadly. I think that there are scholars and teachers who, even if they're using a traditional case book, they're trying to bring in supplements. That reminds me, I owe an email to someone who was asking me for better supplements on mass incarceration as an issue, to bring into a more traditional class. I'm thinking of teachers who really are very doctrinal—they still want to help their students understand the way the system functions, at least a little bit. Then there are other teachers who I think are still just very, very far removed from reality. Although often they think they're not. They don't realize how distant their understanding is from what's happening. I think it's seen as a positive thing if you're trying to talk to your students about how the law functions in addition to teaching them the formal rules. Don't you think? Even at more traditional schools?

Bill Clune: Mass incarceration . . . How would you define that?

Cecelia Klingele: So, there's this whole literature around mass incarceration as a construct. Really, it focuses on the increasing rates of incarceration that the United States has seen from the mid-1970s through the early years of the twentieth century, looking at the rate of rapid growth and the expansion in our prison population.

Bill Clune: Yeah.

Keith Findley: On a comparative level, compared to the rest of the world, we're just multiple times higher rates of incarceration, but also, the incarceration, it just skyrocketed at the same time the crime rates were actually declining, so there's this disconnect between crime and punishment here.

Bill Clune: Right. Okay. I know it well now that you mention it, it's one of the heartbreaking things that happened to our legal system, three strikes, drug possession, and so on.

Keith Findley: It's mandatory sentences and it's ratcheting up higher sentences.

Cecelia Klingele: Even though some of the harshest policies of the eighties and nineties are being ameliorated or aren't as prevalent as they once were, our rates of incarceration remain fairly unchanged. So we're no longer going up like this on our growth line, but we just sort of leveled off way up here, where our traditional rates of incarceration were down here.

Keith Findley: So this is reflection of that discretion we talked about. It's unmoored, like how do you know what . . . The way the system settles on sentences is, people in the system get to know what the going rate is, like what's the value of this kind of burglary, and the value kept going up and up as the political pressures increased. So now we may have stabilized, but we stabilized where the norm is way up here still. That's how discretionary sentencing is being exercised, and in charging, and all these things, is to be really harsh and punitive because that feels normal now. So, anything less than that feels like you're giving away the store. That's one of the effects of having a completely discretionary system is that when the pressure's pushing up and that becomes the new norm, that becomes the way discretion is exercised.

Bill Clune: Well, thank you. This was terrific.

Keith Findley: Well, good.

Interview of Walter Dickey by Bill Clune

Abstract

Walter Dickey took Criminal Justice Administration as a student when it was an optional three-credit second-semester course and taught the updated required version when he joined the faculty in 1976 and began collaborating with Frank Remington and Herman Goldstein. At the time, both Remington and Goldstein were interested in teaching the course as a study of how to make the criminal justice system more fair and effective in reducing threats to public safety with the least possible harmful side effects. The starting place for both views was the behaviors that came to the attention of law enforcement. The course was organized to encourage analysis of a set of common questions: what is the behavior that attracts law enforcement, how does law enforcement learn of the behavior, what is the response, how fair and effective is the response, and how could authority be conferred in a more effective manner.

With his problem-oriented policing, Goldstein emphasized solutions beyond criminal law, while Remington believed that the system itself must and could be improved, but there was considerable overlap and mutual reinforcement, as illustrated by the problem of public intoxication. With Remington's guidance, Wisconsin became the first state to allow police officers to place intoxicated individuals in detox centers rather than jails. Incarceration of drunks, often for one night, had been one of the most common functions of law enforcement and was essentially a failed social experiment. In an example of problem-oriented policing, Goldstein developed a complimentary solution that did not involve law enforcement—a token system by which bartenders could offer intoxicated patrons a token for a cab ride home and another for retrieving their cars in the morning. Another example fitting the general framework (of law enforcement investigation and response) was stop and question or stop and frisk, an intrusive practice that had been shown to have strong negative effects on public safety due to loss of community goodwill and citizen cooperation with the police. Remington was instrumental in developing Wisconsin legislative guidelines for when such stops were justified, the factual predicate required for police intervention. An example of a particularly harmful policy was the Ramparts program in Detroit where police decoys posed as unconscious victims, and the police ended up chasing and killing people who tried to rob the undercover officers. A parallel example at the federal level was ABSCAM, a much-publicized incident where undercover FBI agents solicited bribes from public officials. U.S. Attorney General

Edward Levi asked Remington what the predicates for such "sting" activities should be, as well as other covert surveillance, leading eventually to a set of federal guidelines (guidelines subsequently diluted after 9/11 by the Patriot Act).

Remington had a legal process view of the criminal justice system, successfully arguing that when legal process was removed as a first-year requirement Criminal Justice Administration should take its place as a required first-year course. He regarded Supreme Court decisions as ineffective because they ruled out specific activities but otherwise left unlimited authority in place. He preferred legislative or administrative rules as long as they were carefully tailored to the behavioral problem and the complexities of criminal justice (for this reason doubting the utility of applying the standard rules of the Administrative Procedure Act).

The Criminal Justice Administration course was (and is) an outstanding example of integrating empirical knowledge about the law into a law course. The large American Bar Foundation survey of criminal justice, which Remington helped direct, was revolutionary in revealing how the system actually operated in practice. Faculty from other prominent law schools visited Wisconsin and attended seminars built around those findings and left with ideas for modifying their own courses. One such seminar attended by Dickey he called perhaps the most intensive learning experience of his life. Social scientists involved in the survey had enormous positive influence, including Herman Goldstein and Don Newman at Wisconsin, and Lloyd Ohlin at Harvard. Goldstein, Remington, and Dickey stressed that "cops know things," as when one officer identified a bookseller on campus who was serving as a fence for stolen course books by not asking for identification and sponsored regulation that required ID, and another officer who sponsored municipal regulation of pool tables, the confined location of which he had determined was responsible for many bar fights. More broadly, Remington viewed empirical facts as essential for problem solving in criminal justice. Remington advised Dickey, early in Dickey's career at UW, that rather than write a doctrinal article on reckless murder, thereby retreating into the ivory tower, "the young professor should, with knowledge of accepted wisdom about an intractable problem, search out new knowledge, previously undiscovered facts, missed connections between facts, and by an act of imagination place that new knowledge in revealing relationship to what is already known."[1]

Clinical programs at Wisconsin offered hands-on experience and many empirical findings. The Legal Assistance to Inmates clinical program (LAIP), directed by Dickey, exposed students and faculty to multiple versions of sentencing systems (guidelines, determinate, indeterminate)

---

[1] Walter Dickey and Michael Smith, "What We Do," *The Gargoyle*, Spring/Summer 2002, https://perma.cc/3Q49-9VH7.

and allowed access to pre-sentencing reports that yielded rich insights into the people who were accused of crimes and their encounters with the system. In LAIP, the pre-sentence report served as the best statement of the factual basis for the crime, usually more complete than the guilty plea. It also was the basis for prison classification and parole decisions, both release and revocation. Staff realized how frequently errors were made and often tried to correct them, particularly in the federal "mandatory" guideline system. Dickey wrote an article about the importance of accuracy in the sentencing report. In later years, presentence reports were used as "problems" in sentencing, and as useful illustrations in the work of Dickey and UW Law Professor Michael Smith on model sentencing. Dickey and Smith developed model sentences as guidance for judges and a "reasoning" process approach to the imposition of sentences, based on the view that sentencing was a legal decision and should be approached by applying facts to a legal standard. This work became nationally and internationally known and influential.

Professor Dickey stressed the importance of listening to clients who often came from different worlds than law students and lawyers, fully informing them, and not overruling their preferences. A common example arose in plea bargaining and probation. Rather than threaten clients that the judge might throw the book at them, Dickey taught students to inform clients about the risks of probation, which could turn into a life sentence on the installment plan due to the many reasons for revocation of probation unrelated to the original crime. Clients should be asked to consider whether a thirty to forty-five day jail sentence might leave them better off. Dickey also stressed the importance of listening and good judgment, qualities not conferred by traditional appellate case analysis.

A point sometimes heard from students was that because of its emphasis on real empirical impacts the course might be viewed as much sociology as law. But many students valued the course greatly, precisely because of the exposure it provided to multiple aspects of the law as actually practiced (far more so than the traditional criminal procedure courses organized around analysis of Supreme Court cases on the Fourth, Fifth, and Sixth Amendments). In addition, the professors emphasized that students would be serving in multiple roles impacted by and impacting criminal law later in their careers, such as legislator, community leader, judge, prosecutor, and public defender. True to that thought, Remington and Dickey sent letters to students who had taken the course, ten to fifteen years after graduation, asking (in effect), "this is what we were trying to do, was it of value?" 100 percent said yes, and most said they had never tried a criminal law case.

Walter Dickey: Some background, Bill, maybe would be helpful to you.

Bill Clune: Yes, background should be first.

Walter Dickey: Yeah. First of all, the timing of this. The original first volume, I think, actually I was a law student when it came out. I was a second-year law student. The course was not required, you only had one required criminal law course. It was four credits in the spring of your first year.

Bill Clune: Was that required course substantive crimes and procedure?

Walter Dickey: Yes, it was, although depending on who taught it. Frank, to a great extent, emphasized the substantive law. Ed Kimble had a mix in there of substantive and procedure, but more on the substantive law. I think substantive law was probably the area of greater emphasis then.

Bill Clune: Okay.

Walter Dickey: Don't forget you had Bob Seidman teaching African criminal law and stuff, so it was a whole other world over there.

Bill Clune: But the procedure course was the big thick book?

Walter Dickey: That was the big thick book. It had John Arthur Wilson in the back. We were the first ones to have the actual hard cover, and that was in '69, the fall of '69. It was not required, but by the time I started teaching in the law school in '76, it was required, and it was required as the second-semester course.

Bill Clune: Mm-hmm (affirmative).

Walter Dickey: You had substantive criminal law then for four credits in the first semester, and you had this for three in the second.

Bill Clune: Criminal justice administration.

Walter Dickey: Exactly. Now I say criminal justice administration, criminal justice administration taught by Frank and I, by Dave Schultz whenever he started teaching it, not by John Robertson who taught the more traditional Fourth, Fifth, and Sixth Amendment course.

Bill Clune: Okay. All at the same time?

Walter Dickey: Yeah.

Bill Clune: Using a different book?

Walter Dickey: Using a different book.

Bill Clune: Yeah.

Walter Dickey: Yeah. The other thing I was going to say, by way of background, is I think one of the things that was going on is Herman did his original problem-oriented studies. I think of them as being published in '82, but Frank and I and Herman sat and talked about his work then, I'm going to say over the course of three years, almost daily. Herman, I think, was coming to the view that the criminal justice system was a wholly inadequate way for dealing with these problems.

Bill Clune: Right.

Walter Dickey: One of his graphic examples was the drunk driving problem in Dane County. One of the things that's revealed in his study, and it's later been confirmed by the Department of Transportation in a statewide look at this, they tried to estimate in partnership with the Madison Police Department the number of drunk drivers on the road in Madison, Wisconsin on Friday from 2 until 4 a.m. The estimate was there are 1,800 drunk drivers on the road during those hours. I'll never forget, they made 3.7 arrests a night. Herman was saying, "And they arrested the wrong guys." First of all, he said the arrests fell into two categories. One category was the people who had crashed and therefore were found to be drunk after the crash. The other category was the people who were driving so carefully, that the cops stopped them, and they got arrested for drunk driving.

Bill Clune: Yeah, or you pull over to the side of the road and you fall asleep and turn your car off.

Walter Dickey: That's still drunk driving. It's still drunk driving. But Herman was, and the other part of what Herman was doing, he was looking at sexual assault in Dane County. Among the things he discovered was this "system" whose parts did not communicate with each other. I think his most graphic illustration of that was the fact that Health and Social Services released the sex offenders who are resident at either at Old Central State Hospital, at that point was just closing, and they're being moved over to Mendota, and they're being almost all released into Dane County without any notification to either the police, or to the Department of Corrections, because they were not corrections clients. They'd been committed under the old sex crimes law.

Then he discovers that a lot of the stranger-on-stranger sexual assaults are being committed by these guys and that the system for apprehension and protection doesn't know about the fact that all these guys are being sort of brought in. Again, I don't want to speak for Herman here, but I've sort of traced his view that the system, criminal justice system, is wholly inadequate for these kinds of things, particularly as it's currently organized.

That was one of the things that was going on there, but Herman was really emphasizing the importance of looking at specific problems as a way of revealing how you might get greater public safety.

Bill Clune: Yes.

Walter Dickey: Frank, on the other hand, was much more wedded to the conventional criminal justice system if it could only be fixed, as a way of dealing with behavioral problems.

Bill Clune: Yeah, interesting.

Walter Dickey: As an overview, maybe I just say, so we had a series of five questions we would ask the class as a way of trying to organize each section. The five questions were, "What is the substantive problem of concern?" Street robbery. "How is authority conferred to deal with the problem?" If you look at the street robbery, all the substantive, all the statute that says is, "Street robbery is a crime if you take the property of another by threatening use of force." How does the system respond to the problem? For this, you get into investigative responses. Well first of all, these are muggings we're talking about.

Bill Clune: Mm-hmm (affirmative).

Walter Dickey: They respond to the call for help. Well, what you immediately discover is that the victims of muggings have called the police long after the mugger is gone, have been stunned by the bang on the head that they got, or whatever it is that happened, cannot describe them at all, and they're a half hour gone. I've got to find a telephone book. Don't forget there were no cell phones or anything like that.

Bill Clune: Yeah.

Walter Dickey: And so as an investigative response, responding to that fact of the crime, it's wholly inadequate.

Bill Clune: Okay.

Walter Dickey: Then you get into decoys and other things. Now, we went through so many freaking drafts of this. The decoy one I remember vividly. At one point we had, and maybe it's still in here, this vivid description of the Ramparts Decoy Program in Detroit, where they basically killed the suspects. The numbers are just incredible. They'd have the decoy, the decoy would be a drunk staggering around or a drunk lying in the street, the street robber would come up to them, the cops would be hiding, and they'd chase the guy down, and most of the time the guys run and then they shot him. I remember being staggered by the number of people who died at the hands of the police as part of this decoy operation.

Stopping and questioning was essential to all of this, and it's been essential to most of what we've done as an investigative response because it's so common, so oppressive, because it has so many implications for safety, because it alienates the community to the nth degree, like in New York City, if you've been following what's been going on in the *New York Times*.

Bill Clune: That investigative technique wouldn't just apply to street robbery, but to almost anything.

Walter Dickey: That's right. So after the, what's the problem, how is authority conferred to deal with the problem, how does the system respond to the problem, the next question was, "How effective is the system's response to the problem?" You see some of that in here. Ineffective is a kind way of putting it, though it does lead you to ask the question, "What's the measure of effectiveness?" That then gets you into questions about alienating the community and what its affect is on other public-safety measures you might be taking where you've alienated the community to the degree where they're not going to be of any help to you.

Bill Clune: I see.

Walter Dickey: Yeah, that gets you to the whole community policing thing, which Herman and Frank were somewhat skeptical of, favoring the more problem-oriented approach to that. I don't want to overstate their skepticism. They obviously felt that good community relations were vital to public safety but were being sacrificed in a lot of the things that the system was doing.

The last question was how could authority be conferred and the system respond in ways that would be more fair and effective. Then you got to ask the question, "What do you mean by fair?" And you've also got the question of what do you mean by effective.

Bill Clune: Mm-hmm (affirmative).

Walter Dickey: This was a reflection, I think, of Frank's view that the system, if we could only do it right, we'd have a much better world. In the how is authority conferred, remember I said we have the substantive law statute, but we used to talk all the time about the fact that if you look at the U.S. Supreme Court decisions, of which Frank was just an utter skeptic, he would say, "So the Supreme Court, basically, is a limitation on governmental authority." It's saying you can search the glove compartment but you can't search the trunk." So we are conferring authority through the least qualified group to be conferring authority, and the way we're doing it is by saying, "You can do anything you want unless the things we tell you you can't do."

What is the meaning of Miranda and all that. You also have some stuff in here on what's the outcome of the motions to suppress and stuff like that, you find that the outcomes are almost always the evidence isn't suppressed. It was called the law of the kilo, the law of search and seizure depends on the amount of drugs.

One of the things I would say, and it's responsive to your question what topics does the course cover, one of the topics the book was directed at was the legal process. You may remember that we dropped the legal process course as a requirement, and Frank persuaded whoever the curriculum folks were at the time, to make this the legal process course. That's why it became required in the second semester. This is also Frank's way of getting more criminal law into the curriculum, which was always one of his goals.

I don't say that in a cynical sort of way. He truly believed that the legal process ought to be one of the things that we should be studying here, and the absence of administrative controls, the absence of the application of the Administration Procedure Act to the police agencies, parole and probation agencies and the like, was one of the things he had mixed feelings about. He wanted the rule of law to apply, but he realized how diverse and rich the universe of behaviors were, how hard it was to control, and the limits of rules as methods of control.

Bill Clune: Yeah, Herman, whom I interviewed a couple weeks ago, said it was a revelation to people that the police department would have any internal rules governing anything other than you having your shoes shined.

Walter Dickey: I don't know if you remember but in '78 I started working on the administrative rules for the department of corrections. While I was still a quarter time at the law school . . .

Bill Clune: I do remember.

Walter Dickey: . . . my quarter time was almost all devoted to this book. I was working on the administrative rules for corrections, and we, Frank and I, in particular Herman, were looking at the question of how useful rules might be in a setting such as this. What had happened was the legislature overruled Pat Lucy's veto. There was a statute on the books that exempted the parole board and the department of corrections from the administrative procedure act in Wisconsin.

Bill Clune: Hmm.

Walter Dickey: The veto was overridden when the legislature passed the law removing the exemption, and now corrections was in the situation of having to make administrative rules.

Bill Clune: He vetoed the exemption or he vetoed the—?

Walter Dickey: No, he vetoed the removal of the exemption.

Bill Clune: Oh.

Walter Dickey: So you had a Democratic legislature. Democratic governor. Democratic legislature removes the exemption.

Bill Clune: That was supposed to be the great progressive governor.

Walter Dickey: Yeah. There was this distrust, and so they turned to the law school thinking we would be neutral and bring a degree of objectivity to the effort to make the rules. That's how I came to be the person who was responsible for developing the administrative rules.

Bill Clune: Okay.

Walter Dickey: And realize we're undertaking this at about the same time, so there's a lot of interplay as we talked about the usefulness, or lack thereof, of rules and their application in different situations.

Bill Clune: Okay. By the way, do you remember taking the legal process course using the Garrison and Hurst book?

Walter Dickey: Yes.

Bill Clune: You're saying it was discontinued about the time you started teaching.

Walter Dickey: When I was a student, and I graduated in '71, it was a required course in the first year. Margo Melli taught me it in room 260.

Bill Clune: You remember that course somewhat at all?

Walter Dickey: Oh yeah. It was a great course. Unlike most of the other students, I thought it was fascinating because I knew so little about this. You start with a guy on the railroad who gets hurt, and you take it all the way through the regulatory state. You know what I mean?

Bill Clune: Yeah.

Walter Dickey: I don't even think I'd ever met a lawyer until I came to law school, so this was all just fascinating to me. That was certainly one of the things Frank thought was important and wanted this course to be.

Bill Clune: Yeah, I can see the parallels.

Walter Dickey: The other thing we used to do is we used to talk so much about the teaching of it, collaborate on how we could do it. The five questions I mentioned was one of the products of our discussions.

Bill Clune: Mm-hmm (affirmative).

Walter Dickey: If you look at the first chapter here, Don Newman wrote a lot of this. We would begin with what we called a class or two on the behaviors of concern to the criminal justice system.

Bill Clune: Mm-hmm (affirmative).

Walter Dickey: So much of it was non-criminal, the drunk on a cold night, the frightened old lady, the cat in the tree. So much of it did not invoke the formal system. Now realize one of the directions this took, and it is consistent with what I said before about conferring authority, is Frank and Herman and I mostly then went through a period where we thought a more specific conferral of authority would lead to more effective measures. All of this stuff about detoxification that Wisconsin was the first state to adopt, where you didn't have to arrest the drunk, you could take him to the detox. That was an effort to unload, in a sense, from the criminal justice system stuff that we used the system to deal with. So we took the drunk to jail, and it was an inappropriate use of the jail. Jails are getting crowded, all that stuff is going on, and jail isn't really what this guy needs. Detox is what he needs.

Bill Clune: They were just spending the overnight drying out anyway.

Walter Dickey: Exactly. Now, that was effectively a sort of failed experiment . . .

Bill Clune: The detox thing was?

Walter Dickey: Yeah. I think in its early years it worked fairly well, but then people started to game it. I'm not sure it sort of ever reached the kind of potential that we were thinking it had. Realize too, with respect to the drunk driving, we're really fighting against the tide here because what we are basically saying is, "Look, arrest is not the solution to this problem." Herman invented the token system, I don't know, did he tell you about that?

Bill Clune: I don't think so.

Walter Dickey: The token system was the bartender has two tokens. The drunk is drunk and the bartender pushes the two tokens across to the drunk and says, "Look, I'm going to call you a cab and one token is going to get you home. The other token is going to get you back here in the morning to pick up your car." What eventually Herman came to say was, "You have to have a person own the problem who actually has the capacity to solve it." That was trying to get that bartender to own the problem of the drunk driver and to give him a mechanism by which they could solve it. Get this drunk driver off the road that you've been serving too many drinks.

Herman is really . . . Here's what I would say. This is my observation. Herman, out of respect for Frank, is unwilling, or maybe he doesn't yet believe, that the criminal justice system is not the answer here. Frank is struggling to make the criminal justice system a more effective solution, and Herman is getting more and more, if not agnostic, he becomes an unbeliever.

I was floored by some of the stuff that Herman was finding in this problem-oriented stuff. But I wanted the system to be, "If you could only make it better." I spent my life trying to do that. If we could only make it better, it'll work.

Bill Clune: Exactly. There has to be a criminal justice system, there will be. There will be arrests. There will be encounters between the police and . . .

Walter Dickey: Citizens. Sure.

Bill Clune: . . . and citizens. Some of which are enormously serious. The police are put under all kinds of pressure in the community to solve problems, I guess, or to be the first responder thing.

Walter Dickey: Herman and Frank, one of the things we used to say in our classes, I took this from Herman and Frank, was, "So why do people call the police?" The answer is first of all, they're open twenty-four hours a day. Second, they actually come when you call. And third, they come clothed with legal and moral authority to act even if their authority has actually nothing to do with the problem you've called them about."

We used to say this in our introductory classes as a way of saying, "Look, you have to begin with an understanding of the range of behaviors with which the police are called upon to deal. Realize this slice of arrest, prosecution, and conviction is really a little slice of the range of behavior." Then if you looked at the, we still got the chart in this book I bet. Herman and Frank did not like this chart very much. The one that shows the funnel.

Bill Clune: Mm-hmm (affirmative).

Walter Dickey: The funnel shows how few arrests actually end up in convictions. It gets smaller and smaller as you go along, and then finally you have this little bit that comes out at the end, that's the people who are actually convicted of offenses and sanctioned in some way or another. Again, I'm going all over the place, but before we get off the investigation, one of the things that really interested us at this time, and it was in part because of Frank's involvement in Washington, and remember Abscam?

Bill Clune: Oh, Abscam. Members of Congress and other public officials convicted of corruption and taking bribes in a sting operation.

Walter Dickey: Yes. Abscam was the FBI dressed up as Saudi princes in Philadelphia and they invited congressmen, then bought their votes and handed them suitcases of money. They recorded it all. '78, '79?

Bill Clune: Yeah.

Walter Dickey: So I'm sitting in Frank's office. Abscam has happened. The Attorney General calls Frank. He asks him to come to Washington . . .

Bill Clune: Levi, was that the Attorney General?

Walter Dickey: Levi, right. Ed Levi. The question that was, the legal question we were dealing with, and Frank then came back and involved my research assistance in looking at it, is because the congressmen said, "How did you pick me?" Now, Martin Luther King said the same thing, and we made that point. Why did I become the subject of investigation, which lead into what I thought was a fascinating question, and that is what factual basis, if any, is necessary before you undertake an investigation. Then when you really start to look at it, if you believe you can have a meaningful low factual threshold, it may limit what the nature of the investigation you can undertake.

Bill Clune: Is this like a predicate for a sting?

Walter Dickey: Exactly. Not only was it a predicate for a sting, but the Patriot Act after 9/11 actually repealed the limitations that had been put on undercover. The FBI wanted to put undercover people in the mosques, but they had no factual predicate for doing so. Their own rules forbade them from doing it. Patriot Act wiped all that out.

This whole question of why single me out, the congressman out, because I'm a Democrat, Republican, Black, Hispanic, come from a crucial district, all that sort of stuff, and the FBI hadn't thought any of this stuff through. The Attorney General was calling on Frank to think about the question of whether there ought to be rules governing the FBI and what rules ought to, if any, govern undertaking an investigation, and whether there had to be, as I said, a factual predicate and etc.

Bill Clune: Can't resist saying this is exactly what Trump's lawyers are saying, "Why'd you start investigating me?"

Walter Dickey: Yeah.

Bill Clune: It's the same equitable problem they're trying to raise, but there seems to be plenty of predicate in his case.

Walter Dickey: Yeah.

Bill Clune: I guess in criminal justice theory, the idea was, well, if you're a criminal, you don't have any right to contest that we've picked you up because arrest is always random. We happen to observe somebody or we happen to catch somebody.

Walter Dickey: We can do anything we want on the absence of a law that says we can't. That was, I don't know want to oversimplify Frank's thinking about this, but that was his, to call Frank cynical is not fair, but his cynical view of Supreme Court-made law, because really it is so lacking a perspective on what the real issues are and judges are particularly unsuited to be lawmakers, and so he really believed that the legislature ought to be far more active here. He would point to the stop and questioning law that we've got in Wisconsin statutes as a victory for the way things should be because there you've got the legislature specifying the circumstances in which stopping and questioning is permissible.

Bill Clune: So it lists a number of suspicious behaviors or predicates or something?

Walter Dickey: It talks about the factual predicate for it. Well, now so again, in later iterations of this book, we put out a whole bunch of new editions of it. Some of them are kind of interesting, which we self-published because we bought the copyright in about '89 or '90, I can't remember when. We bought the copyright from Bobbs Merril, which was being eaten up by some big company. So we tried different approaches. We introduced different problems. We even had a much more overt section, we called it "The Search for a More Plausible Future."

In that section, which we spent about the last three or four weeks of the semester on, we used as a springboard this, "How do you confer authority," to move, really, two questions, suppose you look at the whole enterprise differently and you ask yourself government's limitations here are substantial. Its objectives ought to be more modest. How would you go about trying to create greater public safety if you didn't use some of the predicates that we've been using so far as the way to do business? This relied, to a certain extent, on some of Herman's work, and also some work that Michael Smith and I did. A lot of it had to do with sentencing because we were really interested in working on sentencing at that time. It was sort of schizophrenic. It had a police section to it and it had a correctional sentencing section to it because those were the places in which we thought a more plausible future had some possibility. We were working like crazy on trying to get sentencing reformed, and Herman obviously was doing what all he was doing with his problem orientation.

So Herman, one of the things we used to say is cops know stuff. Just two quick illustrations. One from this campus, there was the problem of stealing books from the various buildings in which students study. This is in the days when you had books, obviously, instead of computers.

So the kids would go out and leave their books in classrooms because you had two, three kids in a classroom at 10:00 at night studying, but they'd leave their books and go out. There were people who were systematically stealing these books. A cop here on campus decided he was going to solve this problem. He decided that the way to solve the problem was to go to the places where the books were being sold. He did. He discovered that there were three of four bookstores that were buying all these books, and then either reselling them somewhere, maybe here or maybe somewhere else.

Bill Clune: He was looking at them as fences?

Walter Dickey: They were fences. I think all but one were naive fences, and they readily agreed to effectively operate like pawn shops, so they took the name and address and demanded identification from anybody who came in to sell a book. The last one, the one that knew exactly what they were doing, said, "No, we're not doing that."

The cop goes to the city council and he gets an ordinance passed requiring all bookstores to do what the three or four are doing, including this one, and apparently it had a substantially preventative effect on the stealing of books.

Bill Clune: So he was a one-man social engineer.

Walter Dickey: Exactly. Exactly. Now, so the cop is the point of contact here. He doesn't use his traditional legal authority. He does that. Have you ever read the monograph *Fights in Bars*?

Bill Clune: Not recently anyway.

Walter Dickey: So the problem-oriented stuff yields all of these monographs on specific problems. They are fascinating. They are just terrific. One of the ones I remember most vividly is *Fights in Bars*. You know what the number one cause of fights in bars is?

Bill Clune: Women?

Walter Dickey: The pool table.

Bill Clune: Oh, really.

Walter Dickey: Yes. Fights over who's turn it is and fights over bumping guys who are about to shoot.

Again, we're not going to solve all the fights in bars problems, but if you can get the pool table into the place and have this order of things squared away, you can make a difference.

Bill Clune: Yeah.

Walter Dickey: Again, there's a cop, who apparently had been called back to this place time after time after time and it was always for a fight, and the fight always had to do with the pool table. Eventually a study was undertaken about this in a much more expansive sort of a way.

But they started with the placement of the pool table in the room that's causing the bumping problem.

Bill Clune: Yeah, don't bump into me.

Walter Dickey: This is Herman's problem-solving, consistent with his get stuff out of the system. This is a cop noticing repeated calls for service.

Bill Clune: Do you think that that kind of cop entrepreneur social problem-solving was in anyway influenced by the climate of problem-solving around here? Or is that something cops always did?

Walter Dickey: I think Herman's work blessed and allowed what a lot of instinctive cops were doing.

Bill Clune: Sure, cops know stuff, yeah.

Walter Dickey: That's right, but at a low visibility level. I don't know if you followed his work. If you have a minute, you ought to go to the problem-solving website because they've got all the monographs there.

Bill Clune: Is that the one Mike Scott's the head of?

Walter Dickey: Yeah. One of the other things, though, we were trying to do with these courses, again one of the subjects, was teach problem-solving.

Bill Clune: Mm-hmm (affirmative).

Walter Dickey: Because we were asking, "Well, how could you confer authority and how could the systems finally be more fair and effective? In order to really delve into that, you need facts. In here, I think it's in here, we've got something from Vera on the question of . . .

Bill Clune: Michael Smith's work.

Walter Dickey: . . . yeah, street robbery. This had arisen because the New York city cops were complaining about the Manhattan DA's office reduction of robberies to low-level misdemeanors. They are saying, "The DA's over there are just a bunch of lazy bastards who aren't willing to take on the cases that they ought to be taking on." Vera was brought in to study what the DA's office was doing.

Bill Clune: Okay.

Walter Dickey: So what they discover is that they're reducing about 40 percent of the cases, and the other 60 they stick with no matter what. So what are the 40 percent that they're reducing? Well, it turns out almost all of them are disputes about money owed from one person to the other.

Bill Clune: Hmm.

Walter Dickey: And that when you take that perspective about it and you realize what the case is going to look like if it ever goes to trial, you don't have what you think you have.

Bill Clune: It's a criminalized kind of small claims thing . . . A dispute over a debt.

Walter Dickey: Yes. I don't remember where we've got it in here, but so you've got this question, I think it's in the evaluation section on street robbery, how effective is the system? There, it actually is sorting out cases. What looks like they're excusing all these goddamn street robberies and not really getting what we would call fair, is actually is a rough sort of justice. You know?

Bill Clune: Efficiency and fairness.

Walter Dickey: Yeah. Yeah.

Bill Clune: I'm interested in what you said about problem-solving as a skill, because of the students being unhappy with broad scale legal courses, for lack of a better term, legal process, which they got discontented with. "Why are we doing this," you know. A disgruntled student could say, "I didn't come here to learn problem-solving."

Walter Dickey: I'm not going to put this on Frank, I'll just say it about myself. I had contempt for what I used to call instant practicality.

In terms of the students' discontent, I think the students' discontent had more to do with the fact that their friends in other law schools were getting the Fourth, Fifth, and Sixth Amendment and they weren't. They were wondering, "If Harvard's teaching the Fourth, Fifth, and Sixth Amendment, why are these Wisconsin guys giving us this sort of stuff?"

Bill Clune: You think they knew that kind of stuff?

Walter Dickey: Oh, I think they did.

Bill Clune: Or, like you say, John Robertson was teaching another section of it.

Walter Dickey: That's right.

Bill Clune: Why aren't we learning this good book stuff?

Walter Dickey: That's right. That's right. On the what to do when you go into the police station, I used to tell them, Look, you're going to learn what to do in the police station the first time you go in there. The idea that I can sort of prepare you for that, other than with an understanding of what this is really all about, is kind of ridiculous. The world's going to change so many times between now and the end of your career that the idea that I'm going to prepare you for one moment is ridiculous.

The second thing I would say is, Look, you're going to be a leader somewhere. Either you're going to be in a big law firm, you're going to be a judge, you're going to be a legislator, there are all kinds of people, careers, you're going to have over the course of your lives.

Bill Clune: Not to mention public administration itself.

Walter Dickey: We believe that you may have a moment in which what you learn in here matters, but even if you don't have such a moment, we think your position is one where a perspective like the kind we want to try to give you is going to be vital.

Bill Clune: Mm-hmm (affirmative).

Walter Dickey: Now I would also add to them, one of the things that we're trying to teach here is judgment. That's a very hard and elusive sort of thing to either pin down or to try to convey. If what you want to try to teach is judgment, one of the things you have to be aware of is how what you're saying and doing is going to be received by another.

Bill Clune: Mm-hmm (affirmative).

Walter Dickey: . . . how it's going to be received by another, then you need to know a lot of the things that we're talking about here because you're learning about worlds that are, for the most part, foreign to you. But if you're going to operate in them, you need an appreciation of what the perspective of the people is from those worlds. Now, they didn't necessarily like those answers.

But realize, Bill, we thought we were teaching and were devoting most of our energy into people who were not going to go into the criminal justice system.

Bill Clune: Right.

Walter Dickey: We wanted to get the Foley & Lardner types. Some of my, the people I'm proudest of are people who have gone in that direction.

Bill Clune: That's a very good point.

Walter Dickey: We felt we were preparing them. John Skilton, that's who we thought we were preparing.

Bill Clune: I was in a meeting with him the other day. I was in a meeting with him. What a great guy.

Walter Dickey: Yeah. With respect to the people who were going to go into the criminal justice system, and it goes to one of your questions, one of the other things we thought we were trying to do here, what we were trying to teach was professional responsibility. Professional responsibility, not the rules of the code of professional responsibility, but the obligation of the lawyer to the client. We used to say, and again here were taking some stuff that we were doing in LAIP and applying it in this course. We used to say one of the problems with legal education is that the professor asks you to brief the case and you say the facts are and the issues are and the holding laws and the concurring opinions said this and the dissent was right and they criticized the majority for the following . . . We said the problem with that is it situates you in the place of being the critic.

We said, quite honestly in our experience, the critic is not the place most of you are going to be. You may be judges at some time or another in your lives, but that's a long way off. You're going to be in situations in which you are going to be representing people. Therefore, we want to explore with you what your obligations are to those people. The other thing we'd say is, one of the other problems with legal education is it doesn't necessarily teach you to listen to another person.

Bill Clune: Mm-hmm (affirmative).

Walter Dickey: What we want to do is introduce you to worlds in which you're going to realize how vital it is that you listen because their value system, and their life experience is likely to have been so different from yours, that they are going to want things that you don't think they should want. If you don't think they should want them, there's a powerful belief that you should impose your values.

Bill Clune: Stigma.

Walter Dickey: Exactly. One of the things we were trying to do was introduce ideas of professional responsibility. That later became prominent in later editions of the book where we tried to give emphasis to those things, for example, like sentencing. We used to say, "Look, here's one of the outcomes you've learned from this." One of the outcomes you've learned is you get probation for your first drug offense, and you know your guy's a druggie. He gets revoked, and he basically ends up doing something resembling life on the installment plan.

Bill Clune: Mm-hmm (affirmative).

Walter Dickey: Now, one, you need to ask yourself whether or not you have some obligation to that client to try to put them in a situation in which the repetitive nature of what they do isn't sort of inevitable. And failing your ability to do that, you really ought to consider asking the client whether instead of taking probation, which is what they all want, they wouldn't be better off going to jail, for thirty days or forty-five days, or whatever the hell it is, because with a long, imposed, in-state probation sentence, revocation is virtually inevitable.

Bill Clune: For everything and anything beyond anything to do with the original crime.

Walter Dickey: That's right. Again, it's understanding the client. Now you've got to deliver some bad news, and you've got to ask yourself, "How am I going to tell this guy not to take probation?" And why should I tell him not to take probation? Well, I've looked at what the outcomes are, and the outcomes are all bad, if you take probation.

Bill Clune: What you're saying is that they at least could ask the question based on the course.

Walter Dickey: Yeah. As you trace the dispositions of the case, this is the law in action part, what you see is that dispositions, 70 percent of them end up in revocation. So now, again, the statistics is a statistic. But you know this guy, or the woman who's been arrested for prostitution when really it's drug use, you've got to also confront the professional responsibility question. You've got to introduce this foreign idea, take jail now, without imposing your values on the person. You've got to put an array of options in front of them. Try and make them as informed as possible, and allow them to make the decision that's in accord with where they are and their values, and not overrule by exaggerating, because that's one of the typical ways you can get a guy to take a plea. "Look, this judge is going to give you fifty years if you don't take the plea."

You've also got the whole question of commitment as not guilty by reason of mental disease or defect, and a prison sentence. Everybody thinks, "Oh, well I'll take the mental disease or defect," could be a life sentence, you know.

Bill Clune: Mm-hmm (affirmative).

Walter Dickey: That's where specific knowledge really matters.

Bill Clune: No one could complain about understanding sentencing choices.

Walter Dickey: Yes. In fact, it was, Bill. I think in the teaching of the course, they loved the sentencing stuff.

Bill Clune: Okay.

Walter Dickey: They, for the most part, realized this was of use to them. This was usable knowledge of a fairly concrete kind. Because you could . . . I used to draw on the board, lay out, "Here's how a sentence is implemented." And then we'd look at all the consequences, collateral consequences, life on the installment plan, subject of revocation, all that sort of stuff. I think they thought that was the melding of law and life in a way that developed useable knowledge for them. They were much more open to that then they were to a lot of the other stuff.

I don't have much more time, but let me just tell you, one of the things that Frank and I did was we decided we were going to get student evaluations five years after graduation, ten years after graduation, and fifteen years after graduation. We weren't going to send them a form. We were going to send them a letter. The letter said, "Here's what we were trying to do. Did you find the course of value as you've experienced life since law school?" We've got two big thick volumes of the letters somewhere, but they're really rewarding and satisfying, and to a person, appreciative. 80 percent of them are from people who said, whose first sentence is, "I've never done a criminal law case in my life."

Bill Clune: Fascinating.

Walter Dickey: Yeah. The perspectives, the leadership ones certainly comes through, but it opened my eyes. Just a lot of really cool things.

Bill Clune: Now that we're running out of time, do you remember whether the book stayed the same over the years or were there changes?

Walter Dickey: We did a lot of different things with the book. I've got a lot of the editions, since this edition where the board of regents got the copy. We gave greater emphasis to the Fourth, Fifth, and Sixth Amendment, but we basically maintained the structure of beginning with the substantive problem. Now we shifted the substantive problems over the years.

Bill Clune: Mm-hmm (affirmative).

Walter Dickey: Now this edition you brought with you doesn't have sexual assault in it. This has got street robbery, organized crime, and drugs.

Bill Clune: Yeah, I think sexual assault became such a hot button issues, even while we were there in the seventies and the eighties, I guess. I remember when the degrees of sexual assault law were introduced and things like that.

Walter Dickey: Right. One year, maybe more than one now as I think back, we tried an experiment where we ended the substantive law course with sexual assault, and it was the law, the substantive law. Then we began the administration course with the problem of sexual assault in all its many many manifestations, as a way of trying to bring some degree of integration and appreciation for whether the substantive law was useful, applicable, when you saw the range of behaviors to which one tried to apply it. We fooled around with a bunch of different problems.

One of the questions you had here was where does the descriptive stuff, basically is the way I think of it, where does it come from. If you look at it, you see a lot of it comes from the American Bar Foundation Survey and Wayne LaFave and Don Newman and Frank Miller's books, but we had research assistants working hard at finding descriptions of substantive problems. The street robbery stuff, as I said, we went through a lot of drafts. Sometimes I get a headache thinking about how many drafts we went through.

Bill Clune: Yeah, it's hard work. So you had research assistants. You also had a clinical program.

Walter Dickey: Right.

Bill Clune: How much did the Legal Assistance to Inmates program feed back into the course?

Walter Dickey: A lot, for sentencing. We do three sentencing systems. We do the federal with its federal sentencing guidelines, we do the Wisconsin indeterminate, and then we do a straight determinant sentencing system, as a way of sort of applying and helping them learn how a sentence would be executed. I used to say what a sentence means.

We had a lot of LAIP stuff. We got pre-sentence reports galore. In fact, we have some pre-sentences in this book. In later editions of the book, we relied even more on pre-sentence reports, both for the factual predicate for the investigatory and arrest and plea bargaining stage, and try to trace them all the way through the sentencing.

One of the other things that's going on here is the alterations we're making in the books are reflecting our interests at the moment.

Bill Clune: Yeah. Kind of natural with a problem-solving mentality.

Walter Dickey: Yes.

Bill Clune: New problems come . . .

Walter Dickey: That's right. Now Frank never said this, but I believed Frank wanted to use the table of contents and the organization of this book as a way of educating law professors all over the country about what's really going on, and a different way of thinking about what's really going on. He was committed to that.

Bill Clune: Yeah, Herman said that he had, they had summer seminars at which professors from other major schools were coming here to learn about at the American Bar Foundation study, they were stunned by a lot of the stuff.

Walter Dickey: Right. Then we had another series of seminars in '95, '96. Lloyd Ohlin and Frank led them. I still regard them as maybe the most intense learning experience of my life. I just sat and listened as we went from the Bar Foundation survey through the current moment and tried to trace the ideas of the Bar Foundation and what had become of them in the meantime.

Bill Clune: Wow.

Walter Dickey: it was a fascinating intellectual history experience.

Bill Clune: That must have been amazing.

Walter Dickey: Did you know Lloyd Ohlin?

Bill Clune: I didn't.

Walter Dickey: Lloyd, he was at Harvard. He wasn't a law professor. He was a sociologist. Newman wasn't a law professor either, you know. Newman was a social worker.

Bill Clune: Yeah, and Herman had a degree in public administration.

Walter Dickey: And Herman, exactly.

Bill Clune: Yeah, so there were a lot of interdisciplinary people.

Walter Dickey: Exactly.

Bill Clune: Tons of interdisciplinary stuff worked into this, into the where does the knowledge come from, and into how does the teaching of it get informed, created, and changed over the years.

Walter Dickey: Realize, Lloyd Ohlin and Frank were the co-directors of the Bar Foundation survey.

Bill Clune: Okay.

Walter Dickey: Right, and so that, and Lloyd and Frank. Lloyd was such a gentleman, such an old-school . . .

Bill Clune: I was thinking about gentleman Frank, you mentioned him as skeptic but he was always open-minded and kind.

Walter Dickey: I was thinking about it because I've been thinking a lot about this after your inquiry. I have, at home, I've got to get it to the Remington family, the correspondence between Erwin Griswold and

Frank and George Young. Erwin Griswold write Frank, I'm going to say it's '55 or so, saying, "We've done a complete check on you and we are inviting you to take a full professorship with tenure at Harvard." The date on it is a Monday. So Frank's response is dated the following Thursday. "Thank you very much. I like it here at Wisconsin. I'm not leaving."

Walter Dickey: Then there's a response from Griswold that says, "We'll double your salary." Frank graciously says, "Maybe I come out and give a talk sometime, but this is where I'm going to be."

Bill Clune: He was another Willard in that sense. Willard turned down Harvard.

Walter Dickey: Right. George Young learns of this after it's all happened. He's the dean of law school. He writes to Griswold, "Thanks for copying me on the letter. Frank let me know about it after he'd sent it off. I'm sure glad he's not going." So Frank did not use the letter for leverage.

Bill Clune: For a raise?

Walter Dickey: Exactly.

Bill Clune: That would be very like Frank.

Walter Dickey: Yeah.

Bill Clune: Yeah. This is fabulous. I'll get the recording transcribed, and I'll send you a copy of the transcript.

Walter Dickey: Sure. I love trying to remember all this stuff.

Bill Clune: I've got to let you go because you've got some other things to do, I'm sure, so thank you.

Walter Dickey: Yep. I do. Great, and we'll hear from each other.

Made in United States
Orlando, FL
04 November 2026

90200630R00154